"WHAT CAN'T BRAVE AMERICANS ENDURE?"

The New Jersey Infantry at the Valley Forge Encampment

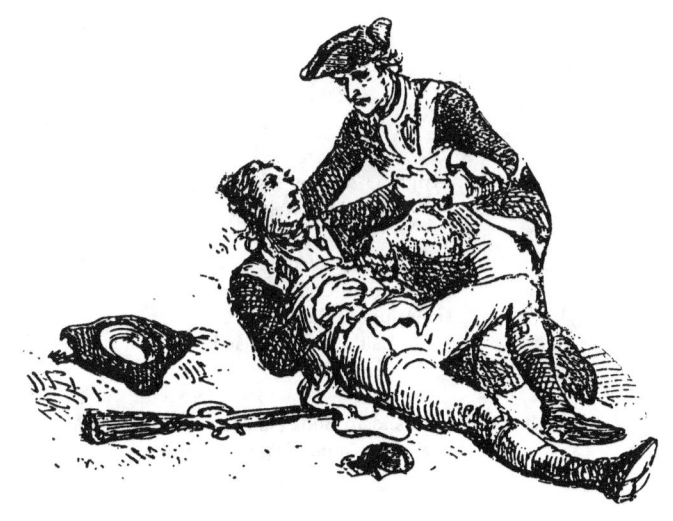

Joseph Lee Boyle

CLEARFIELD

Copyright © 2001 by Joseph Lee Boyle
All Rights Reserved.

Printed for
Clearfield Company, Inc. by
Genealogical Publishing Co., Inc.
Baltimore, Maryland
2001

International Standard Book Number: 0-8063-5113-6
Made in the United States of America

TABLE OF CONTENTS

Preface……………………………………………………………………..iv

Introduction……………………………………………………………….vii

Glossary…………………………………………………………………..xii

Locations Mentioned……………………………………………………..xvi

Name Index…………………………………………………………………1

Bibliography……………………………………………………………144

PREFACE

While the six month encampment of the Continental Army at Valley Forge in 1777-1778 has been part of America's folklore for generations, most of the men who served there have remained anonymous. The names of over 30,000 men of all ranks appear on the surviving monthly muster and payroll records. This compilation is the second volume of an effort to recognize some of these heroes of the Revolutionary War.

The information in the Name Index has been abstracted from Record Group 93, "Revolutionary War Rolls, 1775-1783," at the National Archives in Washington, D.C. Microfilm copies can be found at the branches of the National Archives and at some larger libraries. Microfilm rolls 55-57 pertain to the First New Jersey from 1777-1783; rolls 57-60 the Second; rolls 60-62 the Third; rolls 62-63 the Fourth; roll 123 Forman's; and rolls 127-29 Spencer's. This list does not include men in the cavalry and artillery regiments.

It must be noted that men were not required to enlist in a regiment from their home state. There was always competition for recruits, and as the Continental Army wintered in New Jersey several times, New Jersey men can be found in the regiments of other states. The Speaker of the New Jersey General Assembly complained "many of the inhabitants inlisted into the established regiments of other States, and a still greater number into what are commonly called the sixteen additional, two of which [Forman's and Spencer's] especially were almost entirely levied...in New Jersey."[1] It should not be assumed that all of the men listed were from the State of New Jersey. As these six regiments spent over a year in New York and Pennsylvania, it is likely that some men from these states joined the New Jersey ranks.

The information which follows in the Name Index has been taken from the muster and payrolls. The muster rolls were usually compiled in the early part of each month for the preceding month. Men are shown by company, with name and rank. Any alterations which happened during the month are shown, usually with the date it occurred. These include men joining and leaving the company for various causes and being promoted. Though the reports are for the preceding month, it cannot be assumed that a man who appears as "on command" for example, was in that status for an entire month. Such annotation indicates a soldier's status on the day a given roll was compiled.

---

[1]. Joseph Hart to Congress, 3 April 1778, George Washington Papers, Roll 48, Library of Congress.

The rolls were not compiled within consistent periods after the end of the month. Most of the rolls for December 1777 are dated January 3, 1778. However, the rolls for June 1778 are largely dated July 22. The latter can be accounted for by the fact that the Army had been on the move for several weeks after leaving Valley Forge and had fought the Battle of Monmouth on June 28. As these were status reports, a man who appears as "sick absent" on a June roll may not have been sick at all in June, but become sick in July.

The payrolls were derived from the muster rolls. These were also kept on a monthly basis and ideally, though rarely, the men were paid on a monthly basis for the preceding month. In practice, the pay was usually several months behind and the non-financial notations on payrolls may be less accurate. Where discrepancies are noted on the date a man enters or leaves the service, the payroll is probably more accurate than the muster roll, as the regimental paymaster was audited on his disbursements.

The companies are known by the name of the company captain. In a few cases the company commander left the army, but his company continued to be listed for some months under the former captain's name. This sometimes causes confusion. Captain Jonathan Kinsey died in November 1777, and Lt. Bateman Lloyd commanded the company through June 1778, but the company continued to be called Kinsey's. In cases where a captain left the army and no new captain took over, the captain's name remains the one listed.

For the most part the original rolls are reasonably legible. However in some cases they are extremely poor. Brackets indicate illegible or questionable words. Private William Jones of the First New Jersey is quite clearly noted for April 1778 as "drunk present." The reader should be very much aware that many of the names on the original lists have multiple spellings. For last and first names, the two most common spellings are represented. However, some names appear with more than two variations. For example, the last name of the man shown on the following list in the Fourth New Jersey as Eliphalet Hebbard/Hibbard, also appears Hebbirt/Hebard/Hebbert/Hebirt. There are probably other variations for the time periods before and after Valley Forge. In cases where no dominant spelling appears, the rolls have been checked forwards or backwards from the Valley Forge time period to find the most common variations. Additional variations can be found for some men on the rolls before and after the Valley Forge period. In these cases only the names shown on the rolls from December 1777 through June 1778 inclusive are used.

A common problem was that the record keeping was often months behind for men who had been sent to distant hospitals or were left behind on special duty. Some men were fortunate in being resurrected from the grave by the Army's paperwork. Hugh Doyal of the Fourth is listed dead for March 1778, but for April 1778 he appears as deserted. There are other irregularities that can be reasonably explained. Captain Daniel Baldwin appears as wounded on December, present in January, and wounded absent for the remainder of the period. It is probable that Baldwin was wounded earlier in 1777, and the recorder for January simply failed to make note of it.

A number of men appear as deserting and then returning. This may account for some of the gaps in the records for other men. Some may have deserted for a month or two, then returned, and the officer preparing the roll never noted the soldier's absence. Those who are interested in a particular individual before or after the Valley Forge Encampment should check the rolls for the months before or after Valley Forge or request a copy of the soldier's service record from the National Archives in Washington.

There are some men who appear on a single roll and then disappear without notation. They may have enlisted and then rapidly deserted or died. Some of these notations could be clerical errors or extreme errors in spelling, and some of these mysteries will never be clarified. In other cases a man may have changed companies. James Whitehead is listed only in April as a drummer in Flahavan's Company. A man of the same name appears as a private in Angel's Company for the months before and after April, but not for April itself. It may be conjectured that Whitehead received a temporary post as a drummer but was not satisfactory in the work and returned to his original company.

Only Spencer's Regiment, which was part of Conway's Brigade, was at Valley Forge for the entire encampment period. The Second New Jersey under Colonel Israel Shreve was ordered on March 19, 1778, to "march immediately" for New Jersey as Washington was concerned about British raiding parties.[2] On April 10 the "detachment" from Forman's Regiment was ordered to prepare for immediate departure to New Jersey to join the Second New Jersey. The date they actually left Valley Forge is not certain. In turn the First New Jersey was sent to New Jersey on May 8. Finally, on May 25, Washington ordered Maxwell to proceed immediately to New Jersey with the Third and Fourth Regiments.[3]

---

[2]. Washington to Israel Shreve, 19 March 1778, *Writings of George Washington*, 11:109-110.

[3]. General Orders, 10 April 1778, *WGW*, 11:232; Washington to William Livingston, 14 April 1778, Ibid., 256. George Ewing, *The Military Journal of George Ewing (1754-1824) a Soldier of Valley Forge*. Yonkers, N.Y. Privately printed, 1928, 52; Washington to Maxwell, 25 May 1778, *WGW*, 11:448.

INTRODUCTION

There are few regimental histories for units in the Revolutionary War. In several cases there are histories of the regulars, then called the Continental Line, of a given state. However, none has been completed for the regiments which served from the State of New Jersey. The best single source is Robert K. Wright's *The Continental Army*. This gives a short sketch of each regiment with an excellent bibliography for further reading.

In June 1775, the Continental Congress adopted the army of New Englanders besieging the British in Boston and appointed George Washington of Virginia as Commander in Chief on the Continental Army. Washington inherited what were essentially state armies with short terms of enlistment. Throughout the Fall of 1775 into the Spring of 1776, Congress authorized the formation of various regiments by the states in a piecemeal fashion while Washington and his officers strove to establish a coherent organization. These new units also had short term enlistments.

At the end of 1776, most of the enlistments for Continental troops expired. Congress had anticipated the problem of a disappearing army and had passed a resolve for eighty-eight battalions, or regiments, on September 16, 1776. This was intended to be an army for the duration of the war. However, efforts to recruit the new organization were ineffectual, and in January 1777 Washington was left with only a small cadre of veterans.

New Jersey's quota for the new army in 1777 was four regiments, the same it furnished in 1776. The New Jersey legislature reorganized its officer corps and made strenuous efforts to fill the regiments. However, most of the regiments did not achieve substantial numbers until April and May 1777.[4]

On December 27, 1776, Congress authorized "sixteen additional regiments" to be organized directly by Continental authority instead of by the state governments. Two of these were to be raised by Oliver Spencer and David Forman, veteran militia leaders. Forman's Regiment was never more than a "detachment" and was eventually merged with Spencer's in 1779. Though not assigned to a specific state, these regiments were raised in New Jersey.[5]

---

[4]. Robert K. Wright, Jr., *The Continental Army*, (Washington: Government Printing Office, 1986), 110.

[5]. Wright, *The Continental Army*, 321, 324.

The British plan in 1777 was to cut the United States in half with a British army advancing south from Canada under General John Burgoyne. Burgoyne was to advance to Albany while other British troops moved up along the Hudson River from New York to meet him. After defeat in two engagements against an American Army under Horatio Gates, Burgoyne was forced to surrender at Saratoga in October, the biggest American victory to that date.

The second major British initiative of the year found General William Howe in late August with a British fleet at the head of the Chesapeake Bay. Howe landed in Cecil County, Maryland, and began the advance which would lead to the capture of the American capital of Philadelphia a month later.

All six of the regiments of New Jersey men were with George Washington's "Grand Army" for the entire campaign. The four numbered regiments comprised "Maxwell's Brigade" under Brigadier William Maxwell of New Jersey. Spencer's Regiment was part of Conway's Brigade, and Forman's detachment was part of the garrison of Fort Mercer in New Jersey.

These men fought at the Battle of Brandywine and were part of those who attacked the British right wing at Germantown on October 4.[6] In an audacious surprise attack on the encampment of the British Army, the Americans initially routed the Redcoats but lost momentum and cohesiveness and were forced to retreat. Despite the losses, Washington's men were in high spirits from having initially rocked the British back on their heels.

After Germantown, the opposing armies licked their wounds. The British withdrew and fortified themselves in Philadelphia. They also began their "river assault" of nearly six weeks to clear the Delaware of obstructions and subdue the American strong points of Fort Mifflin south of Philadelphia and Fort Mercer on the New Jersey side of the river. This was critical for the British to be able to communicate with their fleet and bring up supplies and reinforcements.[7]

Meanwhile the commander of the New Jersey Brigade, Brigadier William Maxwell, had to undergo a Court of Enquiry, the results of which were announced in General Orders on October 26. The Court decided "it appears, he was once during said time disguised with liquor in such a manner, as to disqualify him in some measure, but not fully from doing his duty, and that once or twice besides his spirits were a little elevated by spirituous liquor." The

---

[6]. General Orders, 3 October 1777, *WGW*, 9:307.

[7]. John F. Reed, *Campaign to Valley Forge*, (Pioneer Press, 1965), 269-87.

Court passed this on to George Washington to decide if a court martial was necessary. A court martial was held, and on November 4 they acquitted Maxwell as he "was not at any time disguised with liquor, so as to disqualify him in any measure from doing his duty."[8]

On December 4, General Howe led his army out of Philadelphia to confront Washington. By this time the Americans were well fortified on the hills at White Marsh in present day Montgomery County. They had also been reinforced by four more brigades of men, fresh from victory over Burgoyne at Saratoga. Howe looked things over for three days, and tried to maneuver for an engagement, but Washington was too wise to leave his stronghold and engage the British in the open field.

After the British retired to Philadelphia, Washington remained at White Marsh until December 11. The army crossed the Schuylkill River to a place called the Gulph and remained there from December 12 until December 19. Exactly when it was decided to encamp the army at Valley Forge for the winter is not certain, but it was on December 17 that Washington told the men in General Orders that the army would take post in the neighborhood. On December 19 the army left Continental Army left the Gulph and marched into Valley Forge.

Some idea of the rigors of the campaign can be gained by a troop return of Maxwell's Brigade on December 23. The four regiments had a total of 573 privates present fit for duty. This was less than a single regiment was supposed to muster.[9]

The tale of the Continental Army at Valley Forge has often been told. The most thorough recent study is John Jackson's *Valley Forge*. However, a body folklore and myth has so encompassed the six-month encampment that the historical facts are sometimes difficult to discern.

The first few days of the Valley Forge Encampment and mid February 1778 were the hardest times for the troops. Worn out after a hard campaign, they had to build log huts for their winter lodging. At the same time a food shortage so severe occurred that Washington wrote to the President of Congress on December 22 that if something was not done immediately "this Army must

---

[8]. General Orders, 26 October 1777, *WGW*, 9:438; Ibid., 10:4.

[9]. Return of General Maxwell's Brigade, 23 December 1777, RG 93, M 247, Roll 136, f 124, National Archives.

dissolve."[10] The General was forced to send details out from the camp to take food from the citizenry to feed his men.

Thousands of other troops were too ill-clad to be out of doors or participate in any work details. William Gifford wrote on January 24 that "we lay in Tents until the 20 instant; an instance of the kind hardly ever known in any Country whatever, but what can't brave Americans endure, Nobly fighting for the rights of their injured Country."[11]

Many men left the Army in January 1778 as their terms of service were up. For the next few months few new enlistments appear. However, by April the number of recruits began to increase. Some historians have remarked that General Howe missed a golden opportunity to attack Washington at Valley Forge when the Continental Army was at a low ebb. This might be so, but even if Washington could have kept a full complement of men at Valley Forge, there would have been no chance of feeding them.

There were few opportunities for glory or excitement at Valley Forge. After the huts were constructed, many of the soldiers were given the opportunity to go home on furlough. Those who remained stood guard duty, cut firewood, drilled, and were sometimes sent out of camp "on command." This catchall term might mean guarding stores at an outlying post, collecting forage for the army's horses, or guarding prisoners. Throughout the six months the British were in Philadelphia and the Continental Army at Valley Forge, detachments were rotated to the "lines"–the area close to the British fortifications to stop civilians going into the city and harass enemy patrols. These assignments were probably a welcome break from the tedium of camp, but they were not without risk as men were killed, wounded, or captured in skirmishes.

There was much discontent among the officer corps at Valley Forge, and some was directed against Maxwell. On March 2, seven field officers signed a complaint to a committee of the Continental Congress, then at Valley Forge. The seven wished to have Maxwell removed as "from a natural incapacity of genius, he is, and ever will be unable to discharge the duties of his exalted Station, with advantage to his country, and reputation to its arms...he remains

---

[10]. Washington to Henry Laurens, 22 December 1777, *WGW*, 10:183.

[11]. William Gifford to Benjamin Holme, 24 January 1778, Revolutionary Era Documents, #50, New Jersey Historical Society.

totally ignorant of military discipline....He is destitute of address, and without fortitude."[12] Despite this lack of confidence, Maxwell remained with the Army.

In March the arrival of "Baron" Frederick von Steuben brought a new drill for the army. The Commander in Chief's guard was enlarged to serve as the model company. Some New Jersey men were transferred to the guard at this time. Steuben introduced a simple but highly efficient drill which was critical to the success of American arms.[13]

The high point of the Encampment was reached on May 6, 1778. Word of the American alliance with France was announced a few days before, and the entire army celebrated with an orchestrated *feude de joie*. Further good news arrived shortly after this when it became certain that the British were preparing to evacuate Philadelphia. No one knew what the new British commander Henry Clinton was planning to do, but the simple fact that the American capital would be free was enough reason for joy.

Philadelphia was evacuated on June 18, and the Continental Army left Valley Forge the next day. Maxwell, already in New Jersey with his brigade, was ordered to keep up a "correspondence as the movements of this Army must be governed wholly by the intelligence I receive." Maxwell was further ordered to stay on the left of the enemy and "give them all the annoyance you can." [14]

At the Battle of Monmouth on June 28, the New Jersey troops were unfortunate in being under the command of General Lee. Lee mishandled his troops and as a result Washington had to settle for a drawn battle when he might have had a clear victory. One officer wrote they formed the second line "whilst the Front line commanded by our illustrious Genl. in person....Drove the proud King's-Guards & haughty British-Grenadiers."[15]

The New Jersey regiments in the Continental Line were reorganized several times before the Revolutionary War finally ended. The last remaining, the First and Second, were formally disbanded on November 15, 1783, at West Point.

---

[12]. "Memorial of Jersey Field Officers agt. Genl. Maxwell," 2 March 1778, RG 360, M 245, Roll 51, i41, vol. 7, 177-80, National Archives.

[13]. Wright, *Continental Army*, 141-42.

[14]. Washington to Maxwell, 24 June 1778, *WGW*, 12:113-14.

[15]. Mark Lender & James Kirby Martin eds., *Citizen Soldier: The Revolutionary War Journal of Joseph Bloomfield* (Newark: New Jersey Historical Society, 1982), 139-37.

GLOSSARY

Absent Without Leave	Missing from his regiment without authorization.
Armorer/Armoring	Armorers were responsible for repairing weapons and keeping them in service.
Artificer	Artificer was a generic term for skilled specialists such as blacksmiths, carpenters, and leather workers who made and repaired articles required by the army.
Attending Sick	See tending sick.
At the Lines	See on the lines.
Baggage	The clothes, tents, provisions, and other stores of an army, carried by wagon or packhorse.
Batman	An officer's servant. The term was more common in the British Army.
Boatman	In service in a small boat on the Schuylkill River, bringing food, forage, or other supplies to Valley Forge.
Brigade	A tactical unit of four or more regiments.
Brigade Guard	On guard duty at the brigade level, probably guarding the stores or arms of the brigade.
Bullock Guard	The guard detailed to watch over the cattle herd kept available to feed the army.
Buying Horses	On temporary duty out of camp purchasing horses for the army.
Cadet	A man serving without pay until he can be appointed as a commissioned officer.
Cloathier General	The man appointed to head the department that purchased and distributed clothing to the army.
Command	See on command.
Commander-in-Chief's Guard	See General Washington's Guard.
Commissary Guard	The guard detailed to protect the food supply of the army.
Confined in Guard House	Under arrest for one or more infractions of the army's regulations.
Deserter/Deserted	A man who left his regiment with authorization and may have gone over to the enemy, or left for his home.
Detached Artillery	On temporary assigned to an artillery unit.
Discharged	Released from the army either due to a physical infirmity or completion of the required term of service.

Driving Wagon	See wagoner.
Drum Major	The lead drummer in a regiment who teaches the other drummers the proper drum calls and their usage.
Enlisted	The man has joined the army as a private or non-commissioned officer.
Ensign	The lowest ranking officer in the infantry, who carried the colors, or ensign, into battle.
Exchanged	An exchange was the trading of prisoners with the enemy for those of equal rank, or based on a mutually agreed on set of values by rank.
Fatigue/On Fatigue	Assigned to a work detail in camp such as building fortifications or cleaning the encampment.
Fife Major	The lead fifer in a regiment who teaches the other fifers the proper calls and their usage.
Forage Master	Forage refers to the grain and hay fed to the livestock. The forage master purchased and distributed the forage.
Furlough	See on furlough.
Gaol/Goal	This term was usually used when a man was confined in a civilian jail outside of the camp.
General Maxwell's Guard	Serving in the personal guard of General William Maxwell.
General Scott's Guard	Serving in the personal guard of General Charles Scott.
General Washington's Guard/ His Excellency's Guard	Washington's personal guard, usually called the Commander in Chief's guard. Originally all Virginians, in March 1778, one hundred men from the other ten states represented at Valley Forge were added. These men protected Washington's person, the official papers, and the army's cash.
Guard	See on guard
Huts	Huts at Valley Forge.
Inoc Small Pox	Under inoculation for smallpox.
In Provost	See provost.
Invalids/Invalid Corps	A special unit of men who were physically unfit for field duty, but who were capable enough to serve as guards for prisoners and supplies.
Jersies/Jersys	New Jersey had been divided into the colonies of East and West Jersey. Well before of the Revolution it had been unified into one colony, but was still frequently called the "Jersies."
Joined	The date the man reported to his regiment at camp.

Not Joined	The soldier has not joined his regiment. This is usually noted when he has not reported when expected.
Oath	On February 3, 1778, Congress resolved that every officer who held a commission from Congress was required to take an oath of allegiance. Many of oaths do not survive. Details on the oaths can be found in Waldenmaier, *Some of the Earliest Oaths of Allegiance*
On Command/Command	On assignment outside the camp for a periods of a day, up to several months. Most of the time where, or what the assignment was, does not appear in the records.
On Furlough	Given permission to be absent from military duty. Forty-five to sixty days leave seem to have been the most common periods.
On Guard/Guard	The men detailed to protect the encampment.
On Picket/Picket	An advanced guard posted outside the camp to keep watch for the approach of the enemy.
On the Lines/At the Lines	On assignment with other soldiers close to the British line of fortifications at Philadelphia. Men on the lines were to harass British patrols, and stop civilians from carrying supplies into Philadelphia for sale to the enemy.
Orderly Sergeant	The man responsible for writing down the daily orders.
Prisoner on Parole/Parole	An officer who had been captured by the enemy, and had been given liberty by the enemy, after signing a promise not to take up arms until exchanged.
Provost/In Provost	In the camp jail for a violation of regulations.
Provost Guard	A man who was serving as a guard at the camp jail.
Quartermaster's Department	The department responsible for setting up an encampment, supplying wagons for transportation, and providing items such as tents, knapsacks, and tools for an army
Reduced	Lowered in rank due to incompetence, or an infraction of regulations.
Refiner	On temporary duty, probably serving at a smelter refining lead ore.
Resigned	Officers could resign from the army without completing a specific term of service, However they could not do so without approval from their superiors.

Sick Absent	Sick at an unspecified location outside the camp.
Sick in Hospital	Sick at a hospital either in camp, or at an unspecified location outside the camp.
Sick in Jersey	Sick somewhere in New Jersey.
Sick in Pennsylvania	Sick somewhere in Pennsylvania
Sick Present	Sick in a hut or tent at camp.
Sick Quarters	Sick in a hut or tent at camp.
Sub Inspector	An appointment as an assistant to Baron Friedrich William von Steuben, the Inspector General.
Substitute	A man who was paid to serve in the army in place of another.
Surgeon General	The doctor at the head of the army's medical department.
Taken	Taken prisoner by the enemy.
Taken by prior enlistment	The soldier has enlisted at an earlier time in another regiment, deserted, and enlisted again for the cash bounty. He was caught and returned to his original regiment.
Tending Sick/Attending Sick	Helping to look after the sick at a hospital.
Under Arrest	A man who faced charges for an infraction of army regulations.
Unfit for the Service	Physically unfit to serve as a soldier.
Wagon Master	A man in charge of a group of wagons.
Wagoner	Driving a wagon for the army.
Waiter/Waiting	A man detailed to served as an officers personal servant.
With Baggage	Guarding the baggage of the army
With Doctor Cochran	On assignment with Dr. John Cochran, the Surgeon General.
With Morgan's Regiment	On assignment with Colonel Daniel Morgan of Virginia.

LOCATIONS MENTIONED

Counties listed are those which are on current map. Many of the counties that existed in 1777-1778 are now much smaller, as they were broken up to form new counties. For example, all the land which forms the current Delaware County, Pennsylvania, was then part of Chester County.

Allentown	Monmouth County, New Jersey or Lehigh County, Pennsylvania
Barnegat	Ocean County, New Jersey
Barnards Town	Bernards or Bernardsville, Somerset County, New Jersey
B. Brook	Bound Brook, Somerset County, New Jersey
Bethlehem	Northampton County, Pennsylvania
Brandywine	Chester/Delaware Counties, Pennsylvania. Battle fought there on September 11, 1777.
Bucks County/Buxcounty	Bucks County, Pennsylvania
Chatham	Morris County, New Jersey
Cikiot	See Kakiat
Clove	The Clove, also Smith's Clove, refers to a valley through the mountains on the east side of the Ramapo River and the mountains themselves.
Cooper's Ferry	Now Camden, New Jersey
Easton/Eastown	Northampton County, Pennsylvania
Elizabethtown	Now Elizabeth, Union County, New Jersey
Ephrata	Lancaster County, Pennsylvania
Essex	Essex County, New Jersey
French Creek	Chester County, Pennsylvania
German Town	Philadelphia County, Pennsylvania. Battle fought there on October 4, 1777.
Glocester	Gloucester, Gloucester County, New Jersey
Hanover	Morris County, New Jersey
Hopewell	Mercer County, New Jersey or Cumberland County, New Jersey
Hunterdon Co.	Hunterdon County, New Jersey
Huts	Huts at Valley Forge
Jersey/Jersies	New Jersey
Kakiat	Now New Hempstead, Rockland County, New York
Kingwood	Hunterdon County, New Jersey
Lancaster	Lancaster County, Pennsylvania
L. Island	Long Island, New York
Longwood	Probably Longwood, Morris County, New Jersey

Monmouth	Now Freehold, Monmouth County, New Jersey
Morestown	Moorestown, Burlington County, New Jersey
Morris County	Morris County, New Jersey
Morristown	Morris County, New Jersey
M Town	Probably Morristown, Morris County, New Jersey
Newark	Essex County, New Jersey
New Mills	Burlington County, New Jersey
Princeton/Princetown	Mercer County, New Jersey
Quibbletown	Now New Market, Middlesex County, New Jersey
Radnor	Delaware County, Pennsylvania
Reading	Reading, Berks County, Pennsylvania
Rockaway	Morris County, New Jersey
Salem	Salem County, New Jersey
Schaefers	Schaefferstown, Lebanon County, Pennsylvania
Short Hills	Essex County, New Jersey
Springfield	Union County, New Jersey or possibly Burlington County, New Jersey.
Sussex	Sussex County, New Jersey
Trap	Trappe, Montgomery County, Pennsylvania
Trenton	Mercer County, New Jersey
Turkey	Now New Providence, Essex County, New Jersey
Westfield	Union County, New Jersey
Woodbridge	Middlesex County, New Jersey
Yellow Springs	Now Chester Springs, Chester County, Pennsylvania

Name	Rank	Regiment/ Company	Remarks
Aaron/Aron, Thomas	Private	Third, Ross	March-April 1778; May 1778-sick absent; June 1778.
Abbot, Richard	Corporal	Fourth, Anderson	Dec 1777; Jan 1778-on furlough; Feb-April 1778; May 1778-sick in hospital; June 1778
Able, John	Private	Second, Hollingshead	May 27, 1778-enlisted; June 1778.
Adams/ Addams, Abel	Private	Third, Ross	Dec 1777-Feb 1778; March 1778-on command; April 1778; May 1778-on command; June 1778.
Adams, Jacob	Private	Fourth, Forman	Dec 1777-wagoner; Jan 24, 1778-joined; Feb 1778-wagoner; March 1778; April 1778-wagoner; May 1778; June 1778-wagoner.
Adams, Mathew	Private	Second, Luse	May 5, 1778-enlisted; June 1, 1778-joined; June 1778.
Additor/ Adderton, Consider	Private	Second, Cummings	Dec 1777-June 1778.
Agar, Hugh	Private	Third, Gifford	Dec 1777-Feb 1778; March-April 1778-on command; May 1778; June 1778-on guard.
Ager, Archibald	Private	First, Piatt	Dec 1777-Feb 1778-sick in Jersey; March 1778; April 1778-sick present; May-June 1778-sick absent.
Aimes/Ames, John	Private	Second, Phillips	May 14, 1778-enlisted; May 28, 1778-joined; May-June 1778.
Airey, Nathaniel	Private	First, Piatt	Dec 1777-March 1778-sick in Jersey.
Akers, Amos	Private	Second, Phillips	May 14, 1778-enlisted; May 28, 1778-joined; May-June 1778.
Alby/Albee, Jabez	Sergeant	First, Baldwin	Dec 1777-sick Pennsylvania; Jan-March 1778; April-June 1778-sick present
Alexander, William. Usually called Lord Stirling.	Major General		Oath at Valley Forge on May 12, 1778, witnessed by Washington.
Allcutt/Alcutt, Israel	Private	Second, Hollingshead	Dec 1777; Jan 1778-sick in hospital; Feb-April 1778; May 1778-on command; June 1778-sick hospital.
Alcutt/Alcut, Jacob	Private	Second, Cummings	Dec 1777; Jan 1778-sick absent; Feb-April 1778; May 1778-sick absent; June 1778.

Name	Rank	Company	Service Record
Allcut, John	Private	First, Angel	May 31, 1778-joined; May 1778; June 1778-sick absent.
Allen/Alen, Benjamin	Sergeant/ Private	Spencer's, Pierson	Dec 1777-April 1778; May 1778-sick camp; June 1778-Yellow Springs sick; June 1778 reduced to private.
Allen, David	Private	Second, Bowman	Dec 1777; Jan 1778-sick absent/wounded absent; Feb 1778-wounded absent; March-June 1778.
Allen, Enoch	Private	First, Morrison	March 1778-confined; April 1778; May 10, 1778-deserted.
Allen, Jacob	Corporal	Forman's, Burowes	Dec 1777-June 1778.
Allen, John	Private	Third, Paterson	Dec 1, 1777-enlisted; Dec 12, 1777-deserted.
Allibey/ Alaby, Isaac	Private	Second, Cummings	Dec 1777-April 1778; May 25, 1778-deserted.
Allin, James	Private	First, Longstreet	Dec 1777; Jan 26, 1778-dead.
Allin, Samuel	Private	Fourth, Martin	Dec 1777-sick in hospital; Jan 1778-sick absent; Feb 1778-sick in hospital; March 1778-sick hospital; April 1778-unfit for service.
Alman, John	Quarter-master Sergeant	First, Mead	Dec 1777-Feb 1778; March 1778-with Forage Master. Alman appears as quartermaster sergeant for Dec 1777-March 1778. He is also listed as a sergeant in Mead's Co. for the months of Feb-March 1778.
Allson/Alson, Powell/ Thowell	Corporal	First, Baldwin	Dec 1777-Jan 1778-command Reading; Feb 1778-on command Bethlehem; March 1778-on command; April-June 1778-on command Bethlehem.
Alwood/ Elwood, Richard	Private	Spencer's, Lyon	Dec 1777-sick in country; Jan-May 1778; June 7, 1778-died.
Amey/Amy, David	Private	Fourth, Forman	Dec 1777-April 1778; May 1778-sick in hospital; June 1778.
Anderson, Andrew	Private	Third, Cox	March 15, 1778-enlisted; April 1778; May 1778-on command at the lines; June 1778-sick at Princeton Hospital.
Anderson, Darius/Durias	Private	Third, Anderson	Dec 1777-June 1778.
Anderson, Elijah	Private	Second, Bowman	Dec 1777-April 1778; May 1778-on command; June 1778.
Anderson, Francis	Private	First, Mead	April 1778-not joined.
Anderson, James	Private	First, Morrison	May 31, 1778 joined according to May 1778 muster roll but May payroll shows he joined on May 27; May-June 1778.

Name	Rank	Company	Service
Anderson, John	Captain	Fourth, Anderson	Dec 1777-Feb 1778; March-April 1778-on command; May 1778; June 5, 1778-resigned.
Anderson, Joseph Inslee	Captain	Third, Anderson	Dec 1777-Jan 1778; Feb 1778-sick absent; March-June 1778. Oath at Valley Forge on May 11, 1778.
Anderson, Samuel	Private	First, Polhemus	Dec 1777-Jan 1778; Feb-March 1778-sick present; April-May 1778; June 1778-sick Princeton.
Anderson, William	Corporal	First, Polhemus	Dec 1777-Jan 1778; Feb-April 1778-on command; May 1778; June 1778-reduced to private, on furlough.
Andrews, William	Corporal	Third, Ross	Dec 1777-June 1778.
Angel, John V.	Captain	First, Angel	Dec 1777-May 1778; June 1778-on command.
Anson, James	Private	Spencer's, Brittin	Dec 1777-Jan 1778; Feb-March 1778-on furlough; April 1778-sick Cikiot; May-June 1778.
Applegate, Daniel	Private	First, Polhemus	Dec 1777-Feb 1778; March 1778-on command; April 1778-Yellow Springs; May-June 1778; July 10, 1778-deserted.
Applegate, Moses	Private	First, Polhemus	Dec 1777-Jan 1778-sick; Feb 1778-sick present; March 1778-sick present; April 1778; May 1778-guard; June 1778-on command.
Applegate, Robert	Private	First, Longstreet	May 24, 1778-joined; May 1778; June 1778-on command.
Applegate/ Appelgate, William	Private	Fourth, Anderson	May 28, 1778-enlisted; June 1778.
Appleton, Abraham	2nd. Lt./ 1st. Lt.	Second, Phillips	Dec 1777; Jan 1, 1778-promoted to 1st. Lt.; Jan-June 1778.
Arey, James	Private	Second, Luse	May 6, 1778-enlisted; June 1778.
Armstrong, James	Private/ Cadet	Third, Gifford	June 7, 1778-joined. He is listed as a cadet on the June 1778 payroll and receives a private's pay.
Arnold, Stephen	Private	First, Morrison	May 1778; June 1778-sick Newark.
Arnold, Sylvanus	Sergeant	First, Morrison	Dec 1777-Feb 1778-sick absent; March 1778-on command in Jersey; April 1778; May 1778-sick at Princeton; June 1778.
Arvin/Arwin - see Erwin			
Atkinson/ Atkson, William	Private	Fourth, Kinsey	Dec 1777-Feb 1778-sick hospital; March 24, 1778-dead.

Name	Rank	Company	Notes
Augustain/Augustin, George	Private	First, Angel	Dec 1777-April 1778; May 1778-sick at Princeton; June 1778.
Austin, James	Private	Forman's, Combs	Dec 1777-June 1778.
Ayres/Eyers, Benjamin	Private	Spencer's, Brittin	Dec 1777-Jan 1778-sick absent; Feb 1778-sick present; March 1778-sick absent; April 1778-sick Elizabethtown; May 15, 1778-discharged.
Ayres, Reuben	Private	Fourth, Forman	Dec 1777-Feb 1778; March 1778-on command; April 1778 muster roll shows he was imprisoned on April 30. May 1778-imprisoned; July 1778 muster roll shows he was "taken" April 10 and exchanged on July 18.
Back, Robert	Private	Third, Hennion	Dec 1777-Feb 1778; March 1778-on command; April-June 1778.
Badcock, Joshua	Private	Fourth, Holmes	July 1778 payroll shows him as a "pris^r. from the 30th. June 1777 to the 1st Augt. 1778."
Badgely, Joseph	Private	First, Morrison	May 1778; June 1778-sick Westfield.
Baily/Baly, Barney	Drummer	Spencer's, Bonnel	Dec 1777-March 1778; April 1778-on command; May-June 1778.
Baker, David	1st. Lt.	Spencer's, Brittin	Dec 1777-March 1778; April 6, 1778-resigned.
Baker, Jonathan	Private	First, Baldwin	May 1778; June 1778-on command.
Baker, Miliam/Milon	Private	Third, Paterson	May 27, 1778-joined. May-June 1778.
Baker, Thomas	Private	Third, Gifford	Dec 1777-Feb 1778-sick absent; March-June 1778.
Baker/Backer, William	Private	Fourth, Kinsey	Dec 1777-Feb 1778-sick hospital; March 1778; sick hospital; April 1778.
Baldwin, Benjamin	Fifer	First, Baldwin	Dec 1777-Jan 1778-sick at Sussex; Feb 1778-sick in Essex; March 1778-sick in Jersey; April 1778-deserted; May 1778-"returned since last muster." June 1778.
Baldwin, Daniel	Captain	First, Baldwin	Dec 1777-wounded; Jan 1778; Feb-March 1778-wounded; April-June 1778-wounded absent.
Baldwin, Daniel	Private	First, Morrison	May-June 1778.
Baldwin, Jesse	2nd. Lt./Quartermaster	First, Flahavan	Dec 1777-Feb 1778; March-April 1778-on furlough. Appointed quartermaster in May. Appears on both staff and company muster rolls for May-June 1778.

Name	Rank	Company	Service
Ball, Adam	Private	First, Piatt	March 1778-joined; March-April 1778; May 1778-with baggage; June 12, 1778-deserted.
Ball, Cornelius	Private	Spencer's, Brittin	Dec 1777-April 1778; May 1778-on guard; June 1778.
Ball, Enos	Corporal	Spencer's, Brodrick	Dec 1777-Jan 1778; Feb 1778-sick present; March 4, 1778-died.
Ball, Joshua	Private	First, Angel	Jan-Feb 1778; March 1778-deserted; May-June 1778.
Ball, Justus	Private	Third, Gifford	Dec 1777-June 1778.
Ball, Samuel	Private	First, Morrison	May 27, 1778-joined; May 1778-on picket; June 1778.
Ball, Stephen	Surgeon's Mate	First	Dec 1777-sick absent; Jan 1778-absent without leave; Feb-June 1778.
Ballard, James	Corporal/ Sergeant	First, Polhemus	Dec 1777-March 1778; April 1778-Yellow Springs; May 1778-on command; June 20, 1778-promoted to sergeant; June 1778-on guard.
Ballard, Jeremiah	Captain	Third, Ballard	Dec 1777-June 1778. Oath at Valley Forge on May 21, 1778.
Bambridge, John	Private	Third, Ballard	June 3, 1778-enlisted; June 1778.
Bandel/ Bandle, John	Private	Fourth, Martin	Dec 1777-Feb 1778; March 1778-on guard; April 1778; May-June 1778-on command.
Bangheart, Barney	Private	Third, Cox	Dec 1777-April 1778; May 1778-at Princetown Hospital; June 1778.
Banks/Bank, Jamison	Private	Fourth, Lyon	Dec 1777-Jan 1778-sick absent; Feb-May 1778; June 1778-on command.
Banthom, John	Private	Forman's, Combs	Dec 1777-June 1778.
Barber, Francis	Lt. Col.	Third	Dec 1777-Feb 1778; March 1778-on furlough; April 1778; May 1778-Sub Inspector; June 1778. Oath at Valley Forge on May 11, 1778.
Barber, William	Adjutant	Spencer's	Dec 1777-March 1778; April 1778-promoted. On May 7, 1778 he was promoted to Major and appointed aid-de-camp to Lord Stirling (William Alexander). Oath at Valley Forge on May 16, 1778.
Barcalow, Cornelius	Sergeant/ Private	Forman's, Burowes	Dec 1777; Jan 5, 1778-reduced to the ranks; Jan-April 1778; May 1778-sick in New Jersey; June 1778 muster roll shows he deserted on July 1, 1778.
Bardon/ Barden, John	Private	First, Mead	Dec 1777-March 1778-sick in Jersey; April 1778-deserted.

Barker, Thomas	Private	Second, Luse	Dec 3, 1777-enlisted; March 1778; April 10, 1778-deserted.
Barnet/ Barnett, William M.	Surgeon	First	Dec 1777-Jan 1778-sick absent; Feb 1778; March 1778-sick absent; April-June 1778.
Barr/Bar, Adam	Private	First, Flahavan	Dec 1777-Feb 1778; March 1778-command; April 1778; May 1778-Princeton Hospital; June 1778-sick in hospital.
Barr, William	Sergeant Major	Second	Dec 1777-June 1778.
Barrel, Thomas	Private	Fourth, Kinsey	Dec 1777-April 1778; May 1778-on command; June 1778.
Barrell, William	Private	Second, Phillips	Feb 4, 1778-enlisted; March-April 1778; May 1778-on guard; June 1778.
Barton, William	1st Lt.	Fourth, Holmes	Dec 1777-Feb 1778; March 1778-sick absent; April 1778-sick at Allen Town; May-June 1778.
Bates/Beats, William	Private	Spencer's, Weatherby	Dec 1777-June 1778.
Batling, James	Private	Fourth, Anderson	Dec 1777-Feb 1778; March 1778-sick present; April 1778-command [buy]ing horses; May 1778; June 1778-on guard.
Bayly, Samuel	Private	Fourth, Mitchell	June 1778.
Bayley, Aaron	Private	Second, Luse	May 10, 1778-enlisted; June 1, 1778-joined; June 1778.
Beach, Janish	Private	First, Morrison	May 27, 1778-joined; May 1778-on command; June 1778-sick Newark.
Beach, Stephen	Private	Third, Ballard	Dec 1777-March 1778; April 1778-on week's command; May 1778-sick in M Town; June 1778-sick Newark.
Beach, William	1st. Lt.	Spencer's, Brodrick	Dec 1777-Jan 1778; Feb 1778-on command; March 1778-sick present; April-May 1778; June 1778-on furlough. Oath at Valley Forge on May 11, 1778.
Beadle, Joseph	Private	First, Morrison	May 27, 1778-joined; May 1778; June 1778-sick Newark.
Beadle/ Beedle, Simeon	Private	First, Baldwin	Dec 1777-Feb 1778-sick Bethlehem; March 1778-sick in Jersey; April 1778-deserted.
Beagle/ Beedle, Absalom	Corporal	First, Morrison	Dec 1777-Feb 1778; March 1778-General Scott's Guard; April 1778-sick present; May 13, 1778-died.
Beagle/ Beadle, Benjamin	Corporal	First, Flahavan	April 1778; May 1778-on furlough; June 1778.

Name	Rank	Company	Service
Beagle/Bedle, Jacob	Private	First, Flahavan	Feb 15, 1778-joined; Feb-March 1778; May 1778-command; June 1778.
Beardwine/ Beardawine, Peter	Private	First, Piatt	May 26, 1778-joined; May-June 1778.
Beck/Beeck, Robert	Private	Third, Holmes	Dec 1777-Feb 1778; March 1778-on command; April-June 1778
Beckner/ Bickner, John	Private	First, Piatt	May 31, 1778-joined; May 1778; June 1778-on furlough.
Bedeau/ Bedaw, Elias	Sergeant	Spencer's, Ward	Dec 1777-Feb 1778; March-April 1778-on furlough; May 1778-on duty; June 1778-on furlough.
Bedford, Joseph	Private	Third, Cox	June 1, 1778 enlisted; June 5, 1778-joined; June 1778.
Beedle/Bigle, Moses	Private	First, Mead	March-June 1778.
Beegle/Begal, Thomas	Private	Third, Ballard	Dec 1777; Jan 1778; Feb-April 1778-on furlough; May 4, 1778-deserted.
Belden/ Beldin, Joseph	Private	Second, Cummings	Dec 1777; Jan 1778-on furlough; Feb-April 1778; May 1, 1778-deserted.
Bell, John	Private	Forman's, Burowes	Dec 1777-April 1778; May 1778-on command; June 1778.
Bell, John	Corporal	Spencer's, Edsall	Dec 1777-Jan 1778; Feb 1778-sick present; March 1778-on furlough; April-June 1778.
Bell/Bill, Josiah	Private	Second, Luse	Dec 1777-June 1778.
Bell, Peter	Private	Fourth, Holmes	December 1, 1777-deserted.
Bell/Bill, Phineas	Private	Second, Luse	Dec 1777-June 1778.
Bell, William	Corporal	Spencer's, Brittin	Dec 1777-Jan 1778; Feb 1778-wounded absent; March 18, 1778-died.
Belles/Bellis, John	Private	Fourth, Anderson	May 28, 1778-enlisted; June 1778.
Benham, Joseph	Sergeant	Third, Paterson	Dec 1777-Jan 1778; Feb 1778-on furlough; March 1778-sick absent; April-May 1778; June 1778-on furlough.
Bennet, Samuel	Private	Forman's, Wikoff	Dec 1777-June 1778.
Bennett, Jeremiah	Private	Second, Phillips	May 8, 1778-enlisted; June 1, 1778-joined; June 1778.
Bennett, John	Private	Second, Hollingshead	Dec 1777-June 1778.
Bennett, Joseph	Private	Second, Hollingshead	Dec 15, 1778-enlisted; Jan-April 1778; May 1778-on command; June 1778.
Bennett, Matthias	Private	Second, Cummings	Dec 1777-April 1778; May 10, 1778-deserted.

Name	Rank	Company	Notes
Bennett, Nehemiah	Private	Second, Phillips	May 5, 1778-enlisted; June 1, 1778-joined; June 1778.
Bennett/ Bennet, Silas	Private	First, Angel	Dec 1777-March 1778.
Bennett, Silas	Private	First, Flahavan	April 1778-sick present; May-June 1778.
Bennett, Thomas	Private	Second, Cummings	June 1, 1778-joined; June 1778.
Berkstaler/ Barracksteller, Joseph	Private	Second, Hollingshead	Dec 1777-May 1778; June 1778-on command.
Berry, John	Private	Forman's, Burowes	Dec 1777-April 1778; May 10, 1778-taken prisoner. August 1778 muster roll shows he was exchanged on August 9.
Bertron/ Bertrom, David	Fifer	First, Piatt	Dec 1777; Jan-Feb 1778-on furlough; March 1778-absent in Jersey; April-June 1778.
Besley, James	Private	Third, Mott	April 1778; May 19, 1778-deserted.
Beth, Archibald	Private	Second, Phillips	May 14, 1778-enlisted; May 28, 1778-joined; May-June 1778.
Bevans, Davis	Private	Third, Gifford	June 7, 1778-joined; June 1778.
Bevin/Bivin, Moses	Private	Spencer's, Ward	Dec 1777-Feb 1778-sick in hospital; March 1778-wounded absent; April 1778-sick hospital.
Bevins/ Bevens, Mathew	Sergeant	First, Mead	Dec 1777-June 1778.
Bigelow/ Begalow, Jabez	Private/ Fife Major	Third, Cox	June 1778 muster roll for Cox's Co. shows him enlisted as a private on June 1, 1778. June 1778 Field & Staff roll shows him appointed as fife major on June 1. Later rolls show him as fife major for the regiment.
Bilbury/ Bilberry, Wooldrick/ Woolder	Private	Third, Ballard	Dec 1777-June 1778.
Biggers/ Biggars, William	Corporal	Second, Helms	Dec 1777-June 1778.
Bird, William	Private	First, Baldwin	Feb 8, 1778-enlisted; March 1778-sick present; April 1778-sick Yellow Springs; May 1778-sick present; June 1778-on the bullock guard.
Birkins/ Burkins, John	Private	Second, Hollingshead	Dec 1777-April 1778; May 1778-on command; June 1778.

Name	Rank	Company	Service
Birney/ Burney, Peter	Private	Third, Mott	Dec 1777-March 1778; April-May 1778-on command; June 1778.
Bishop, John	Sergeant/ Sergeant Major	First, Piatt's for Dec only.	Dec 1777; Jan 1 1778 promoted to sergeant major; Jan-April 1778; May 1778-sick present; June 1778-sick absent.
Bishop, William	Private	Third, Ballard	Dec 1777-June 1778.
Black, Adam	Private	First, Flahavan	May 25, 1778-joined; May-June 1778.
Blackford, Anthony	Private	First, Piatt	June 1778.
Blackney/ Blackner, Godfrey	Corporal	Fourth, Martin	Dec 1777; Jan 1778-on command; Feb-April 1778; May 1778-on command; June 1778-on guard.
Blackston/ Blackstone, John	Private	Second, Helms	Dec 1777-June 1778.
Blair, John	2nd Lt.	Fourth, Holmes	Dec 1777-March 1778; April-May 1778-sick at Princeton; June 1778.
Blair, Robert	Private	Second, Hollingshead	Dec 1777-Feb 1778; March-April 1778-on Gen. Washington's Guard.
Blair, William	Drummer	Second, Hollingshead	Feb 1, 1778-enlisted; May-June 1778.
Blany, Robert	Private	Fourth, Anderson	Dec 1777-Feb 1778-sick in hospital; March-April 1778-Invalids.
Blanchard/ Blancher, William	Private	First, Longstreet	May 24, 1778-joined; May-June 1778.
Blaracom/ Blaricom, Henry	Private	Spencer's, Ward	Dec 1777-deserted; Jan 1778 [ ]; Feb 1778-confined gaol Morristown; March-April 1778-gaol Morristown; May 1778-broke gaol and deserted; June 1778.
Bleekman/ Blackman, Thomas	Private	Third, Mott	Dec 1777-Feb 1777; March 1778-on guard; April-June 1778.
Blew/Blue, Daniel	Private	First, Baldwin	Jan 31 1778-enlisted; Feb 1778-boatman; March-April 1778-on command; May 1778; June 1778-on command.
Blizard, Morgan	Private	Second, Cummings	May 20, 1778-enlisted; May 24, 1778-joined; May-June 1778.
Bloom/ Blume, Barnt/Baunt	Private	Spencer's, Brodrick	Dec 1777-on command; Jan 1778; Feb 1778-on command; March 1778-on command at hospital; April 30, 1778-deserted.
Bloom, George	Sergeant	Spencer's, Brodrick	Dec 12, 1777-died.

Bloomfield, Jarvis	Ensign	Third, Gifford	Dec 1777-Jan 1778-wounded absent; Feb- June 1778.
Bloomfield, Joseph	Major	Third	Dec 1777-Jan 1778-furlough; Feb-June 1778. Oath at Valley Forge on May 11, 1778.
Blowers, Robert	Private	Second, Baldwin	Dec 1777-sick Jerseys; Jan-Feb 1778; March-April 1778-sick present; May 1778-on the lines in Jersey; June 1778-on guard.
Blumfield/ Bloomfield, Charles	Private	Fourth, Mitchell	Dec 1777-Feb 1778; Mar 1778-on command; April-June 1778.
Bogart/ Bogard, James	Private	Third, Paterson	Dec 1777-March 1778; April-sick present; May 1778-on guard; June 1778-sick absent.
Boggs, Thomas	Private	Second, Phillips	Dec 1777; Jan 1778-on command; Feb-May 1778; June 27, 1778-killed.
Bolton, John	Private	Forman's, Burowes	Dec 1777-April 1778; May 1778-on command; June 1778.
Bolton, Robert	2nd. Lt.	Forman's, Combs	Dec 1777; Jan 7, 1778-resigned.
Bond, Nathaniel	Private	First, Morrison	June 1778.
Bond, William	Private	Third, Hennion	March 15, 1778-enlisted; April 1778; May 1778-on command; June 1778-sick absent.
Bond, William	Captain	Fourth	Dec 2, 1777-resigned. His company was combined with Forman's.
Boney/Baney, Michael	Private	Third, Mott	Dec 1777; Jan-Feb 1778-sick absent; March 1778; April-June 1778-on command.
Boney, Simon	Private	Third, Ross	Dec 1777-Feb 1778; March 1778-on command; April 1778-command Bucks County; May 1778-sick absent; June 1778.
Bonham, Absalom	2nd Lt.	Fourth, Anderson	Dec 1777-Feb 1778; March 1778-on furlough; April 1778-on command; May-June 1778. Oath at Valley Forge on May 11, 1778.
Bonham, Ephraim	Private	Third, Paterson	Dec 1777-Feb 1778; March 1778-on command, April 1778; May 1778-on guard; June 1778.
Bonnel/ Bonnell, James	1st. Lt.	Spencer's, Lyon	Dec 1777-June 1778.
Bonnel/ Bonnell, Samuel	Private	Fourth, Lyon	March 25, 1778-enlisted; April 12, 1778-joined; April 1778; May 1778 sick absent; June 1778.
Bonnill/ Bonnell, Abner	Private	Third, Paterson	May 27, 1778-joined; May 1778; June 1778-on furlough.

Name	Rank	Company	Notes
Bonta, Joseph	Private	First, Morrison	May-June 1778.
Boosey/ Boozey, Daniel	Private	First, Baldwin	Dec 1777-sick present; Jan-April 1778-sick in Jersey; May 1778-sick at Elizabethtown; June 1778.
Boozey/ Bosley, Mathias	Private	Third, Paterson	June 1778-on furlough.
Boston/ Borton, Jonathan	Corporal/ Private	Fourth, Holmes	Dec 1777-Jan 1778; Feb 16, 1778-reduced to private; March 1778-sick present; April-June 1778.
Bordeaux, Jacob	Private	Second, Luse	Dec 15, 1777-dead.
Borden/ Burdon, Abraham	Private	Fourth, Forman	Dec 1777-March 1778-sick in hospital; April 1778-sick absent; May-June 1778-hospital Reading.
Borum/ Boram, Hendrick	Private	Second, Bowman	Dec 1777-April 1778; May 1778-on command; June 1778.
Boston, John	Private	First, Baldwin	December 1, 1777-enlisted; Jan 1778; Feb 1778-on command; March-April 1778; May 1778-sick at Princeton; June 1778-on command.
Boston, Thomas	Private	Second, Cummings	Dec 1777; Jan 1778-on command; Feb-April 1778; May 8, 1778-deserted.
Bostwick, William	1st Lt.	Third, Anderson	Dec 1777-March 1778; April 1778-on furlough; May-June 1778.
Bound, John	Private	Second, Phillips	May 26, 1778-enlisted; June 1, 1778-joined; June 1778-on command.
Bowells/ Bowels, Richard	Private	First, Baldwin	Dec 1777-Jan 1778-sick in Jerseys.
Bowen, Joseph	Private	Second, Cummings	May 21, 1778-enlisted; May 24, 1778-joined; May 1778-sick present; June 1778.
Bowen/ Bowin, Nathan	Private	Forman's, Burowes	May 1778-on command; June 1778; July 1, 1778-deserted.
Bowen, Samuel	Private	Fourth, Kinsey	June 1778 muster roll states: "Taken prisoner 1 Dec 1777 exchanged June 1778."
Bowers Powers, James	Drummer	Third, Gifford	Dec 1777-April 1778; May 1778-sick at P Town Hospital; June 1778.
Bowers, John On the March payroll he appears as Powers	Private	First, Angel	Dec 1777-Jan 1778-on command Newark; Feb-March 1778-on command; April 1, 1778-deserted; May 1778; June 1778-on furlough.
Bowers, Samuel	Private	First, Baldwin	June 1778.

Name	Rank	Company	Notes
Bowman, Aman	Private	Fourth, Mitchell	June 1778.
Bowman, Nathaniel	Captain	Second, Bowman	Dec 1777-June 1778; May-June 1778.
Bowman, Thomas	Private	Third, Paterson	May 27, 1778-joined; May-June 1778.
Boyd/Boyde, John	Private	First, Angel	Dec 1777-April 1778; May 1778-sick at Princeton; June 1778-on furlough.
Boyd/Boyde, John	Private	Second, Reading	May 1, 1778-enlisted & joined; May 1778; June 1778-on guard.
Boyd, Jonathan	Private	Second, Hollingshead	Dec 1777-June 1778.
Boyars, John	Private/ Corporal	Spencer's, Maxwell	Dec 1777-Jan 1778; Feb 1, 1778-promoted to corporal; Feb-March 1778; April 1778-sick present; May 10, 1778-died.
Boylan, Aaron	Private	First, Piatt	May 21, 1778-joined; May 1778-on guard; June 1778.
Boyles/Boiles, James	Private	Fourth, Kinsey	Dec 1777; Jan 1778-on command; Feb 1778; March 1778-on guard; April 1778; May 1778-on command; June 1778.
Braderick/Bradrick, Daniel	Private	First, Angel	Dec 1777-March 1778; April 1778-on command at the lines.
Bradford, James	Private	Second, Cummings	May 20, 1778-enlisted; May 27, 1778-joined; May-June 1778 on command.
Bradford/ Bradshaw, Thomas	Private	Third, Mott	Dec 1777; Jan-June 1778-sick absent.
Bradock/ Badrick, William	Corporal	Fourth, Lyon	Dec 1777-June 1778.
Bradshaw, William	Private/ Corporal	First, Mead	Dec 1777-April 1778; April 30, 1778-promoted to corporal; May-June 1778.
Brady/Bready, Daniel	Private	First, Mead	June 5, 1778-joined; June 1778-"Butchard." As he appears on later rolls it apparently refers to working as a butcher.
Brady, Edward	Private	Third, Ross	Dec 1777-Feb 1777; March 1778-on command; April 1778-on picket; May 1778; June 1778-missing.
Brady/Bradey, Patrick	Private	Fourth, Holmes	Dec 1777-Jan 1778-furlough; Feb 1778; March 1778-on command; April-June 1778.
Brand, Joseph	Private	Second, Cummings	May 24, 1778-joined; May-June 1778.
Brant, John	Private	First, Mead	June 5, 1778-enlisted; June 1778.

Name	Rank	Company	Notes
Brant, Mathias	Private	First, Mead	June 5, 1778-enlisted; June 1778.
Brasted, Isaac	Private	Spencer's, Brodrick's	Dec 1777-Feb 1778; March 1778-on fortnight command; April-June 1778.
Bratey/Braley, David	Private	First, Piatt	March-June 1778.
Bray, Andrew	Private	Second, Luse	May 10, 1778-enlisted; June 1, 1778-joined; June 1778.
Brearley, David	Lt. Col.	Fourth	Dec 1777; Jan 1778-on furlough; Feb 1778-sick present; March-June 1778. Oath at Valley Forge on May 11, 1778.
Brearly, John	Private	Second, Reading	May 14, 1778-enlisted; June 1778. The June 1778 muster roll shows he joined on May 1, but the June 1778 payroll shows his pay beginning on May 14.
Breed, George	Sergeant	Third, Mott	Dec 1777-March 1778; April-May 1778-on command; June 1778.
Brees, Henry	Private	Second, Luse	May 5, 1778-enlisted; June 1778.
Breese, Timothy	Private	First, Mead	May-June 1778.
Brewer/Bruer, Henry	Private	Second, Cummings	May 21, 1778-enlisted; May 24, 1778-joined; May 1778-on guard; June 1778.
Brewer/Bruer, John	Private	Third, Anderson	Dec 1777-June 1778.
Brewer, Paul	Private	Third, Ross	Dec 1777; Jan 1778-on command; Feb-May 1778; June 1778-sick present.
Brewster/Bruster, Daniel	Private	Third, Mott	Dec 1777-April 1778; May 1778-on command; June 1778.
Briant, Escob	Private	Third, Anderson	Dec 1777-June 1778.
Brillo, Barnabas	Private	Second, Bowman	Dec 1777-Feb 1778; March 1, 1778-deserted to the enemy.
Brink, Aaron	Private	Spencer's, Edsall	Dec 1777-sick hospital; Jan-March 1778; April 1778-on command; May 1778-on guard; June 1778.
Brink, Haramonous	Sergeant	First, Edsall	May-June 1778.
Brink, Peter	Private	Second, Helms	May 10, 1778-enlisted; June 14, 1778-joined; June 1778.
Britain/Britton, Joseph	Private	First, Morrison	Dec 29, 1777-joined; Dec 1777-Feb 1778; March 1778-sick in camp; April 1778; May 1, 1778-deserted.
Brittain, Jeremiah	Private	First, Piatt	May 1778-sick absent; June 1778.
Brittin, William	Captain	Spencer's, Brittin	Dec 1777-March 1778; April 10, 1778-resigned.
Britton, Daniel	Private	Second, Luse	May 10, 1778-enlisted; June 1, 1778-joined; June 1778.

Britton/Britin, Daniel	Private	Spencer's, Pierson	Dec 1777-Jan 1778; Feb 1778-sick present; March 1778; April 1778-on command; May 1778-sick camp; June 1778.
Britton/Brittin, John	Sergeant	Spencer's, Pierson	Dec 1777-April 1778; May 1778-sick in camp; June 1778-on furlough.
Britton, William	Private	Forman's, Burowes	Dec 1777-April 1778; May 1778-sick at Princeton; June 1778.
Brodrick, James	Captain	Spencer's, Brodrick	Dec 1777-Feb 1778; March 1778-on furlough; April-May 1778; June 1778-wounded Sussex. Oath at Valley Forge on May 11, 1778.
Brodrick, William	Private	Fourth, Lyon	Dec 1777-June 1778.
Brooks, Almarin	Sergeant	Second, Sparks	Dec 1777-June 1778.
Brooks, James	Private	First, Morrison	June 14, 1778-[joined]; June 1778.
Brooks, John	Private	Third, Gifford	May 27, 1778-joined; May-June 1778.
Brown, Asher	Private	Forman's, Burowes	Dec 10, 1777-deserted.
Brown, David	Corporal	Third, Cox	Dec 1777; Jan-Feb 1778-sick in hospital; March 4, 1778-died in Reading Hospital.
Brown, David	Private	Second, Phillips	April 11, 1778-enlisted; April 1778; May 1778-on command; June 1778-on furlough.
Brown/Browne, Edward	Private	First, Baldwin	Dec 1777-sick present; Jan 1778-sick Pennsylvania; Feb-April 1778; May 1778-sick at Princeton; June 1778.
Brown, George	Private	First, Mead	April-June 1778.
Brown, George	Private	Second, Luse	May 5, 1778-enlisted; June 1778.
Brown, Henry	Private	Fourth, Kinsey	December 21, 1777-died.
Brown, Job	Corporal	Third, Mott	Dec 1777-Feb 1778; March 1778-on guard; April 1778-sick present; May-June 1778.
Brown, John	Private	First, Baldwin	Dec 1777-sick Bethlehem; Jan 1778-dead.
Brown, John	Private	First, Morrison	Dec 29, 1777-enlisted; Jan-Feb 1778.
Brown, John	Private	Second, Cummings	Dec 1777-April 1778; May 1778-sick absent; June 1778.
Brown, John	Private/Sergeant	Forman's, Forman	Dec 1777-March 1778; April 20, 1778-promoted to sergeant; April-June 1778.

Name	Rank	Company	Notes
Brown, Malichi/ Malaky	Private	Spencer's, Edsall	Dec 1777-Jan 1778; Feb 1778-sick absent; March 1778-sick present; April-June 1778.
Brown, Peter	Drummer	Second, Reading	Jan-April 1778; May 1778-sick absent; June 1778.
Brown, Samuel	Fifer/ Private	Third, Ballard	Dec 1777; Jan 9, 1778-reduced to private; Jan-April 1778; May 1778-on guard; June 1778.
Brown, Samuel	Private	Third, Gifford	Feb 8, 1778-enlisted; Feb 1778; March 1778-sick present; April 20, 1778-died.
Brown, Thomas	Private	Second, Sparks	May 3, 1778-enlisted; June 1778.
Brown, Thomas, Jr.	Private	Second, Sparks	Dec 1777-March 1778; April 5, 1778-taken; July 17, 1778-exchanged.
Brown, Thomas	Private/ Corporal	Forman's, Wikoff	Dec 1777; Jan 1, 1778-promoted to corporal; Jan-June 1778.
Brown, Timothy	Private	Second, Luse	June 5, 1778-enlisted; June 1778.
Brown, Zebulon	Private	Fourth, Kinsey	Dec 1777-June 1778.
Browne/ Brown, William	Private	Fourth, Mitchell	Dec 1777-at hospital sick; Jan 1778-sick hospital; Feb 1778; March 1778-sick hospital; April 1778-sick Allentown; May 1778-died in Allentown.
Bruchaw/ Brechaw, Peter	Private	Third, Ross	Dec 1777-Feb 1778, March 1778-on command; April-June 1778.
Brush, Israel	Private	First, Polhemus	May 1778 muster roll shows he joined on May 25, but the payroll shows he joined May 29. June 1778-sick Jerseys.
Bryan, John	Drummer	Fourth, Anderson	Feb 1778-June 1778.
Bryan/ O'Bryan, Patrick	Private	Fourth, Anderson	Dec 1777-Feb 1778; March 1778-sick present; April-June 1778.
Bryant, Archibald	Private	First, Angel	Dec 1777-March 1778; April 1, 1778-deserted.
Bryant/Briant, Benjamin	Private	First, Angel	Dec 1777-April 1778; May 1778-on command; June 1778,
Bryant/Briant, Jacob	Private	Third, Anderson	Dec 1777-June 1778.
Bryant, John	Private	First, Polhemus	March 30, 1778-enlisted; April 22, 1778-joined; April 1778; May 1778-guard; June 1778-on command.
Bucannon/ Bucannan, Samuel	Private	Fourth, Martin	Dec 1777-March 1778; April 1778-sick present; May 1778-sick Yellow Springs; June 1778-Yellow Springs.
Buck, Henry	Private	Third, Gifford	May 27, 1778-joined; May-June 1778.

Buck, Joseph	Private	Second, Hollingshead	May 4, 1778-enlisted; June 1, 1778-joined; June 1778.
Buckley, Cornelius	Private	Fourth, Anderson	June 1778-on guard.
Budd/Bud, Conklin	Private	Third, Paterson	Dec 1777; Jan 1778-on command; Feb-June 1778.
Bull, Charles	Sergeant	Spencer's, Edsall	Dec 1777-June 1778.
Bull, William	1st. Lt.	Spencer's, Edsall	Dec 1777-Feb 1778; March 1778-sick present; April-June 1778. Oath at Valley Forge on May 11, 1778.
Bullard/ Bulard, Joseph	Private	Spencer's, Pierson	Dec 1777-sick hospital; Jan 1778-sick absent; Feb 12, 1778-died.
Bunn, Levi	Private	Third, Ross	May 1778; June 1778-on guard.
Bunnel/ Bunnels, Benjamin	Private	First, Mead	Dec 1777-deserted; March-April 1778; May 1778-on guard; June 1778-on command.
Bunnell, Gilbert	Private	First, Mead	June 5, 1778-enlisted; June 1778.
Bunnell, Henry	Private	First, Mead	June 5, 1778-enlisted; June 1778-on command.
Bunting/ Buntin, Abel	Private	Fourth, Anderson	Dec 1777-June 1778.
Bunting, Ramoth	Private	Second, Phillips	May 10, 1778-enlisted; June 1, 1778-joined; June 1778.
Bureau/ Barcase, Adam	Private	First, Piatt	May 21,1778-joined; May-June 1778.
Burchan, Richard	Ensign	Fourth, Anderson	Dec 1777-Jan 1778.
Burgess/ Burges, James	Quartermaster Sergeant	Spencer's	Dec 1777-Feb 1778-sick absent; March 1778; April-May 1778-sick at Kakiat; June 1778.
Burgher/ Burger, Henry	Private	Third, Ross	Dec 1777; Jan 1778-on command; Feb 1778; March 1778-on command; April-on command with Engineers; May 1778-on command; June 1778.
Burk/Burke, Henry	Private	Second, Helms	Dec 1777-March 1778; April 5, 1778-taken prisoner; July 17, 1778-exchanged.
Burk/Burch, James	Sergeant	Third, Anderson	Dec 1777-April 1778; May 1778-on command; June 1778.
Burk, Thomas	Private	Third, Anderson	Dec 1777-Jan 1778; Feb 21, 1778-died.
Burlew, Jacob	Private	First, Longstreet	May 24, 1778-joined, May 1778-on command; June 1778.
Burlew, Peter	Private	First, Longstreet	May 24, 1778-joined; May-June 1778.

Name	Rank	Company	Service
Burlew, Thomas	Private	First, Longstreet	June 1778.
Burmingham, Daniel	Private	Forman's, Forman	Dec 1777-June 1778.
Burnet/ Burnett, John	Private	First, Mead	Dec 1777-March 1778; April 1778-on guard; May 1778-sick in Pennsylvania; June 1778.
Burnett/ Burnet, Squire	Private	First, Morrison	May 1778; June 1778-furlough.
Burns, Daniel	Private	Second, Luse	June 11, 1778-joined; June 1778.
Burns, Daniel	Private	Fourth, Forman	May 20, 1778-joined; May-June 1778; July 1 taken by prior enlistment.
Burns, James	Private	Second, Luse	Dec 1777; Jan 1778-sick absent; Feb-April 1778; May 1778-sick absent; June 1778.
Burns/Baurns, Malachi/ Malikia	Private	First, Mead	Dec 1777-sick in hospital; Jan 1778; Feb 1778-sick in Jerseys; March 1778-sick absent; April 1778-sick quarters; May 1778-sick in Pennsylvania; June 1778-deserted.
Burrell/ Burwell, Jedediah	Private	Third, Paterson	Dec 1777-April 1778; May 1778-on guard; June 1778.
Burrell/ Burrel, Zachariah	Private	Third, Ballard	Dec 1777-March 1778; April 1778-on picket; May 1778-sick at Princeton; June 1778-sick Morristown.
Burroughs/ Burrows, James	Fifer	Third, Mott	Dec 1777-June 1778.
Burroughs/ Burrows, John	Private	Third, Mott's	Dec 1777-Feb 1778, March 1778-on furlough; April 1778; May 1778-on command; June 1778-on guard.
Burowes, John	Captain	Forman's, Burowes	Dec 1777-June 1778.
Burrows, Eden	2nd. Lt./ 1st. Lt./ 2nd. Lt.	First, Piatt/ Longstreet	Dec-1777-Jan 1778-2nd. Lt. in Piatt's Co.; Feb-April 1778-1st. Lt. in Longstreet's Co.; May-June 1778-2nd. Lt. in Piatt's Co.
Burtless, William, Jr.	Drummer	Second, Phillips	Dec 1777-June 1778.
Burtless, William, Sr.	Drum Major	Second	Dec 1777-June 1778.
Burton, John	Sergeant	Third, Anderson	Dec 1777-March 1778-wounded absent; April 1778-muster roll states sick absent but pay roll states he returned to the company since muster; May 1778-June 1778.

Name	Rank	Company	Service Record
Burtt, John	Private	Second, Hollingshead	July 9, 1777-deserted; March 1, 1778-returned from desertion; March-April 1778; May 15, 1778-deserted.
Butler, Edward	Private	Third, Cox	Dec 1777; January 23, 1778-deserted.
Butler, John	Sergeant	Spencer's, Maxwell	Dec 1777; Jan-March 1778-on furlough; April 1778; May 1778-on guard; June 1778.
Butts/Buts, Alexander	Private	Fourth, Anderson	May 28, 1778-joined; May-June 1778-on command.
Byard, John	Private	Fourth, Forman	Dec 1777-Jan 1778; Feb 1778-dead.
Cagan, Solomon	Private	First, Piatt	May 26, 1778-joined; May 1778; June 1778-on command.
Cain, Francis	Private	First, Baldwin	Jan 14, 1778-enlisted; Feb 9, 1778-deserted.
Cain/Cane, Michael	Private	First, Longstreet	April 1778; May 1778-on command; June 1778.
Caldier, Ninean	Private	Third, Ross	May 25, 1778-joined; May 1778 on guard; June 1778-on command.
Callehen/Kellehen, Thomas	Private	Second, Luse	Jan 1, 1778-enlisted; Feb-March 1778; April 5, 1778-deserted.
Camble, Joseph	Private	First, Morrison	June 1778-sick present.
Cambrum, Nathaniel	Private	Second, Phillips	May 8, 1778-enlisted; June 1, 1778-joined; June 1778.
Cammick/Carmick, James	Private	Second, Reading	Jan-Feb 1778; March 17, 1778-deserted.
Cammil, Andrew	Private	Fourth, Martin	Dec 1777-March 1778; April 1778-on guard; May-June 1778-on command.
Cammil/Camill, James	Sergeant	First, Flahavan	Dec 1777-April 1778; May 1778-on command; June 1778.
Camp, see DeCamp			
Campabell, John	Private	Fourth, Kinsey	June 1778.
Campbell/Camble, Aaron	Private	Second, Helms	Dec 1777-March 1778; April 5, 1778-taken prisoner.
Campbell, Andrew	Private	Fourth, Martin	Dec 1777-March 1778; April 1778-on guard; May-June 1778.
Campbell, Frederick	Private	Third, Ross	Dec 1777; Jan 30, 1778-deserted.
Campbell, James	Sergeant	First, Flahavan	Dec 1777-June 1778.
Campbell, John	Private	Second, Sparks	Dec 1777-June 1778.

Name	Rank	Company	Notes
Campbell, Lewis	Private	Fourth, Forman	Dec 1777-Feb 1778; March 1778-on command; April 1778-on his Excellency's Guard.
Campbell, McDonald	Fifer	Fourth, Forman	May 20, 1778-joined; May-June 1778.
Campbell/ Cambell, Robert	Private	Third, Gifford	Dec 1777-April 1778; May 1778-on furlough; June 1778-sick absent.
Campbell, Robert	Private	Second, Sparks	May 8, 1778-enlisted; June 1778.
Campbell/ Cambell, Simeon	Drummer/ Private	First, Morrison	Dec 1777-Feb 1778; March 1778-sick in Jersey. April muster roll 1778 shows him as deserted but April payroll reads "mustered deserted thro mistake." May 1778-reduced to private; June 1778-missing since June [ ].
Campbell/ Campabell, William	Private/ Corporal	Fourth, Anderson	May 28, 1778-joined; May 1778; June 1778-promoted to corporal.
Campfield/ Camfield, Jabez	Surgeon	Spencer's	Dec 1777; Jan-March 1778-on furlough; April 1778-on command; May-June 1778-sick Morristown.
Campfield, John	Private	First, Baldwin	May 1778; June 1778-on command.
Cannady - see Kennedy			
Cape, John	2nd. Lt.	First, Angel	Dec 1777-Jan 1778; Feb 1778-on command in Jersey; March-June 1778.
Carbury/ Carberry, Francis	Private	Third, Ross	Dec 1777-Feb 1778; March 1778-on command; April-June 1778.
Carhart, Thomas	Corporal	Third, Paterson	Dec 1777-Jan 1778; Feb 1778-on furlough; March 1778-June 1778.
Carl, Ephraim	Private	First, Angel	June 1778.
Carle, Adreyan	Private	First, Longstreet	June 4, 1778-joined; June 1778-on command.
Carlile/ Carlisle, Ebenezer	Sergeant	Fourth, Anderson	Dec 1777; Jan-Feb 1778-absent without leave; March 1778-deserted; April-May 1778; June-on guard.
Carmichael/ Carmihell, James	Private	Second, Bowman	Dec 1777-June 1778.
Carney, Lawrence	Private	Third, Gifford	June 7, 1778-joined; June 1778.
Carnine, Cornelius	Private	First, Piatt	Dec 1777-Feb 1778; March 1778-on command at the lines.
Carnine, Edward	Private	First, Piatt	Dec 1777-June 1778.

Name	Rank	Company	Service
Carr/Kerr, Daniel	Private	First, Piatt	April 30, 1778-joined, April 1778; May 1778-on command; June 10, 1778-deserted.
Carr, James	Private	Spencer's, Maxwell	Dec 1777-June 1778.
Carr, William	Private	Spencer's, Maxwell	Dec 1777-June 1778.
Carrick, James	Corporal	Spencer's, Maxwell	Dec 1777-June 1778.
Carroll, Jeremiah	Private	Second, Phillips	May 8, 1778-enlisted; June 1, 1778 joined; June 1778.
Cartmell, John	Private	Second, Sparks	December 6, 1777-dead.
Carter, David	Corporal	Fourth, Mitchell	Dec 1777-April 1778; May 1778-sick Yellow Springs Hospital; June 1778.
Carter/Cartor, George	Corporal	First, Angel	Dec 1777-March 1778; April 1778-brigade guard; May 1778-sick at Princeton; June 1778.
Carter, Richard	Private	Fourth, Forman	Dec 1777-Feb 1778; March 1778-unfit for service; April 29, 1778-discharged. One roll lists him as Carter Richard.
Carter, Samuel	Private	First, Mead	June 5, 1778-joined; June 1778-on guard.
Cartrecht/Cahucht, Aaron	Private	Second, Helms	May 10, 1778-enlisted; June 14, 1778-joined; June 1778.
Cartwright/Cartright, Thomas	Private	First, Piatt	March 1778; April 1778-on picket guard; May 1778-with baggage; June 1778.
Carty/Cartee, Daniel	Private	Second, Cummings	Jan 1, 1778-joined; Jan-June 1778.
Carty/Cartey, Isaac	Corporal	Second, Cummings	Dec 1777-April 1778; May 1778-on command; June 1778.
Carty/Cartee, John	Private	Second, Cummings	Feb-May 1778-on command; June 1778-on guard
Carty, William	Private	Second, Sparks	May 10, 1778-enlisted; June 1778.
Case, Thomas	Private	Second, Phillips	May 14, 1778-enlisted; May 28, 1778-joined; June 1778-on command.
Caseby/Keesby, Richard	Private	Second, Helms	Dec 1777-March 1778; April 5, 1778-taken prisoner; July 17, 1778-exchanged.
Casey, Henry	Sergeant	Third, Ballard	Dec 1777-June 1778.
Casey, John	Private	Fourth, Mitchell	June 1778.
Casey, William	Sergeant	Spencer's, Maxwell	Dec 1777-Feb 1778; March 1778-on guard; April-May 1778; June 1778-command Clove.

Name	Rank	Company	Service
Casterlin, Hiram	Private	First, Morrison	Dec 1777-Feb 1778-sick present; March-April 1778-Lord Stirling's Guard; May 1778-sick New Mills; June 1778-sick Princeton.
Castle, John	Private	Second, Phillips	Dec 1777-April 1778; May 1778-on guard; June 1778.
Castor, Isaac	Private	Second, Helms	May 10, 1778-enlisted, June 14, 1778-joined; June 1778.
Catanch/ Cotanch, William	2nd Lt.	Third, Hennion	Dec 1777-Feb 1778; March 1778-on furlough; April 28, 1778-resigned.
Caterline/ Caterlin, Abraham	Private	Fourth, Forman	Dec 1777-Feb 1778; March 1778-on command; April-May 1778; June 1778-on guard.
Cato, John	Private	Fourth, Forman	Dec 1777-June 1778.
Cavanagh/ Cavannah, John	Sergeant	Third, Hennion	Dec 1777-June 1778.
Cavannah, John	Private	Fourth, Lyon	Sept 25, 1777-deserted; March 28, 1778-joined; March-June 1778.
Cealey - see Seely			
Ceasar/Cezar, John	Private	Fourth, Forman	Dec 1777-June 1778.
Cezar/Sezar, Thomas	Private	Spencer's, Edsall	Dec 1777-on furlough; Jan 1778; Feb-March 1778-sick present; April 30, 1778-died.
Chaimbors, David	Private	Fourth, Martin	May 30, 1778-joined; May 1778; June 1778-on guard.
Chamberlain/ Chamberlin, Lewis	Private	Fourth, Anderson	May 28, 1778-joined; May 1778-on command; June 1778.
Chambers/ Chaimbors, James	Private	Fourth, Martin	Dec 1777-Feb 1778; March 1778-sick present; April-June 1778.
Chambers, Robert	Private	First, Angel	March 1778-sick at Princeton; April 1778.
Chandler, James	Private	First, Baldwin	May-June 1778.
Chandler, Martin	Drummer	Third, Mott	Dec 1777-June 1778.
Chandler, Samuel	Private	Third, Anderson	Dec 1777-June 1778.
Chanel, Michael	Private	Spencer's, Edsall	Dec 1777-Feb 1778; March 1, 1778-died.
Chaneywoolf/ Chanewolf, Joseph	Private	Spencer's, Wilkins/ Edsall	Dec 1777; Jan-May 1778-on furlough; June 1778. In May he transferred to Edsall's Co.

Chaplin, Philip	Sergeant	Forman's, Combs	Dec 1777-June 1778.
Chapman, Adam	Private	First, Longstreet	May 24, 1778-joined, May-June 1778.
Charles, John	Private	Fourth, Forman	June 5, 1778-joined; June 1778.
Charter, John	Private	Second, Sparks	June 8, 1778-enlisted; June 1778.
Chasey/ Chacey, John	Sergeant	Fourth, Forman	Dec 1777-March 1778; April 1778-on command at the lines; May-June 1778.
Cheeks, John	Private	Fourth, Forman	June 5, 1778-joined; June 1778.
Cherry/Chery, Henry	Private	Spencer's, Pierson	Dec 1777-Jan 1778; Feb 1778-sick present; March 1778-on furlough; April 1778-on command; May 1778-driving wagons; June 1778-wagoner.
Chester, Hiram	Private	Second, Cummings	May 20, 1778-enlisted; May 27, 1778-joined; May 1778-on command; June 1778.
Chester, John	Private	Second, Helms	Dec 1777-April 1778; May 1778-on command; June 1778.
Chew, Richard	Private	Second, Cummings	Dec 1777-April 1778; May 1778-sick absent; June 1778.
Chew, Richard	Private	Forman's, Burowes	Dec 1777-May 1778; June 3, 1778-deserted; June 15, 1778-joined; June 1778.
Childs/ Chields, William	Private	Second, Bowman	Dec 1777; Jan-June 1778-sick absent.
Chiverall - see Shavaral			
Christy, James	Private	Fourth, Kinsey	Dec 1777-Feb 1778-sick hospital; April-June 1778.
Chubb, John	Private	Second, Luse	Dec 1777; Jan 1778-on command; Feb-March 1778; May 1778-on command; June 1778.
Chumard - see Shumard			
Churchwood, William	Private	First, Flahavan	May 25, 1778-joined; May-June 1778.
Clark, Andrew	Private/ Sergeant	First, Baldwin	May 30, 1778-joined; May 31, 1778-promoted to sergeant; June 1778-with the artillery.
Clark, Bird	Private	First, Baldwin	May-June 1778.
Clark, Daniel	Private	First, Baldwin	Dec 1777; Jan 1778-sick present; Feb 21, 1778-dead.
Clark, Eli	Private	First, Morrison	May-June 1778.

Clark, Michael	Private	Second, Bowman	June 1778 payroll states he was "taken 26 June '77 & returned."
Clark, Norris	Private	Spencer's, Pierson	Dec 1777; Jan 1778-on command; Feb 1778-on furlough; March 1778-on guard; April 1778-sick hospital; May 1778-sick at French Creek Hospital; June 1778-Yellow Springs sick.
Clark, Richard	Private	First, Mead	Feb 3, 1778-enlisted; Feb-June 1778.
Clark, Samuel	Private	First, Baldwin	Dec 1777-April 1778; May 1778-on the lines in Jersey; June 1778.
Clark/Clarke, Samuel	Sergeant	Fourth, Lyon	Dec 1777-Jan 1778; Feb 1778-sick present; March-April 1778; May 1778-on command; June 1778.
Clark, William	Private	First, Baldwin	Dec 1777; Jan 1778-sick [Pennsylvania]; Feb-April 1778; May 1778-on the lines in Jersey; June 1778-on guard.
Clark, William	1st Lt.	Third, Ross	Dec 1777-Feb 1778; March-April 1778-on command; May-June 1778.
Clark/Clerk, William	Private	Second, Sparks	Dec 1777-sick in hospital; Jan 1778-sick absent; Feb-June 1778.
Clawson, John	Private	Second, Luse	May 6, 1778-enlisted; June 1778.
Clayton, Henry	Private	Third, Hennion	Dec 1777-March 1778-sick absent; April-June 1778.
Clayton, Samuel	Private	Forman's, Burowes	Dec 2, 1777-deserted.
Cleavenger, Thomas	Private	Forman's, Burowes	Dec 1777; Jan 1, 1778-deserted.
Clemhorn, Henry	Private	Second, Helms	October 4, 1777-taken; July 17, 1778-exchanged.
Clemmons/Clemons, John	Private	Second, Cummings	Dec 1777-March 1778; April 4, 1778-dead.
Clemons, John	Private	Second, Hollingshead	Dec 1777-March 1778; April 5, 1778-taken prisoner at Cooper's Ferry; July 17, 1778-exchanged.
Clifton, George	Private	Fourth, Mitchell	Dec 1777-at Rockaway sick; Jan 1778-sick Rockaway; Feb-April 1778; May 1778-sick Princeton Hospital; June 1778.
Cliftonfield, Charles	Private	Fourth, Mitchell	May 1778-sick Princeton Hospital, June 1778.
Cline, Nicholas	Private	First, Baldwin	Dec 1777-April 1778-on furlough; May-June 1778.
Clinger, Frederick	Private	First, Flahavan	Dec 1777 muster roll shows he deserted on Dec 31, but the Dec 1778 payroll shows Dec 18 as the date he deserted.

Name	Rank	Company	Service
Clintick, John	Private	Spencer's, Brodrick	Jan 1778-on command; Feb 1778-sick present; March 6, 1778-died
Clutch, Obadiah	Private	Second, Hollingshead	Dec 1777-June 1778.
Clutter/Cluter, Peter	Private	Spencer's, Edsall	Dec 1777-Jan 1778; Feb-March 1778-on furlough; April 1778 [ ]; May 1, 1778-deserted.
Cobb, Christopher	Fifer	Second, Bowman	Dec 1777-Jan 1778; Feb 14, 1778-discharged.
Cobb, Matthias	Private	Third, Cox	May 21, 1778-enlisted; June 1778-sick at Princeton Hospital.
Cobb, Thomas	Private	Third, Cox	Dec 1777-June 1778.
Cocker, Samuel	Private	First, Morrison	May-June 1778.
Cockrum/Cockrom, Squire	Fifer	Spencer's, Brittin	Dec 1777-sick hospital; Jan 1778-sick present; Feb-June 1778.
Coddington/Codington, Robert	Private	Fourth, Forman	Dec 1777-May 1778-sick absent; June 1778.
Cogswell/Cogsel, Joseph	Private	Fourth, Martin	Dec 1777-March 1778; April 10, 1778-deserted.
Cole/Coale, Aron	Private	Fourth, Martin	Dec 1777-Feb 1778-sick absent; March 5, 1778-deserted.
Cole, Cornelius	Private	Spencer's, Brodrick	Jan 1778; Feb-March 1778-sick present; April 9, 1778-died.
Cole, Henry	Private	First, Morrison	May 1778; June 1778-picket.
Cole/Coal, John	Private	Spencer's, Lyon	Dec 1777-March 1778.
Coleman/Colman, Dennnis	Private	Second, Luse	Dec 1777; Jan 1778-sick absent; Feb-April 1778; May 1778-sick absent; June 29, 1778-missing.
Coleman/Coalman, Jobe	Private	First, Angel	Dec 1777-Feb 1778; March 1778-on command; April 1778-bullock guard; May 1778-on command; June 1778-sick absent.
Coleman, John	Private	Second, Phillips	March 30, 1778-enlisted; April 1778; May 1778-confined to guardhouse; June 1778.
Collins, John	Private	Fourth, Mitchell	Dec 1777-June 1778.
Collins, William	Private	Third, Anderson	June 6, 1778-enlisted; June 1778.

Name	Rank	Company	Service
Combs/ Combes, Campbell	Corporal	Fourth, Forman	Dec 1777-Jan 1778-sick absent; Feb 1778; March 1778-sick absent; April 1778; May 1778-sick present; June 1778-sick in hospital.
Combs, John	Captain	Forman's, Combs	Dec 1777-June 1778.
Compton/ Cumpton, John	Private	First, Piatt	May 26, 1778-joined; May-June 1778.
Condict, Daniel	Private	First, Morrison	May 27, 1778-joined; May 1778-on picket; June 1778.
Condon, James	Private	Second, Hollingshead	Dec 1777; Jan 1778-on command; Feb-June 1778.
Conger, Daniel	Private	Third, Ballard	June 5, 1778-enlisted; June 1778.
Conkelton/ Congleton, David	Corporal	Spencer's, Brodrick	Dec 1777-sick in hospital; Jan 1778; Feb-March 1778-on furlough; April-May 1778; June 1, 1778-taken by a prior enlistment.
Conklin/ Conkland, Cornelius	Private	Spencer's, Pierson	Dec 1777-sick in hospital; Jan-June 1778.
Conklin/ Conkling, John	Private	Spencer's, Brodrick	June 4, 1777-deserted; April 23, 1778-joined; April-May 1778; June 1778-hospital near Yellow Springs.
Conklin, John	Private	Spencer's, Lyon	Dec 1777-Jan 1778; Feb 1778-sick camp; March 1778-sick present; April-June 1778.
Conkling/ Conklin, Jonathan	Private	Third, Ballard	Dec 1777-April 1778; May 1778-sick in Hopewell; June 1778.
Conn, Samuel	2nd. Lt.	Fourth, Kinsey	Dec 1777-June 1778. Oath at Valley Forge on May 11, 1778.
Connell, Charles	Private	Third, Paterson	Dec 1777-Feb 1778; March-April 1778-on command; May 1778-on guard; June 1778-sick present.
Connelly/ Conoley, Thomas	Private	Third, Anderson	September 11, 1777-taken prisoner; Dec 1777-Jan 1778; Feb 1778-waiting on Dr. Draper; March-April 1778; May 18, 1778-deserted.
Conner, Edward	Private	Fourth, Anderson	May 28, 1778-joined; May-June 1778.
Conner, John	Private	Second, Phillips	May 8, 1778-enlisted; June 1, 1778-joined; June 1778.
Conner, Mathew	Private	Second, Luse	May 6, 1778-enlisted; June 1778.
Conner/ Coner, Timothy	Private	Fourth, Kinsey	Dec 1777-May 1778; June 1778-sick hospital.

Name	Rank	Company	Service
Connery/ Conery, Nicholas	Sergeant	Second, Sparks	Dec 1777-Feb 1778; March 20, 1778-deserted.
Connors/ Conors, Casper	Private	Fourth, Martin	Dec 1777-sick in hospital; Jan-Feb 1778-sick absent; March 1778-sick hospital; April 30, 1778-deserted; May 1778-sick in Jersey; June 1778-sick hospital.
Conoly, John	Private	First, Longstreet	June 4, 1778-joined; June 1778.
Conrod/ Conrad, Henry	Private	First, Mead	Jan 1, 1778-joined; Jan-May 1778; June 1778-dead.
Consalee, Avry, Jr.	Private	First, Morrison	May 1778; June 1778-sick at Woodbridge.
Consalee, Avry	Private	First, Morrison	May-June 1778.
Conway, John	Major	Fourth	Dec 1777-March 1778; April 1778-on furlough; May 1778-at Headquarters on command; June 1778. Oath at Valley Forge on May 11, 1778.
Cook, George	Private	First, Piatt	May 21, 1778-joined; May-June 1778.
Cook, George	Private	Second, Phillips	March 11, 1778-enlisted; March-April 1778; May 1778-on command; June 28, 1778-deserted.
Cook, Jacob	Private	Fourth, Forman	Dec 1777-March 1778-sick in hospital; April-June 1778.
Cook, William	Private	First, Morrison	May-June 1778.
Coombs/ Combs, Lawrence	Sergeant	Third, Holmes	Dec 1777-Feb 1778-sick absent; March 1778-deserted.
Coon, Daniel	Private	Fourth, Forman	May 20, 1778-enlisted; June 1778.
Cooper, Alexander	Private	Third, Anderson	June 7, 1778-enlisted; June 1778.
Cooper, David	Private	First, Mead	June 5, 1778-enlisted; June 1778.
Cooper, William	Private	Fourth, Anderson	May 28, 1778-enlisted; May 1778.
Cooper, William	Private	Second, Luse	May 10, 1778-enlisted; June 1, 1778-joined; June 1778.
Corgan/ Corgen, Henry	Private	Fourth, Kinsey	Dec 1777-June 1778.
Corman/ Cormon, Moses	Private	Spencer's, Ward	Dec 1777-sick absent; Jan 26, 1778-dead.
Cornelius, John	Private	First, Longstreet	May 24, 1778-joined; May 1778-on command; June 1778.

Cornick/ Cornock, Joseph	Private	Second, Sparks	Dec 1777-June 1778.
Correy/Corry, Timothy	Private	Fourth, Lyon	May 31, 1778-joined; May-June 1778.
Corrington/ Correnton, Benjamin	Private	First, Baldwin	Dec 1777; Jan 1778-sick [Pennsylvania]; Feb 1778; March-April 1778-sick present; May-June 1778.
Corson/ Cosen, Abel	Fifer	Second, Hollingshead	July 9, 1777-deserted; April 1778-June 1778.
Corwine, George	Private	Third, Ballard	Dec 1777-April 1778; May 1778-on guard; June 1778.
Corwine, John	Private	Third, Ballard	May 28, 1778-enlisted; June 1778.
Cory, David	Private	First, Baldwin	May-June 1778-on command.
Cory, Peter	Private	Fourth, Forman	June 15, 1778 enlisted; June 16, 1778-joined; June 1778.
Cosart/ Causart, John	Private	First, Mead	Dec 1777-March 1778; April 1778-sick present; May 1778-sick in Pennsylvania; June 1778-Westfield.
Cosgrove/ Calsgrove, Charles	Private	Third, Paterson	Dec 1777-April 1778; May 1778-on command; June 1778.
Courtney/ Corteny, Luke	Private	Fourth, Lyon	Dec 1777-April 1778; May 1778-on command; June 1778.
Covenhoven/ Counover, Albert	Private	Fourth, Anderson	May 1778-joined; June 1778-on command.
Covenhoven, Covinhover, William	2nd. Lt.	First, Longstreet	Dec 1777-April 1778-sick in Jerseys; May 1778; June 1778-dead.
Covert, Peter	Private	Fourth, Forman's	May 30, 1778-joined; May-June 1778.
Covett, Tunis	Private	First, Polhemus	Dec 1777-Jan 1778; Feb-April 1778-sick present; May 1778; June 1778-on guard.
Cox/Coxe, Abraham	Private	Second, Sparks	Dec 1777-June 1778.
Cox, Andrew	Private	Fourth, Holmes	Dec 1777-Feb 1778; March 30, 1778-taken prisoner; April-May 1778-prisoner; June 1778.
Cox, Hance/ Hans. On the Feb 1778 payroll the name appears as Hancocks.	Private	First, Mead	Dec 1777-Jan 1778; Feb-March 1778-sick Yellow Springs; April 1778-supposed at Yellow Springs; May 1778-sick in Pennsylvania; June 1778-deserted.

Cox, Richard	Captain	Third, Cox	Dec 1777-Feb 1778; March 1778-on command; April-June 1778. Oath at Valley Forge on May 11, 1778.
Cozzens/ Cozzans, Samuel	Private	Third, Anderson	Dec 1777-Jan 1778; Feb 20, 1778-died.
Crafton, John	Private	Second, Cummings	May 27, 1778-joined; May-June 1778.
Cramer, Andrew	Private	Second, Cummings	Dec 1777-April 1778; May 1778-on command; June 1778.
Cramer, Israel	Private	First, Flahavan	May 26, 1778-enlisted; June 1778.
Cramer, William	Private/ Fifer	First, Polhemus	Dec 1777-with Major Morris; Jan 1778; Feb 1778-promoted to fifer; March 1778; April 1778-Yellow Springs; May-June 1778.
Crammer/ Cramer, Josiah	Private	Fourth, Kinsey	March 15, 1778-enlisted; March 31, 1778-joined; March 1778; April 1778-sick present; May-June 1778.
Crammer, William	Private	First, Flahavan	May 20, 1778-joined; May-June 1778.
Crandle, Elihu	Private	Second, Hollingshead	May 4, 1778-enlisted; June 1778-on command.
Crane, Aaron	Corporal	First, Baldwin	Dec 1777-Jan 1778-command Reading; Feb 1778-command Bethlehem; March 1778-on command; April-1778-on command Bethlehem; May 1778-on command at Morristown; June 1778.
Crane, Asea/Eacy	Private	First, Piatt	May 21, 1778-joined; May-June 1778.
Crane, Edmond	Private	First, Baldwin	Dec 1777-sick Jerseys; Jan-March 1778; April 1778-sick present; May-June 1778.
Crane, Eliakim	Drummer	First, Baldwin	Dec 1777-sick present; Jan-Feb 1778-sick Morristown; March 1778-sick Jersey; April-May 1778; June [28], 1778-killed.
Crane, Ezekiel	Private	Spencer's, Ward	Dec 1777-May 1778; June 1778-on guard.
Crane, John	Private	First, Morrison	May-June 1778.
Crane/Craine, Jonathan/John	Private	Fourth, Mitchell	Dec 1777-March 1778-on command; April 1778-on command at Kingwood; May-June 1778.
Crane, Joseph	Private	First, Piatt	May-June 1778.
Crane, Silas	Private	Second, Phillips	May 8, 1778-enlisted; June 1, 1778-joined; June 1778.

Craven, Joseph	Private	First, Polhemus	Dec 1777-Feb 1778; March-April 1778-on command; May 1778; June 1778-on guard.
Cravan, Stophel/ Stofield	Private	First, Polhemus	Dec 1777-Jan 1778; Feb-March 1778-sick Pennsylvania; April 1778-Yellow Springs; May 1778-sick Princeton; June 1778.
Cravan, William	Private	First, Polhemus	June 1778.
Crealey/ Crealey, Hugh	Private	Fourth, Kinsey	Dec 1777-sick hospital; Jan-June 1778.
Creer, Martin	Private	Third, Ross	June 1, 1778-joined, June 1778-on command.
Cresey/ Crisy, John	Private	First, Piatt	Dec 1777-Jan 1778-sick in the hospital; Feb 15, 1778-dead.
Crill, John	Corporal	Third, Cox	March 1, 1778-enlisted; April 1778; May 1778-at Princeton Hospital; June 1778-sick at Princeton Hospital.
Critzer, Leonard	Private	Third, Ross	May 25, 1778-joined; May 1778; June 1778-on command.
Crofut/ Crowfoot, Joseph	Private	Spencer's, Brittin	Dec 1777; Jan 1778-sick present; Feb-April 1778; May 1778-attending sick; June 1778.
Crome, George	Drummer	Second, Bowman	March 1, 1778-enlisted; April 8, 1778-joined; April-June 1778.
Cromwell, Oliver	Private	Second, Bowman	Dec 1777; Jan 1778-absent with leave; Feb-June 1778.
Crossman, Amos	Private	Third, Anderson	Dec 1777-June 1778.
Crow, Garret	Private	First, Angel	May 31, 1778-joined; May 1778; June 1778-sick absent.
Crowell, David	Private	First, Morrison	Dec 1777; Jan 1778-sick in hospital; Feb 1778-sick absent; March 1778-sick in Jersey; April 1778-deserted. May 1778; June 1778-sick Newark.
Crowell, Joseph	Private	First, Morrison	May 27, 1778-joined; May-June 1778.
Cuff/Cuffie, Negro Also listed as "(Negro) Cuff"	Private/ Fifer	Third, Paterson	Jan 19, 1778-enlisted, Jan 1778-on command; Feb 1778; March-April 1778-on command; May-June 1778. On the June 1778 muster roll Cuff Warner is listed, but not Negro Cuff. Negro Cuff is listed as a fifer for July 1778, but no Cuff Warner is listed. These appear to be the same individual.
Cuffey, William Culleman - see Kullemon	Private	Second, Phillips	May 15, 1778-enlisted; June 1, 1778-joined; June 1778-on command.

Cully/Colly, William	Private	Fourth, Kinsey	Dec 1777-Feb 1778; March 1778-sick present; April 1778; May 1778-on guard; June 1778.
Cummings, John Noble	Captain	Second, Cummings	Dec 1777; Jan 1778-on furlough; Feb-April 1778; May 1778-on command; June 1778-on furlough.
Cummings, William	Private	Third, Paterson	May 1778-sick absent.
Cummins, Theophilus	Sergeant	First, Angel	Dec 1777-Jan 1778-sick absent; Feb 1778; March 1778-sick in Jersey; April 1778-deserted.
Cumpton, Jacob	Private	First, Longstreet	May 26, 1778-joined; May 1778; June 1778-on command.
Cumstok, Ezekiel	Private	Second, Luse	Dec 1777-April 1778; May 15, 1778-deserted.
Cunningham, Henry	Private	Second, Hollingshead	March 28, 1778-enlisted; April-May 1778; June 13, 1778-discharged.
Cunningham, John	Private	First, Piatt	Dec 1777-Feb 1778; March-May 1778-at Lord Stirling's; June 1778-on command.
Cunningham, John	Private	Third, Anderson	June 7, 1778-enlisted; June 1778.
Curley, John	Private	Second, Phillips	Dec 1777-April 1778; May 1778-sick absent; June 1778.
Curry, John	Private	Second, Reading	Jan-April 1778; May 1778-on command; June 1778.
Curry/Currey, John	Private	Fourth, Forman	Dec 1777-Feb 1778; March 1778-on command; April-May 1778; June 1778-on guard.
Curry/Currey, Patrick	Private	Second, Cummings	Dec 1777; Jan 1778-sick absent; Feb-April 1778; May 1778-sick absent; June 1778.
Curtis, John	Sergeant	Second, Hollingshead	Dec 1777-April 1778; May 1778-on command; June 1778.
Curtis, Marmaduke	1st. Lt.	Third, Hennion	Dec 1777-Jan 1778; Feb-March 1778-on command; April 28, 1778-resigned.
Cutter/Cutler, Ebenezer	Fifer	First, Mead	Dec 1777-Feb 1778; March 1778-sick present; April-June 1778.
Cuysor/Kuyser, Frederick	Private	First, Piatt	Dec 1777-April 1778; May 1778-with baggage; June 1778-on command.
Daily, John	Private	First, Piatt	June 1778-sick absent.
Dain, Joseph	Private	Third, Mott	April 1778; May 19, 1778-deserted.
Dale, Richard	Private	Third, Paterson	December 27, 1777-enlisted; January 4, 1778-deserted.
Dalton, James	Private	Fourth, Anderson	September 1777-deserted; March-June 1778.

Name	Rank	Company	Service Record
Dalton, William	Private	Second, Reading	Jan 1778-sick absent. Listed as dead on composite Feb-May muster roll which is dated June 12, 1778. He is last listed on the payroll for Feb 1778.
Danaly/Donnelly, Daniel	Private	Third, Ross	Dec 1777-April 1777; May 1778-sick absent; June 1778.
Daniels, Jeremiah	Private	Second, Cummings	May 20, 1778-enlisted; May 27, 1778-joined; May-June 1778.
Daniels, Jonathan	Private	Second, Cummings	May 20, 1778-enlisted; May 24, 1778-joined; May-June 1778.
Darby, Ephraim	Quartermaster	Fourth,	Dec 1777; Jan 1778-on furlough; Feb-March 1778, April 1778-on command in Jersey; May-June 1778.
Darby/Derby, William	Private	First, Baldwin	Dec 1777; Jan 1778-sick [Pennsylvania]; Feb-April 1778; May 1778-on the lines in Jersey; June 1778.
Darvin, Ebenezer	Private	Second, Hollingshead	Dec 1, 1777-deserted.
Darcey/Dorecy, John	Surgeon's Mate	Spencer's	Dec 1777-June 1778. Oath at Valley Forge on May 11, 1778.
Davidson/Davisson, James	Private	Third, Paterson	Dec 1777-Feb 1778; March 1778-on command; April 1778; May 1778-on guard; June 1778.
Davidson/Davison, Robert	Private	First, Mead	Dec 1777-June 1778.
Davis, Caleb	Private	Spencer's, Pierson	Dec 1777-Jan 1778-wounded; Feb 1778-sick hospital; March 1778-wounded 4th October; April 1778-wounded absent; May 1778-Reading Hospital; June 1778-wounded Bethlehem.
Davis, Daniel	Corporal	Third, Mott	Dec 1777-Feb 1778; March 1778-on guard; April 1778-on command; May-June 1778.
Davis, Daniel	Private	Spencer's, Lyon	Dec 1777-June 1778.
Davis, John	Private	Fourth, Mitchell	Dec 1777-Feb 1778; March 1778-sick present; April 1778; May 1778-sick absent; June 1778.
Davis, John	Private	Spencer's, Lyon	Dec 1777-Jan 1778; Feb 1778-sick in camp; March 1778-sick present; April 1778-French Creek Hospital; May-June 1778.
Davis, John	Private	Spencer's, Pierson	Dec 1777-sick absent; Jan-Feb 1778; March 1778-on guard; April-June 1778.
Davis, Jonathan	Private	Third, Paterson	May 27, 1778-joined; May-June 1778.

Name	Rank	Company	Service
Davis, Nathaniel	Private	Third, Hennion	Dec 1777-April 1777; May 1778-on guard; June 1778.
Davis, Samuel	Private	Fourth, Mitchell	Dec 1777; Jan 10, 1778-deserted.
Davis, Thomas	Private	First, Angel	May 31, 1778-joined; May 1778; June 1778-on guard.
Davis, Thomas	Private	Second, Luse	May 1, 1778-joined, May 1778-on guard; June 1778.
Davis, Vernor/Varner	Private	Spencer's, Wilkins/Edsall	Dec 1777-April 1778-on command; May-June 1778. In May he transferred to Edsall's Co.
Davis, William	Private	Second, Hollingshead	May 8, 1778-enlisted; June 1778-on command.
Davis, William	Private	Forman's, Burowes	Dec 1777-Jan 1778; Feb 15, 1778-deserted.
Day, Aaron	2nd Lt./Quartermaster	Third, Cox	Dec 1777-absent without leave; Jan 1778-under arrest; Feb-March 1778-on command; April 1778; May 1778 promoted to quartermaster; May-June 1778. Oath at Valley Forge on May 11, 1778.
Day, Amos	Private	Spencer's, Brittin	Dec 1777-June 1778.
Day, Jeremiah/Jerry	Private	Fourth, Mitchell	Dec 1777-March 1778; April 1778-sick in camp; May-June 1778-sick in hospital.
Day/Dey, Moses	Private	Fourth, Lyon	Dec 1777; Jan-Feb 1778-sick absent; March 1778-on furlough; April 1778; May 1778-on guard; June 1778-sick hospital.
Day, Samuel	Private	Fourth, Holmes	Dec 1777-Jan 1778; Feb 1778-absent without leave; March 3, 1778-deserted.
Day, Thomas	Private	Second, Hollingshead	May 8, 1778-enlisted; June 1778-sick hospital.
Dayton, Elias	Colonel	Third	Dec 1777-April 1778-on furlough; May-June 1778.
Dayton, Jonathan	Paymaster	Third	Dec 1777; Jan-Feb 1778-on furlough; March-June 1778.
Deacon, Aaron	Private	Third, Ross	Dec 1777; Jan 1778-on command; Feb-June 1778.
Dean/Deain, John	Private	First, Longstreet	Dec 1777-Feb 1778; March 1778-on command on the lines; April-June 1778.
Dean/Deane, John	Private	Spencer's, Wilkins	Dec 1777-Jan 1778; Feb 1778-guard; March 26, 1778-deserted.
Deane, James	Private	Third, Ross	June 1, 1778-joined; June 1778.
Deane, Joseph	Private	First, Longstreet	June 4, 1778-joined; June 1778.

Name	Rank	Regiment, Company	Notes
Dearmon/ Deharman, James	Private	Third, Ross	Dec 1777; Jan-March 1778-sick absent; April 1778-sick in Jersey; May-June 1778-sick absent.
DeCamp, James	Sergeant	Third, Ballard	May 22, 1778-enlisted; June 1778-on furlough.
DeCamp/ Camp, James	Sergeant/ Sergeant Major	Spencer's, Brittin	Dec 1777-Jan 1778-in Captain Brittin's Co. Jan 22, 1778-promoted to sergeant major; Feb 1778-on furlough; March-April 1778.
Decker, Samuel	Private	Spencer's, Brodrick	Dec 1777-wounded; Jan 1778; Feb 1778-absent wounded; March-April 1778; May-June 1778-wounded in Sussex.
Dehart - see Hart			
Delany, Cornelius	Sergeant	Fourth, Kinsey	Dec 1777-Jan 1778; Feb 1778-sick hospital; March 1778-dead.
Delany/ Deleny, James	Corporal	Spencer's, Bonnel	Dec 1777-June 1778.
Delap, James	Private	Second, Reading	May 1, 1778-enlisted and joined; May-June 1778; July 10, 1778-deserted.
Delens, Pero	Private	Forman's, Combs	Dec 1777-May 1778; June 16, 1778-deserted.
Delphor, John	Private	Second, Phillips	May 27, 1778-enlisted; June 1, 1778-joined; June 1778.
Demaries, Adam	Private	Second, Cummings	May 20, 1778-enlisted; May 24, 1778-joined; May-June 1778.
Denean, William	Fifer	First, Longstreet	Dec 1777-June 1778.
Deneway/ Denneway, John	Private	First, Morrison	May-June 1778.
Denight, James	Private	Fourth, Lyon	Dec 1777-sick present; Jan-April 1778; May 1778-on command; June 1778.
Denight, John	Private	Fourth, Lyon	Dec 1777-April 1778; May 1778-sick present; June 1778-sick hospital.
Denman, John	Private	First, Mead	June 5, 1778-enlisted; June 1778.
Denning - see Dunham			
Dennis, Enos/Enis	Private	Third, Ross	May 25, 1778-joined; May-June 1778.
Dennis/ Dennsion, John	Private	First, Mead	The Feb 1778 payroll roll shows he enlisted on Jan 5, 1778. The Feb muster roll shows he enlisted on Jan 20. Feb 1778; March-April 1778-on furlough; May 1778-absent with leave; June 1778-sick absent.

Name	Rank	Company	Service
Dernfield, Phillip	Private	Second, Helms	May 9, 1778-enlisted; June 26, 1778-joined; June 1778.
Derry, John	Private	Second, Bowman	March 18, 1778-enlisted; April 8, 1778-joined; April-June 1778.
Devoor, John	Private	Second, Luse	May 5, 1778-enlisted; June 1778.
Devore, Luke	Private	Third, Ballard	Dec 1777-March 1778; April 1778-sick present; May 1778; June 1778-wagoner.
Dickinson/ Dickason, Isaac	Private	Fourth, Mitchell	Dec 1777-Feb 1778; March 1778-sick absent; April 1778; May 1778-on command; June 1778.
Dickson, Daniel	Private	Fourth, Forman	May 1778 payroll shows he joined on May 20, but he does not appear on the muster rolls.
Dickson/ Dixon, Joseph	Private	First, Angel	Dec 1777; Jan 1778-deserted; Feb-March 1778; April 1778-sick at Yellow Springs; May 1778-sick at Princeton; June 1778-sick absent.
Dickson, William	Private	First, Longstreet	Jan 1, 1778-enlisted; Jan 1778-on command; Feb 7, 1778-deserted.
Dickson/ Dixon, William	Private	Second, Cummings	Dec 1777; Jan 1778-on command; Feb-June 1778.
Dickson, William	Private	Fourth, Forman	May 20, 1778-joined; May 1778; June 30, 1778-died.
Dignan/ Dignum, Patrick	Private	Second, Sparks	Dec 1777-June 1778.
Dillon, James	Captain	Second	Dec 1, 1777-resigned.
Dimer, Joseph. He is also shown as Joseph D. Mer.	Private	First, Longstreet	June 4, 1778-joined; June 1778.
Dimon/ Dimmon, John	Private	Second, Helms	May 17, 1778-enlisted; June 14, 1778-joined; June 1778-on guard.
Disney, John	Sergeant	Second, Reading	Jan-May 1778; June 1778-on furlough.
Dixon, Ashbrook	Private	Second, Sparks	May 26, 1778-enlisted; June 1778.
Dixon, Thomas	Sergeant	Third, Ross	August 1777-deserted; April 1778 payroll only; May-June 1778.
Dixon/ Dickeson, William	Private	First, Flahavan	Dec 1777-on furlough; Jan 1778-deserted; April 1778-deserted; May-June 1778.
Dod, Jesse	Private	First, Morrison	May-June 1778.
Dod, Timothy	Private	First, Morrison	May-June 1778.

Name	Rank	Company	Service
Donaldson/ Donoldson, James	Private	Spencer's, Weatherby	Dec 1777-April 1778; May 1778-on guard; June 1778.
Donaldson/ Donoldson, John	Private	Spencer's, Weatherby	Dec 1777-March 1778; April 1778-sick present; May 1778-on duty; June 1778-sick present.
Donaldson, William	Private	First, Polhemus	Dec 1777-Jan 1778; Feb 1778-command Jersey; March-April 1778-command; May 1778-guard; June 1778-on guard.
Donally/ Donnally, Hugh	Private	Second, Luse	Dec 1777-April 1778; May 24, 1778-deserted.
Donovan/ Dunavan, John	Private	Third, Anderson	Dec 1777-June 1778.
Dorton/ Dolton, Francis	Private	Second, Sparks	Dec 1777-April 1778; May 1778-on guard; June 1778.
Dothevhat/ Dothemat, George	Private	Second, Cummings	Jan 19, 1778-enlisted; April-June 1778.
Doty/Dotty, Daniel	Private	First, Angel	May-June 1778.
Doty/Dotty, Peter	Private	First, Piatt	May 21, 1778-joined; May-June 1778.
Doud, James	Private	Fourth, Kinsey	Dec 1777-March 1778; April 25, 1778-Taken by Prior Enlistment.
Dougherty/ Doherty, Anthony	Sergeant	Spencer's, Brodrick	Dec 1777-April 1778; May 1778-orderly; June 1778-on furlough.
Dougherty, John	Private	First, Longstreet	Dec 1777-March 1778; April 1778-with Major Lee.
Dougherty/ Doherty, John	Private	Fourth, Anderson	Dec 1777-Jan 1778; Feb-March 1778-on furlough; April-June 1778.
Dougherty, Peter	Private	First, Polhemus	Dec 1777-on furlough; Jan 1778; Feb 1778-sick Jerseys; March-May 1778; June 1778-on command.
Dougherty/ Dorkery, William	Private	Fourth, Martin	Dec 1777-April 1778; May 1778-unfit for service.
Doughty/ Doty, John	Private	Fourth, Mitchell	Dec 1777-Feb 1778; March-April 1778-wagoner; May 24, 1778 died.
Douglas/ Duglas, Thomas	Private	Third, Paterson	November 23, 1777-enlisted; Dec 8, 1777-deserted.
Dow, Folkert	Sergeant	First, Piatt	May 1778; June 1778-on command.
Dow, Henry	Private	Spencer's, Brodrick	Dec 1777-Jan 1778 wounded; Feb-March 1778-absent wounded; April-May 1778; June 1778-on furlough.

Name	Rank	Company	Notes
Dowdney/ Dowdley, Samuel	Private	Third, Mott	Dec 1777; Jan 1778-sick absent; Feb 1778; March 1778-sick present; April 1778; May 1778-on command; June 1778-on guard.
Downes, Edward	1st. Lt.	Forman's, Combs	Dec 1777; Jan 7, 1778-resigned.
Downey, William	Private	Third, Paterson	June 1778-on furlough.
Downing/ Downey, Andrew	Private	Second, Luse	Dec 1777-March 1778; April 5, 1778-taken prisoner.
Doyal/Dyol, Hugh	Private	Fourth, Martin	Dec 1777-sick in hospital; Jan 1778-sick absent; Feb 1778-sick in hospital. March 1778 muster roll lists him as dead. April 1778 muster roll shows he deserted on April 30.
Drake, Cornelius	Private/ Corporal	Third, Ballard	Dec 1777-Jan 1778; Feb 21, 1778-promoted to corporal; Feb-March 1778; April 1778-sick Jersey; May-June 1778.
Drake, Nicholas	Private	First, Polhemus	May 1778 muster roll shows he joined May 25 but the May payroll shows he joined on May 29; June 1778-sick Jerseys.
Druer, John	Private	Fourth, Lyon	May 31, 1778-joined; May 1778; June 1778-on command.
Druer, Timothy	Private	Fourth, Lyon	May 31, 1778-joined, May 1778; June 1778-on guard.
Drum, Christafor	Private	First, Longstreet	June 4, 1778-joined; June 1778.
Duclos, Francis	2nd. Lt.	Second, Sparks	Dec 1777-May 1778; June 1778-on command.
Dugan, Robert	Sergeant	Spencer's, Edsall	May-June 1778.
Dugan, William	Private	Third, Anderson	Dec 1777-April 1778; May 1778-on command; June 1778.
Duglass, John	Sergeant	Fourth, Mitchell	June 1778.
Dullemare/ Dullimare, Robert	Drummer	Fourth, Anderson	March-May 1778; June 1778-on command.
Duly, Joshua	Private	Spencer's, Lyon	Dec 1777-sick in country; Jan 1778-sick Springfield; Feb 1778 muster roll shows he deserted on March 1, 1778.
Duncan, Alexander	Corporal	Forman's, Combs	Dec 1777-June 1778. Sept 1778 muster notes he was "taken prisoner 10th May & thro' a mistake returned inlisted with the Enemy."

Name	Rank	Company	Service
Duncan, Joseph	Sergeant/ Private	Third, Gifford	Dec 1777-Feb 1778; March 16, 1778-reduced to private, March 1778-on furlough; April 1778-on command; May 1778; June 1778-on furlough.
Dunfield, Henry/ Hennery	Private	First, Angel	Dec 1777-May 1778; June 1778-on guard.
Dunham/ Danham, Enoch	Private	First, Longstreet	May 26, 1778-joined; May 1778; June 1778-on command.
Dunham, John	Private	First, Mead	June 15, 1778-enlisted; June 1778.
Dunham, Lewis F.	Surgeon	Third	Dec 1777-on furlough; Jan-Feb 1778; March-April 1778-on furlough; May-June 1778.
Dunham/ Dening Nathaniel	Private	First, Morrison	Aug 1, 1777-deserted; March 1778; April 1778-sick present; May 1778-sick at camp; June 1778-left sick at Valley Forge.
Dunlevi/ Dunlavin, Patrick	Private	Third, Mott	March-June 1778.
Dunnigon, John	Private	Fourth, Forman	Dec 1777; Jan 31, 1778-died.
Dunscomb, Dennis	Private	Fourth, Holmes	Jan 1, 1778-enlisted; Jan 3, 1778-deserted.
Dye, James	Private	First, Polhemus	Dec 1777-sick absent; Jan 1778; Feb-March 1778-sick Jersey; April 1778-dead.
Earl/Erle, Israel	Private	First, Mead	Dec 1777-sick in Jersey; Jan 1778; Feb-March 1778-sick in Jersey; April 1778-deserted; May-June 1778.
Earl/Earle, John	Private	First, Morrison	May-June 1778.
Earl/Earle, Moses	Private	First, Morrison	Dec 15, 1777-died.
Early/Earley, Patrick	Private	Second, Hollingshead	Dec 1777-April 1778; May 1778-on command; June 1778-on furlough.
Early, Samuel	Private	Second, Helms	May 13, 1778-enlisted; June 14, 1778-joined; June 1778.
Easton, James	Private	Second, Piatt	March 1778-confined sick in Provost Guard.
Eastwood, Amariah	Private	Fourth, Forman	Only record is the May 1778 payroll which shows he died on March 5, 1778.
Eaton/Eayton, Benjamin	Private	Fourth, Mitchell	Dec 1777-June 1778.
Eaton, James	Private	First, Baldwin	Dec 1777-deserted.

Name	Rank	Company	Service
Eberheart/Eberhert, Adolph	Private	Fourth, Kinsey	Dec 1777-June 1778.
Edmindson, Joseph	Private	Forman's, Forman	Dec 1777-June 1778.
Edsall, Benjamin	Sergeant	Spencer's, Brodrick	Dec 1777-Jan 1778; Feb-March 1778-on furlough; April-May 1778; June 1778-sick Longwood.
Edsall/Edsell, Richard	Captain	Spencer's, Edsall	Dec 1777-Feb 1778; March 1778-on furlough; April-June 1778. Oath at Valley Forge on May 11, 1778.
Edwards/Eadwards, Jacob	Private	First, Baldwin	Dec 1777; Jan-Feb 1778-sick in Jerseys; March 1778-sick in Jersey; April 1778-deserted.
Edwards, Jesse	Corporal	Fourth, Kinsey	Dec 1777-June 1778.
Edwards, John	Private	Second, Hollingshead	May 27, 1778-enlisted; June 1778.
Edwards, Joseph	Private	Spencer's, Weatherby	Dec 1777-June 1778.
Egburd, Abraham	Private	First, Angel	May 31, 1778-joined; May-June 1778.
Egburd, Lewis/Luice	Private	First, Angel	May 31, 1778-joined; May-June 1778.
Ellis, Daniel	Private	Third, Ross	Dec 1777-Feb 1778; March 1778-on command; April 1778; May 1778-Artillery; June 1778-on guard.
Elmer, Ebenezer	Surgeon's Mate/Surgeon	Second	Dec 1777-June 1778; July 6, 1778-promoted to surgeon.
Elmore, John	Private	Second, Reading	Jan 1, 1778-enlisted; Jan 15, 1778-died.
Elwell, Amoriah	Private	Third, Anderson	June 6, 1778-enlisted; June 1778.
Elwell, Samuel	Sergeant	Fourth, Kinsey	Dec 1777-Jan 1778; Feb 1778-on furlough; March-June 1778,
Embley, John	Private/Drummer	First, Polhemus	Dec 1777-Jan 1778; Feb 1778-promoted to drummer; Feb-June 1778.
Emmons/Emmens, John	Private	Third, Ross	Dec 1777-March 1778; April 1778-on weeks command; May-June 1778-sick absent.
Emery/Emry, Thomas	Private	Fourth, Forman	Dec 1777-Feb 1778-sick in hospital; March 1778-dead.
Emmerton, James	Private	Fourth, Kinsey	The payroll for June 1778 shows he was paid for three months service. He does not appear on the muster rolls.
Emons, Benjamin	Private	Second, Phillips	May 18, 1778-enlisted; May 28, 1778-joined; May-June 1778.

English, John	Private	Third, Ballard	Dec 1777-Feb 1778-sick in hospital; March 1778-sick absent; April 1778 muster roll shows he deserted on April 30, 1778; May 1778 muster roll shows he deserted on May 4, 1778; June 1778-sick present.
Enyard, Banjamin	Private	First, Piatt	May 26, 1778-joined; May-June 1778.
Ereckson/ Erexson, Moses	Private	Second, Cummings	May 27, 1778-joined; May 1778-sick absent; June 1778.
Erickson, Michael	Sergeant/ Private	Forman's, Burowes	Dec 1777; Jan 5, 1778-reduced to private; Jan-April 1778; May 1778-on guard; June 1778.
Erwin/Ervin, Peter	Private	First, Longstreet	Dec 1777-June 1778.
Erwin/Arvin, Robert	Private	First, Morrison	Dec 1777-Feb 1778; March 1778-on command; April 1778; May 1778-on command; June 1778-sick Newark.
Erwin/Arwin, William	Private	First, Angel	Dec 1777-sick at Elizabethtown; Jan-March 1778; April 1778-sick present; May 1778-sick at Princeton; June 1778-sick absent.
Erwin/Erwine, William	Corporal	First, Mead	Dec 1777-Feb 1778; March 1778-on command at the lines; April-June 1778.
Esdell/Esdel, John	Private	Third, Gifford	Dec 1777-June 1778.
Eslick/ Easlick, Stephen	Private	Fourth, Forman	Dec 1777-May 1778; June 1778-sick in hospital.
Evans, Emanuel	Private	Third, Ross	Dec 1777-Jan 1778-sick absent, Feb-June 1778.
Evans/Evens, John	Private	Second, Luse	May 5, 1778-enlisted; June 1778.
Evans/Evens, Thomas	Sergeant	Second, Luse	Dec 1777-June 1778.
Evans/Evins, William	Private	First, Angel	May 31, 1778-joined; May-June 1778.
Evens, Obediah	Private	Fourth, Anderson	June 1778-sick in hospital.
Everden, Samuel	Sergeant Major	Spencer's	Dec 1777; Jan 20, 1778-died.
Everingham/ Eviringham, William	Private	Fourth, Anderson	Dec 1777-Feb 1778; March 1778-sick present; April-May 1778; June 1778-on guard.
Ewing, George	Ensign	Third, Hennion	Dec 1777-Jan 1778; Feb 1778-on furlough; March 1778; April 29, 1778-resigned.

Ewing/ Hewing, Julius	Private	Second, Cummings	Dec 1777; Jan 1778-on furlough; Feb 1, 1778-deserted.
Ewing, Remington	Private	Second, Hollingshead	Dec 1777-April 1778; May-June 1778-on command.
Eyers see Ayres			
Fagins/Fagon, Henry	Private	Second, Cummings	Dec 1777-April 1778; May 1778-sick absent; June 1778.
Fagins/Fagon, Michael	Private	Second, Cummings	Dec 1777-June 1778.
Fancy, David	Private	Second, Luse	Dec 1777-June 1778.
Fandler/ Fenler, Joshua	Private	Fourth, Kinsey	Dec 1777-June 1778.
Fanning, James	Private	Second, Cummings	Dec 1777-March 1778; April 1, 1778-deserted.
Fanning, John	Private	Forman's, Combs	Dec 1777-May 1778; June 12, 1778-transferred to Invalid Corps.
Farin/Farrin, Lawrence	Private	Second, Cummings	Dec 1777; Jan 1778-on command; Feb-June 1778.
Faris - see Pharis			
Farmer, George	Private	Fourth, Kinsey	Dec 1777-Feb 1778; March 1778-on his Excellency's Guard.
Farmer, James	Private	First, Piatt	Dec 1777-Feb 1778; March-April 1778-on Lord Stirling's Guard; May 1778-sick absent; June 1778.
Farney, George	Private	Fourth, Kinsey	Dec 1777-on furlough; Jan-Feb 1778; March 1778-on command; April 1778-wagoner; May 1778; June 1778-sick hospital.
Farr, William	Private	Fourth, Forman	Dec 1777-April 1777; May 1778-sick in hospital; June 1778-on guard.
Farrell/Ferol, John	Private	Spencer's, Brittin	Dec 1777-Jan 1778-wounded hospital; Feb 1778-wounded; March 1778-wounded absent; April 1778-wounded Elizabethtown; May 1778; June 1778-sick Elizabethtown.
Farrow/ Farrah, Abraham	Private	First, Piatt	Dec 1777-Feb 1778; March 1778-wagoner; April 1778; May-June 1778-sick absent.
Feathers, George	Drummer	Spencer's, Weatherby	Dec 1777-Feb 1778; March-April 1778-sick present; May 1778-on duty; June 1778-sick Valley Forge.
Fegen/Fegins, John	Fifer	Second, Sparks	Dec 1777-Jan 1778; Feb 26, 1778-died.
Fennerty/ Fenerty, Joseph	Private	Second, Sparks	Dec 1777-June 1778.

Fennimore, Henry	Private	Second, Cummings	May 21, 1778-enlisted; May 24, 1778-joined; May-June 1778.
Fennimore/ Phennimore, John	Private	Second, Phillips	Dec 1777-April 1778; May 1778-on guard; June 1778-on command.
Fenton, Lewis	Private	First, Polhemus	Dec 1777-sick absent; Jan 1778; Feb 1778-deserted.
Fergusin/ Furgison, Alexander	Private	Second, Helms	May 9, 1778-enlisted; June 26, 1778-joined; June 1778.
Ferguson, Thomas	Corporal	Second, Hollingshead	Dec 1777-April 1778; May 1778-sick hospital; June 1778.
Ferol/Ferroll, John	Private	Fourth, Holmes	Dec 1777-April 1778; May 1778-on command; June 1778.
Ferroll/Farrill, James	Private	Fourth, Forman	Dec 1777-June 1778.
Feston, Jonathan	Private	Fourth, Mitchell	June 1778.
Fichenor, John	Private	First, Morrison	May 27, 1778-joined; May-June 1778.
Ficheoner, Aaron	Private	Fourth, Lyon	June 15, 1778-joined; June 1778.
Fiddis/Fiddie, George	Private	Third, Hennion	Dec 1777-April 1778; May 1778-on command; June 1778.
Field, Charles	Private	First, Morrison	Dec 29, 1777-enlisted; Jan 1778-on command; Feb 1778-deserted.
Filimore, Robert	Private	Fourth, Anderson	March 1778.
Finch, John	Private	Second, Bowman	Dec 1777-June 1778.
Findley/ Findley, John	Private	Fourth, Anderson	Dec 1777-Feb 1778-sick in hospital; March 1778-on command; April-June 1778.
Finley, Robert	Private	Second, Cummings	April-June 1778.
Finley, William	Private	Fourth, Mitchell	Dec 1777-June 1778.
Finn, Thomas	Private	Fourth, Kinsey	March 15, 1778-enlisted; March 31, 1778-joined; March 1778; April 1778-on command; May 1778-sick at Trap; June 1778.
Fipps - see Phips			
Fisher, Christopher	Private	Fourth, Anderson	May 20, 1778-joined; May-June 1778.
Fisher, David	Private	Second, Cummings	May 20, 1778-enlisted; May 24, 1778-joined; May 1778-on command; June 1778.

Fisher, Jacob	Private	Third, Ballard	May 28, 1778-enlisted; May 1778 on guard; June 1778.
Fisher, John	Private	Third, Paterson	Dec 17, 1777 enlisted; Dec 1777-absent without leave; Jan-Feb 1778-sick in Jersey; March 1778-sick absent; April 1778-sick absent in Jersey; May 1778; June 1778-killed.
Fisher, John	Private	Forman's, Burowes	Dec 1777-April 1778; May 1778-on command; June 1778.
Fisher, Moses	Private	Fourth, Anderson	May 28, 1778 enlisted; May-June 1778.
Fisher, William	Private	First, Flahavan	Dec 1777 payroll shows he deserted on Dec 18, 1777 but the Dec muster roll shows he deserted on Dec 31. Feb 1778 payroll states he was "left out in former pay rolls as deserted since found sick in hospital." March 18, 1778-discharged.
Fitch, William	Private	Fourth, Anderson	May 28, 1778-enlisted; June 1778.
Fithian, George	Private	Third, Gifford	May 27, 1778-joined; May-June 1778.
Flahavan, John	Captain	First, Flahavan	Dec 1777-Jan 1778-prisoner.
Flake, John	Private	Second, Cummings	Dec 1777; Jan 1778-sick absent; Feb-April 1778; May 1778-on command; June 1778.
Flanagan, Christopher	Private	First, Angel	April 1778.
Flecher/Flicher, James	Private	Fourth, Holmes	Dec 1777-June 1778.
Fleming, Hugh	Corporal	Second, Reading	Jan-Feb 1778; March 10, 1778-deserted.
Fleming/Flemming, Jeremiah	Private	Third, Ballard	Dec 1777-Feb 1778-lame at Easton; March 1778-sick absent; April 1778-sick in Jersey; May-June 1778-sick Eastown.
Fleming, Lawrence	Private	Third, Cox	Dec 1777-March 1778; April 1778-attending the sick; May 1, 1778-deserted.
Flemming, John	Private	Second, Luse	Dec 1777; Jan 1778-attending sick; Feb-April 1778; May 1778-on command; June 1778.
Fletcher/Flicher, William	Private/Sergeant	Fourth, Holmes	Dec 1777-Jan 1778; Feb 1778-sick present; March 1778-promoted to sergeant; March-June 1778.
Flinn/Flin, John	Private	First, Baldwin	Dec 1777; Jan 1778-sick present; Feb 1778; March 1778-on command; April 1778-on command at the lines; May-June 1778.

Flowers, William	Private	Fourth, Martin	Dec 1777-April 1778; May 1778-sick Princetown; June 1778-Yellow Springs.
Floyd, Joseph	Private	Second, Cummings	April-June 1778.
Fogg, Daniel	Private	Second, Reading	Jan 1778-on command; Feb-June 1778.
Folk/Folke, Peter	Private	Fourth, Anderson	May 28, 1778-enlisted; May-June 1778.
Force, Jacob	Private	Second, Hollingshead	Dec 1777; Jan 1778-sick in hospital; Feb-May 1778; June 1778-on command.
Force, Jonathan	Private	First, Morrison	April 20, 1778-joined; April 1778; May 1778-sick Princeton; June 1778-furlough.
Ford, David	Private	Forman's, Combs	Dec 1777-June 1778.
Ford, Mahlon	2nd. Lt.	Third, Mott	Dec 1777-Jan 1778; Feb 1778-on command; March-April 1778-on furlough; May-June 1778-sick absent.
Ford, Thomas	Private	First, Longstreet	May 24, 1778-joined; May-June 1778.
Foregalt, Frederick	Private	First, Piatt	March 1778.
Forman, Jonathan	Captain	Fourth, Forman	In Dec 1777 Forman's Company was combined with Bond's. Dec 1777-Feb 1778; March 1778-on command; April-June 1778. Oath at Valley Forge on May 11, 1778.
Forman/ Foreman, Samuel	Private	Second, Luse	Dec 3, 1777-enlisted. March-April 1778; May 1778-on guard; June 1778.
Forman, Thomas M.	Captain	Forman's, Forman	Dec 1777-June 1778.
Forrester, James	Private	Forman's, Combs	Dec 1777-June 1778.
Forsyth/ Forsithe, James	Ensign	Spencer's, Wilkins	Dec 1777-sick; Jan 1778-sick absent; Feb 1778; March 14, 1778-resigned.
Foster, Andrew	Private	Third, Cox	May 1, 1777 deserted; Jan 11, 1778-enlisted; Jan-April 1778; May 1778-sick at camp; June 3, 1778-died at camp. These entries may refer to two men with the same name.
Foster, Ichabod	Private	Third, Gifford	Dec 1777-April 1778; May 1778-on command; June 1778.
Foster, Jeremiah	Private	Second, Hollingshead	May 4, 1778-enlisted; June 1778.
Foster, John	Private	Fourth, Lyon	Dec 1777-March 1778-sick absent; April 1778; May 1778-on furlough; June 1778-on guard.

44

Name	Rank	Company	Notes
Foster/Forster, Jonathan	Private	Fourth, Anderson	Dec 1777-May 1778; June 1778-on guard.
Foster, Samuel	Sergeant	First, Morrison	May-June 1778.
Foster, Samuel	Private	Fourth, Mitchell	June 1778.
Fowler/Fohler, Isaac	Sergeant	Fourth, Holmes	Oct 4, 1777-wounded at the Battle of Germantown; Dec 1777-dead.
Fowler/Fowlar, David	Private	First, Mead	Feb 1778; March-April 1778; May 1778-on command; June 1778.
Fowler, Joseph	Private	Third, Anderson	Dec 1777-June 1778.
Fowler, Robert	Fifer	Second, Phillips	March 27, 1778-enlisted; April-June 1778.
Fox, Abraham	Private	Third, Anderson	Dec 1777-Feb 1778.
Fox, Jacob	Private	Third, Gifford	June 7, 1778-joined; June 1778.
Fox, Jacob	Private	Third, Anderson	June 7, 1778-enlisted; June 1778.
Fox, Joseph	Private	Second, Luse	Dec 1777-March 1778; April 5, 1778-taken prisoner
Fox, Pattrick/Patt	Sergeant	Fourth, Kinsey	Dec 1777-Feb 1778-sick absent; April 1778-sick in hospital; May roll shows he deserted in April 1778.
Foy, Daniel	Private	Second, Luse	May 5, 1778-enlisted; June 1778.
Francis, William	Private	Second, Hollingshead	Dec 1777-June 1778.
Frazer/Frasher, George	Private	First, Mead	Dec 1777-June 1778.
Frazy/Frezy, Zebede	Private	Spencer's, Lyon	Muster and payrolls for Sept 1777 show him as having been taken prisoner on Sept 11. May 1778 payroll reads: "Zebede Frazy was left sick at Brandawine the day before the action at that place. Was supposed to have been Prisoner but was sent to Trenton Hospital where he remained till a few days ago when he joined the Regiment." May-June 1778.
Fredenburg - see Vredenburg			
Freeland, John	Private	First, Longstreet	June 4, 1778-joined; June 1778.
Freeland - see Vreeland			

Name	Rank	Company	Service
Freeman, Jedediah	Private	First, Morrison	March-April 1778; May 1778-sick Jersey; June 1778-sick at Newark.
Freeman, John	Private	Third, Ross	Jan-March 1778-sick absent; April 1778-sick in Jersey; May-June 1778-sick absent.
Freeman, Lott	Private	Third, Anderson	Dec 1777-March 1778; April 1778-sick in quarters; May 10, 1778 died.
Freeman, Samuel	Corporal/ Sergeant/ Corporal	First, Baldwin	Dec 1777-sick Jerseys; Jan-Feb 1778-sick Morristown; March-April 1778-sick Jersey; April 1, 1778-promoted to sergeant; May 31, 1778-reduced to corporal; May-June 1778-on command.
Freeze, Jesse	Corporal	Forman's, Burowes	Dec 1777-June 1778.
French, Daniel	Private	Fourth, Anderson	May 28, 1778-enlisted; May-June 1778.
French, Jeremiah	Private	Second, Helms	May 10, 1778-enlisted; June 14, 1778-joined; June 1778.
Fricklin, Robert	Private	Second, Reading	Jan 1778-on command; Feb-June 1778.
Fritch, Daniel	Private	Second, Cummings	Dec 1777; Jan 1778-sick absent; Feb 1, 1778-deserted.
Frizelier/ Friolar, Jacob	Private	First, Longstreet	May 24, 1778-joined; May-June 1778.
Frost, John	Corporal	Fourth, Mitchell	Dec 1777-March 1778; April 1778-sick in camp; May 1778-sick Prince Town Hospital; June 1778.
Fulkerson, Caleb	Fifer	First, Angel	May-June 1778.
Fulkerson, Joseph	Private/ Sergeant	First, Angel	Dec 1777-Feb 1778; March 1778-sick present; April 1778; May 1778-on command; June 1778-promoted to sergeant; June 1778.
Fullen, Joseph	Private	Third, Paterson	Dec 15, 1777-enlisted; January 22, 1778-deserted.
Fullerton, John	Private	Third, Holmes	May 1778 muster roll states: "Deserted June 29 Taken up May 3^d." June 1778-sick absent.
Fullmore/ Fulmore, John	Private	First, Angel	March-April 1778; May 1778-on command; June 1778-on guard.
Funderly, John	Private	Second, Hollingshead	March 20, 1778-enlisted; April-June 1778.
Furey/Fury, James	Private	Second, Hollingshead	Dec 1777-June 1778.
Gale, Alexander	Private	Forman's, Wikoff	Dec 1777-June 1778.

Name	Rank	Company	Service
Gale/Gaile, Joseph	Private/Fifer	Third, Ross	Dec 1777 January 1, 1778-promoted to fifer; Jan 1778; Feb-March 1778-on command; April 1778-command in Jersey; May-June 1778-on command.
Gallaudet, Edgar	1st. Lt.	Third, Gifford	Dec 1777-Feb 1778-sick absent; March 1778-on command; April-June 1778.
Gallaudet, Peter	Private	First, Longstreet	June 4, 1778-joined; June 1778.
Galliher/Galleher, Abraham	Private	Second, Luse	Dec 1777; Jan 1778-sick absent; Feb-March 1778; April 5, 1778-taken prisoner.
Galloway, James	Private	First, Piatt	May 26, 1778-joined; May 1778; June 1778-sick absent.
Gamberton/Gambert, Charles	Sergeant	Fourth, Forman	Dec 1777-Jan 1778; Feb 1778-on furlough; March-June 1778.
Gamble, Robert	Private	Second, Hollingshead	June 1778-on command.
Gardner, Cornelius	Private	First, Morrison	May-June 1778.
Gardner/Gardener, Joseph	Private	Fourth, Forman	Dec 1777-March 1778-sick in hospital; April 1778-sick absent; May 1778-hospital at Reading; June 1778.
Gardner, Thomas	Private	Fourth, Forman	He is only on two payrolls - March 1778-sick in hospital; July 14, 1778-discharged.
Garey/Gary, John	Volunteer	First, Polhemus	He is listed as a volunteer on the muster rolls. The payrolls show him receiving private's pay. Dec 1777-Jan 1778; Feb 1778-furlough; March 1778; April 1778-on command; May-June 1778.
Garlinhouse/Garlinhous, Benjamin	Private	Second, Helms	May 21, 1778-enlisted; June 9, 1778-joined; June 1778-on guard.
Garret/Garrit, John	Private	First, Angel	May 31, 1778-joined; May-June 1778.
Garrison, Benjamin	Private	Second, Cumming	May 20, 1778-enlisted; May 24, 1778-joined; May-June 1778.
Garrison/Garison, Bennet	Corporal	Third, Mott	Dec 1777-Feb 1778; March 1778-on guard; April-May 1778-on command; June 1778.
Garrison, Joel	Private	Third, Paterson	May 29, 1778-enlisted; June 1778.
Garrison, Joseph	Private	Third, Mott	Dec 1777-June 1778.
Garrons/Garens, Thomas	Corporal	Spencer's, Weatherby	Dec 1777-March 1778; April 1778-sick present; May 1778-commissary guard; June 1778.

Name	Rank	Company	Notes
Garrson, Joseph	Private	Fourth, Kinsey	March 1778-deserted.
Garvin, George	Private	Third, Anderson	Feb 1778-in Provost; March-June 1778; April 1778 roll states: "Omited from the 26 June to first of Feby he being prisoner."
Garwood, Samuel	Private	Second, Hollingshead	May 27, 1778-enlisted; June 1778.
Gaskill/Geskill, William	Private	Fourth, Kinsey	Dec 1777-Jan 1778; Feb-April 1778-on Lord Stirling's Guard; May-June 1778.
Gaswright/Gasright, John	Private	Second, Helms	Dec 1777-Jan 1778; Feb 1778-on command; March-April 1778; May 1778-on command; June 1778.
Gathright/Garthwait, Henry	Fifer	Spencer's, Pierson	Dec 1777; Jan-March 1778-on furlough; April 1778; May 1778-sick present; June 1778-on furlough.
Gathright, Garthwait Jeremiah/Jerry	Drummer	Spencer's, Pierson	Dec 1777; Jan-March 1778-on furlough; April-May 1778-sick present; June 1778-on furlough.
Gavin, John	Private	Second, Phillips	May 14, 1778-enlisted; May 28, 1778-joined; May 1778; June 1778-on command.
Gegaung, Jacob	Private	First, Mead	June 1778.
George, John	Private	First, Piatt	Dec 1777; Jan 1778-on command; Feb 1778-on command in Jersey; March-June 1778.
Gerrald/Garrell, John	Private	Fourth, Kinsey	Dec 1777-Jan 1778-sick hospital; Feb-June 1778.
Gibbons/Gibbins, John	Private	Third, Anderson	Dec 1777-March 1778; April 18, 1778-died.
Gibbs/Gibs, John	Private	First, Longstreet	May 26, 1778-joined; May 1778-sick present; June 1778-on command.
Gibs/Jibs, William	Private	First, Mead	Jan 22, 1778-joined; Jan-Feb 1778; March 1778-on command; April 1778; May 1778-on command; June 1778.
Gibson, James	Private	Second, Luse	May 5, 1778-enlisted; June 1778.
Gibson, James	Corporal	Second, Sparks	Dec 1777-sick hospital; Jan-April 1778; May 1778-on command; June 1778.
Gibson, Thomas	Private/Sergeant/Private	Second, Hollingshead	Dec 1, 1777-promoted to sergeant; Dec 1777-May 1778; June 1778-reduced to private, June 1778 sick absent.
Gibson, Thomas	Private	Third, Ross	Dec 1777; Jan 1778-sick absent; Feb 3, 1778-died.

Gibson, Thomas	Private	Third, Gifford	March 1778-April 1778; May 1778-sick at Prince Town Hospital. Payroll for May 1778 shows he enlisted on May 1, this is probably supposed to be March 1. June 1778-sick absent.
Gibson, William	Sergeant	Third, Ross	Dec 1777-Jan 1778; Feb-March 1778-on command; April-June 1778.
Gibson, William	Drummer	Third, Anderson	Dec 1777-June 1778.
Gidiman/ Giddeman, John	Private	First, Polhemus	Dec 1777-May 1778; June 1778-on command.
Giffins/ Githins, Joshua	Private	Fourth, Holmes	Dec 1777-sick present; Jan-May 1778; June 1778-on guard.
Gifford, William	Captain	Third, Gifford	Dec 1777-June 1778. Oath at Valley Forge on May 11, 1778.
Gildersleaves, Asa/Asia	Sergeant	Spencer's, Ward	Dec 1777-Jan 1778; Feb-March 1778-on furlough; April 1778; May 1778-on duty; June 1778-on command as wagon master.
Gill, John	Private	First, Polhemus	June 4, 1778-joined; June 20, 1778-deserted.
Gillaspy, William	Private	Third, Ross	June 1, 1778-joined; June 1778.
Gillings/ Gillins, Patrick	Private	Spencer's, Brittin	Dec 1777-March 1778-sick absent; April 1778-deserted.
Gilmore/ Gelmore, David	Sergeant	Second, Reading	Jan-April 1778; May 1778-on command; June 28, 1778-missing.
Gladhill/ Gladell, Eli	Private	Second, Sparks	Dec 1777-March 1778; April 5, 1778-prisoner; July 17, 1778-exchanged.
Glann/ Glamm, James	Private	Second, Cummings	Dec 1777-June 1778.
Glover, Charles	Private	Third, Cox	Dec 1777-Feb 1778-sick in hospital; March 1778-sick absent; April 1778-sick absent in Jersey; May 1778-supposed to be dead.
Glover, Jacob	Private	Spencer's, Edsall	Dec 1777-Feb 1778; March 1778-sick present; April-June 1778.
Gobell, Samuel	Private	Third, Cox	June 11, 1778-enlisted; June 12, 1778-joined; June 1778.
Goble/Gobel, Stephen	Private	First, Flahavan	Dec 1777-sick in Jersey; Jan 1778-wounded and in Jersey; Feb 1778-wounded now in Jersey; March 1778-sick in Jersey; April 1778-wounded in Jersey; May 1778; June 1778-sick in hospital.

Name	Rank	Company	Notes
Goddard, William	Corporal	Second, Cummings	Dec 1777-March 1778; April 19, 1778-died.
Goggin, Philip	Private	Third, Mott	Dec 1777-Feb 1778; March 1778-on guard; April-May 1778-on command; June 1778.
Golden, Samuel	Private	Second, Hollingshead	May 8, 1778-enlisted; June 1778.
Golder/ Goulden, Joseph	Sergeant	Third, Hennion	Dec 1777-March 1778; April 1778-on guard; May 1778-sick Yellow Springs; June 1778-sick absent.
Golder, Samuel	Private	Second, Hollingshead	June 1778.
Goldsworthy, John	Private	Forman's, Forman	Dec 1777-June 1778.
Goldy, John	Sergeant	Second, Hollingshead	Dec 1777-June 1778.
Goodman, John	Private	First, Mead	June 5, 1778-enlisted; June 1778.
Goodman, William	Private	First, Mead	June 5, 1778-enlisted; June 1778.
Goodman, William	Private	Second, Hollingshead	Dec 1777; Jan 1778-sick in hospital; Feb 1778; March 4, 1778-died at hospital.
Gordon/ Gorden, Baranabus/ Burnades	Private	Spencer's, Maxwell	Dec 1777-March 1778; April-May 1778-on Lord Stirling's guard; June 1778-waiter to Major Barber.
Gordon, David	Private	Third, Ballard	Dec 1777-sick in hospital; Jan-April 1778; May 1778-sick Princetown; June 1778.
Gordon, John	Private	First, Longstreet	June 1778-on command.
Gordon, Michael	Private	First, Longstreet	June 4, 1778-joined; June 1778.
Gordon, William	Private	Forman's, Burowes	Dec 1777-June 1778.
Gore/Goore, James	Private	Second, Helms	Dec 1777-June 1778.
Gouger, Stephen	Drummer	Spencer's, Brodrick	Dec 1777-June 1778.
Grace, John	Fifer	Third, Anderson	Dec 1777-June 1778.
Gracy, Mathew	Private	First, Flahavan	Dec 1777; Jan 1778-sick in hospital; Feb 1778-sick in Jersey hospital; March-April 1778; May 1778-Princeton Hospital; June 1778.

Name	Rank	Company	Notes
Gragg, John	Private	Second, Luse	Feb 1778 payroll shows he enlisted on Jan 1, 1778 and deserted Feb 25. Composite muster roll dated June 12, 1778 shows he enlisted on Feb 1, 1778 and deserted on March 1.
Graham/Grayham, George	Private	Spencer's, Brittin	Dec 1777-Jan 1778; Feb 1778-sick present; March-June 1778.
Graham, Henry	Drummer	Second, Cummings	Dec 1777-April 1778; May 1778-sick absent; June 1778.
Graham, John	Sergeant	Second, Sparks	May 10, 1778-enlisted; June 1778.
Grannan/Grannnon, Thomas	Sergeant	Fourth, Martin	Dec 1777-April 1778-sick in hospital; May 1, 1778-deserted.
Grant, George	Sergeant	Third, Ross	Dec 1777-March 1778; April-May 1778-command at Lord Stirling's; June 1778-on command.
Grant, John	Private	Fourth, Anderson	May 28, 1778-enlisted; May 1778; June 1778-on command.
Gray, Garret	Sergeant	First, Polhemus	Dec 1777-Feb 1778; March 1778-sick present; April 1778-sick in Jersey; May 1778-sick absent; June 1778-sick at B. Brook.
Gray/Grey, Henry	Private	Fourth, Forman	Dec 1777-June 1778.
Gray/Grey, Jacob	Private	Second, Cummings	Dec 1777-April 1778; May 1778-on command; June 1778.
Gray, Lemuel/Lamowil	Private	First, Mead	Dec 1777-sick in hospital; Jan 1778; Feb 1778-at Reading; March-April 1778-sick at Reading; May 1778-sick in Pennsylvania; June 1778-dead.
Gray, Samuel	Private	First, Mead	May 1778-on command; June 1778.
Greatwood/Greatewood, Samuel	Private	Third, Mott	Dec 1777-Feb 1778; March 1778-on guard; April 1778; May 19, 1778-deserted.
Green, John	Private	Third, Hennion	June 7, 1778-joined; June 1778.
Green, Nathaniel	Private	Third, Ballard	June 5, 1778-enlisted; June 1778.
Green, Pierson	Private	Spencer's, Bonnel	Dec 1777-sick Hanover; Jan-May 1778; June 1778-sick Morristown.
Greenwood, Daniel	Private/Sergeant	Fourth, Lyon	Dec 1777-Feb 1778; March 1, 1778-promoted to sergeant; March 1778; April 1778-sick present; May-June 1778-sick Yellow Springs

Name	Rank	Company	Notes
Gregory/ Grigory, Arthur	Private	Spencer's, Ward	Dec 1777-April 1778-on furlough; May 1, 1778-deserted; June 1778-sick Elizabethtown.
Gregory/ Grigory, Thomas	Private	Spencer's, Ward	March 13, 1778-enlisted; April 1778; May 1778-sick in camp; June 1778-Valley Forge sick.
Griffe, Edward	Private	Forman's, Burowes	Dec 1777-April 1778; May 1778-sick at Barnegat; June 1778.
Griffen, William	Private	Third, Anderson	May 1778 payroll shows he was taken prisoner on September 11, 1777 at Brandywine and exchanged on July 14, 1778; July 1778 muster roll shows he was exchanged on July 14.
Griffeth, Joseph	Private	Forman's, Burowes	Dec 1777-June 1778.
Grifffie/ Griffa, Levi	Private	Second, Helms	March-April 1778; May 1778-sick present; June 1778 sick absent.
Griffith/ Griffie, William	Private	Fourth, Kinsey	Dec 1777-March 1778; April-May 1778-on command; June 1778.
Griffy, Daniel	Private	Second, Reading	Jan-June 1778.
Grigg, Robert	Private	Second, Hollingshead	March 30, 1778-enlisted; April-June 1778.
Griggs/Grigg, Daniel	Private	First, Longstreet	Dec 1777-Feb 1778; March 1778-command at the lines; April-May 1778-on command; June 1778.
Griggs, William	Private	Second, Reading	Jan-April 1778; May 1778-on command; June 1778.
Grimes/ Grames, George	Private	Fourth, Martin	Dec 24, 1777-deserted.
Grimes/ Graham, John	Sergeant	Second, Sparks	May 10, 1778-enlisted; June 1778.
Grimes/ Graham, Moses	Private	Third, Anderson	Dec 1777-March 1778; April 30, 1778-deserted.
Grimes, Sheperd	Private	Second, Phillips	May 8, 1778-enlisted; May 28, 1778-joined; May 1778; June 1778-on command.
Groteelas/ Groteclass, Gilbert	Private	Spencer's, Lyon	March 1778-sick present; May 1778-on guard; June 1778-on Commissary guard.
Grubb, Edward	Private	Second, Luse	March 4, 1778-enlisted; May 1778 muster roll shows he deserted on May 15, but the May payroll shows May 24 as the desertion date.

Name	Rank	Company	Service
Grummond, John	Private	First, Angel	May 27, 1778-joined; May-June 1778.
Guard, Daniel	Private	Third, Ballard	Dec 1777-sick in hospital; Jan-Feb 1778-sick in Jersey; March 1778-sick absent; April 1778-sick in Jersey; May 1778-on command at lines; June 1778-sick Morristown.
Guinnip/ Guinop, George	Corporal	Second, Luse	Feb 26, 1778-enlisted; March-June 1778.
Guinup/ Grunrip, Benjamin	Private	Fourth, Martin	Dec 1777-May 1778; June 1778-on guard.
Gunen, Hugh	Private	Second, Helms	May 15, 1778-enlisted; June 10, 1778-joined; June 1778.
Gunning, Richard	Private	Third, Cox	Dec 1777-Feb 1778; March 1778-on furlough; April-June 1778.
Gurrel/ Gurrell, John	Drummer/ Private	Fourth, Holmes	Dec 1777-March 1778; April 1, 1778-reduced to private; April-May 1778; June 1778-on guard.
Guttery, John	Private	First, Angel	Dec 1777-sick absent; Jan 1778-deserted from sick quarters.
Guy, John	Private	Third, Ross	Dec 1777-April 1778; May 1778-on command; June 1778.
Hackett, Jeremiah	Private	Third, Anderson	June 7, 1778-enlisted; June 1778.
Hackett/ Hackel, Joshua	Private	Fourth, Kinsey	March 11, 1778-enlisted; March 31, 1778-joined; March 1778; April 1778-sick present; May-June 1778.
Hackett/ Hacket, Patrick	Private	Fourth, Forman	Dec 1777-June 1778.
Hain, Francis	Private	First, Baldwin	Jan 14, 1778-enlisted; Feb 9, 1778-deserted.
Haines/Hains, Daniel	Private/ Corporal	Second, Hollingshead	Dec 1777-Feb 1778; March 1, 1778-promoted to corporal; March-June 1778.
Haines/Hinds, John	Private	Third, Mott	Dec 1777-April 1778; May 1778-on command; June 1778.
Haines/Hains, William	Private	Third, Mott	Dec 1777-April 1778; May 1778-on command; June 1778.
Hains/Haynes, Joseph	Private	Fourth, Lyon	Dec 1777-Feb 1778-sick absent; March 1778; April 1778-sick [ ] hospital; May 1778-on guard; June 1778.
Halbrook/ Hallbrook William	Sergeant	First, Piatt	Dec 1777-March 1778; April 1778-on picket guard; May 1778; June 1778-under guard.
Haldron, Henry	Private	Second, Helms	May 17, 1778-enlisted; June 17, 1778-joined; June 1778.

Name	Rank	Company	Notes
Halfey, William	Private	First, Baldwin	June 1778.
Halfpenny, Thomas	Private	First, Polhemus	Dec 1777-sick absent; Jan 1778; Feb-March 1778-sick Jersey; April 1778; May 1778-guard; June 1778.
Hall, George	Private/ Sergeant	First, Baldwin	Dec 1777; Jan 1778-promoted to sergeant; Jan 1778; Feb 1778-on furlough; March 1778-on command; April-May 1778; June 1778-on command.
Hall, Jacob	Private	Fourth, Lyon	June 1, 1778-joined; June 1778-on guard.
Hall, James	Private	Second, Bowman	Dec 1777-June 1778.
Hall, Nathaniel/ Nathan	Private	First, Baldwin	Dec 1777-Feb 1778; March-April 1778-sick present; May-June 1778-on furlough.
Hall, Seth	Private	First, Baldwin	June 1778.
Hall, William	Private	Third, Paterson	June 1778-on guard.
Hallarway, Elkany	Private	Third, Ballard	June 5, 1778-enlisted; June 1778.
Halsey, Luther	Adjutant	Second	Dec 1777-June 1778.
Halstead, Josiah	Private	First, Polhemus	June 4, 1778-joined; June 28, 1778-missing.
Hambler, John	Private	Second, Luse	May 6, 1778-enlisted; June 1778.
Hambleton/ Hamilton, James	Private	Second, Hollingshead	Muster roll for Dec 1777 shows he joined on Dec 20, 1777. Dec payroll states: "Taken 26 June Short Hills Joined 16 Decr. 1777." Jan 1778 muster roll shows he joined on Jan 20. Jan 1778-on furlough; Feb-June 1778.
Hambleton, William	Private	Third, Ballard	June 5, 1778-enlisted; June 1778-"Riding for the General."
Hamilton/ Hambleton, Andrew	Private	First, Polhemus	May 1, 1778-joined; May 1778; June 1778-wagoner.
Hamilton, Benjamin	Private	First, Flahavan	June 1778.
Hamilton, James	Private	Second, Bowman	Dec 1777-March 1778; April 20, 1778-deserted.
Hamilton, Thomas	Corporal	Second, Sparks	Dec 1777-April 1778; May-June 1778-sick absent.
Hamilton, William	Quartermaster Sergeant	First	March 1, 1778-appointed quartermaster sergeant; March 1778; April 1778-on furlough; May-June 1778.

Name	Rank	Regiment	Notes
Hammitt/ Hamit, John	1st. Lt.	Spencer's, Pierson	Dec 1777-June 1778. Oath at Valley Forge on May 11, 1778.
Hammon, Ezra	Corporal	First, Piatt	Dec 1777-March 1778; April 1778-on picket guard; May-June 1778.
Hampton, John	Private	Third, Paterson	May 1778; June 1778-on guard.
Hamstead, Robert	Private	First, Mead	May-June 1778.
Hance/Hanse, John	Private	Fourth, Forman	Dec 1777-Feb 1778-sick hospital; March-April 1778; May 1778-on command; June 1778.
Hancock, Andrew	Private	Fourth, Holmes	Dec 1777-Feb 1778-hospital; March 1778-sick in hospital; April 1778-deserted.
Hancocks - see Cox, Hance			
Hand, Constantine	Private	Second, Cummings	May 20, 1778-enlisted; May 24, 1778-joined; May-June 1778.
Hand, Cornelius	Private	Second, Cummings	May 27, 1778-joined; May-June 1778.
Hand, Eliaser	Private	Second, Cummings	May 20, 1778-enlisted; May 27, 1778-joined; May-June 1778.
Handley/ Handly, Richard	Private	Third, Paterson	Dec 1777-Feb 1778; March 1778-on furlough; April-May 1778; June 1778-sick absent.
Hankins, Joseph	Private	First, Polhemus	June 4, 1778-joined; June 1778-sick Monmouth.
Hansman/ Hinsman, Henry	Private	Second, Reading	May 1, 1778-enlisted and joined, May 1778; June 26, 1778-missing.
Hardcastle, John	Sergeant	Fourth, Mitchell	Dec 1777-March 1778; April 1778-sick in camp; May 1778-sick Yellow Springs; June 1778.
Hardenbrook, William	Private	First, Morrison	May-June 1778.
Harder, Simon	Private	First, Piatt	Dec 1777; Jan-April 1778-sick in Jersey.
Harding, John	Private	Third, Mott	Dec 1777-March 1778; April 1778-on command; May 1778-sick absent; June 1778-sick at Yellow Springs.
Harker, Abraham	Private	Second, Cummings	May 20, 1778-enlisted; June 1778.
Harker, Nathan	Private	First, Angel	June 1778.
Harker, Joseph	1st. Lt.	Fourth, Lyon	Dec 1777; Jan 1778-absent without leave.
Harlin, Thomas	Private	Third, Anderson	Dec 1777-Jan 1778; Feb 20, 1778-died.

Name	Rank	Company	Notes
Harper, William	Private	Third, Cox	May 1, 1778-joined; May 1778-on command at ye lines; June 1778-on command.
Harriman/ Harreman, Stephen	Sergeant	Fourth, Mitchell	Dec 1777-Feb 1778; March 1778-General Maxwell's Guard; April 1778; May 1778-sick Yellow Springs; June 1778-sick hospital.
Harriott, William	Private	Fourth, Kinsey	April 1778.
Harris, Jacob	Surgeon's Mate	Fourth	Dec 1777-Jan 1778; Feb 1778-on furlough; March-June 1778. Oath at Valley Forge on May 11, 1778.
Harris, John	Sergeant	First, Piatt	Dec 8, 1777-deserted.
Harris, Samuel	Private	Fourth, Forman	May 20, 1778-joined; May 1778; June 1778-sick hospital.
Harris, Walter	Drummer	Second, Sparks	May 10, 1778-enlisted; June 1778.
Harris, William	Private	First, Morrison	Dec 1777-March 1778; April 1778-sick Pennsylvania; May 1778-sick Jersey; June 1778-sick at Quibbletown.
Harris, William	Private	Second, Helms	May 4, 1778-enlisted; June 28, 1778-joined, June 1778-on guard.
Harrison, Isaac	Private	First, Morrison	May 1778-with blacksmiths; June 1778.
Harrison, William	Major	Forman's	Dec 1777-June 1778.
Harrod/ Harrot, James	Private	Fourth, Martin	Dec 1777-sick in hospital; Jan 1778-sick absent; Feb 1778-sick in hospital; March 1778-sick absent.
Hart/Dehart, Cyrus D.	1st. Lt./ Paymaster	First, Flahavan	Dec 1777-on furlough; Jan-April 1778; April 22, 1778-appointed paymaster; May-June 1778.
Hart, Jacob	Cadet	First, Flahavan	Dec 1777-June 1778.
Hart, Patrick	Private	Fourth, Martin	Dec 1777-deserted; April 1778-sick present; May 1778; June 1778-on guard.
Hart, William D.	Lt. Col.	First	Dec 1777; Jan 1778-on command; Feb-June 1778.
Hartman, Michael	Private	First, Morrison	May-June 1778.
Hartwick/ Hortwick, Baunt/Burnt	Private	First, Longstreet	May 24, 1778-joined; May-June 1778.

Name	Rank	Company	Notes
Harvey/ Hervey, Isaac	Private	First, Brittin	Dec 1777-Jan 1778-sick absent. Feb 1778 payroll states he was left sick at the Clove on June 20, 1777 "and has Never been heard of Since till Last week and it is Said that he is gone to the Enemy."
Hasbrook/ Hosebrooke, John	Corporal	First, Baldwin	Dec 1777-Feb 1778-sick Morristown; March-April 1778-sick Jersey; May 1778; June 1778-sick absent.
Hatfield/ Hetfield, Stephen	Drummer	Fourth, Lyon	Dec 1777-May 1778; June 1778-sick hospital.
Hathaway, Phillip	Private	Fourth, Mitchell	Dec 1777-March 1778; April 12, 1778-deserted.
Hathaway/ Hatheraway, Theophilus/ Theofilas	Private	Third, Ballard	Dec 1777-Feb 1778-sick at the hospital; March 1778; April 1778-on picket; May 1778; June 1778-on weeks command.
Hatter, John	Private	First, Mead	Dec 26, 1777-enlisted; Jan 1778-deserted.
Hawkins, John	Private	Second, Cummings	Dec 1777-April 1778; May 1778-on command; June 1778.
Hawkins, John	Corporal	Spencer's, Combs	Dec 1777-June 1778.
Hawkins/ Hawkings, William	Private	Third, Hennion	Dec 1777-June 1778.
Haycock/ Heycock, Daniel	Private	Spencer's, Brittin	Dec 1777-Jan 1778; Feb 1778-on command; March-April 1778; May 1778-on duty; June 1778.
Hayes, David	Private	Fourth, Mitchell	June 1778.
Hayes, Dennis	Private	First, Morrison	Feb 14, 1778 enlisted, "but sick till 14 July" according to the June 1778 payroll.
Hayes, Joseph	Private	Forman's, Burowes	Dec 1777-June 1778.
Hayley, Hugh	Private	Fourth, Martin	Aug 15, 1777-deserted; March 27, 1778-joined, March 1778 on guard; April 1778; May 1778-on command; June 1778.
Hayman/ Haman, William	Private	Third, Hennion	Dec 1777; Jan 1778-sick absent; Feb-June 1778.
Hayning/ Hannin, George	Private	Fourth, Martin	Dec 1777-Feb 1778; March 1778-on command; April 1778; May 1778-sick present; June 1778-Yellow Springs.

Hays, James	Private	Third, Gifford	June 26, 1778-joined; June 1778.
Hays, John	Private	Second, Hollingshead	Dec 1777-May 1778; June 1778-on command.
Hays/Haze, Michael	Private	First, Mead	Dec 15, 1778-joined; Dec 1777; Jan 1778-sick in Jersey; Feb 1778-deserted; March-April 1778: May 1778-confined; June 1778.
Hays/Hase, Timothy	Private	Third, Mott	April-June 1778.
Hazleton, Abraham/ Abram	Private	Third, Mott	Dec 1777; Jan 1778; Feb-March 1778-sick absent; April 1778-wagoner. April 1778 payroll states he "has bin Neglected in the pay Roll for this seven Months which pay is now Due him as he was prisoner for that space of time." May 1778; June 1778-refiner.
Headley, Moses	Private	First, Baldwin	June 1778-sick absent.
Hebbard/ Hibbard, Eliphalet	Private	Fourth, Anderson	Dec 1777-June 1778.
Hecher - see Ketcher			
Hedges, Joseph	Private	Spencer's, Ward	Dec 1777-March 1778; April 1778-sick hospital Yellow Springs; May 1778-sick French Creek; June 1778-Yellow Springs sick.
Hedges/ Hegges, Nathan	Private	First, Baldwin	Dec 1777-sick Pennsylvania; Jan 1778-sick general hospital; Feb 1778-sick absent; March-April 1778-sick in Jersey; May 1778-sick Morris County; June 1778-sick absent.
Hedrick, John	Private	Third, Ross	June 1, 1778-joined; June 1778-on guard.
Hefener/ Hepner, John	Private	Third, Anderson	Dec 1777; Jan-Feb 1778-wounded absent; March 1778; April 1778 wounded absent Jersey; May 1778-wounded absent Salem; June 1778-wounded absent.
Hegathy/ Hagarthy	Private	Spencer's, Pierson	Dec 1777-Jan 1778; Feb-April 1778-sick present; May-June 1778.
Helmes, Job	Private	Forman's, Wikoff	Dec 1777-April 1778; May 1778-sick at Yellow Springs; June 1778.
Helms, William	Captain	Second, Helms	Jan-June 1778.
Henderson, Isaac	Private	Forman's, Forman	Dec 1777-June 1778.

Name	Rank	Company	Notes
Henderson/Handerson, John	Private	Spencer's, Wilkins	Dec 26, 1777-deserted or taken.
Henderson, Patrick	Private	Fourth, Forman	Dec 1777-Feb 1778; March-April 1778-on furlough; May 1778-on command; June 1778-on guard.
Henderson, William	Sergeant	Fourth, Holmes	Dec 1777-Jan 1778-hospital; Feb 1778-dead.
Hendrickson, John	Private	Forman's, Burowes	Dec 1777-April 1778.
Hendry, Samuel	1st. Lt.	Second, Hollingshead	Dec 1777-June 1778.
Hennion, Cornelius	Captain	Third, Hennion	Dec 1777-absent wounded; Jan 1778; Feb-March 1778-absent wounded; April 1, 1778-resigned. Captain Gifford commanded this company April-June 1778.
Henry, John	Private	Fourth, Anderson	Dec 1777-Feb 1777-sick in hospital; March 1778-deserted.
Henry/Hennery, Joseph	Corporal	First, Angel	Dec 1777-Jan 1778; Feb 1778-on furlough; March 7, 1778-deserted.
Hewitt/Hewit, Benajah	Corporal	Second, Cummings	Dec 1777; Jan 1778-on command; Feb-June 1778.
Hichler/Hiler, Henry	Private	Spencer's, Weatherby	Dec 1777; Jan 1778-waiter; Feb-March 1778-on command; April 1778-deserted; May 22, 1778-deserted.
Hickey/Hicky, John	Private	Second, Helms	Dec 1777; Jan 1778-sick absent; Feb-March 1778; April 5, 1778-taken prisoner.
Hicks, James	Private	First, Baldwin	May 1778; June 1778-sick present.
Hickson, Jonathan	Private	Second, Luse	Dec 3, 1777-deserted; Feb-June 1778.
Hickson, Mathew	Private	Second, Reading	Jan 1778-sick absent; Feb 1, 1778-deserted.
Higgins, John	Private	Third, Ross	Dec 1777-Feb 1778; March 1778-on guard; April 1778-on command; May-June 1778.
Higgins/Heagins, Michael	Private	First, Baldwin	Dec 1777-command at Reading; Jan-April 1778-sick in Jersey; May 1778-sick at Elizabethtown; June 1778-on command.
Higgins, Timothy	Private	Spencer's, Brittin	Dec 1777-March 1778-on command; April 1778-sick Jersey; May 1, 1778-discharged.
Hill, James	Fifer	Fourth, Kinsey	Dec 15, 1777-deserted.

58

Hill, John	Sergeant	Third, Ballard	Dec 1777-Feb 1778; March 1778-on furlough; April 1778; May 1778-sick at Yellow Springs; June 1778-sick at Reading.
Hill, Martin	Sergeant	Second, Phillips	Dec 1777-June 1778.
Hill/Hillin, Samuel	Private	First, Angel	Jan-Feb 1778; March 1778-sick present; April-May 1778; June 1778-on command.
Hillebrant/ Hillabrant, Henry	Private	Second, Sparks	March-June 1778.
Hilliard/ Hillyard, Thomas	Private	Third, Gifford	Dec 1777-June 1778.
Hillin/ Hilaman, Henry	Private	Fourth, Martin	Dec 1777; Jan 1778-on command; Feb 1778; March 1778-on command.; April-May 1778; June 1778-on command.
Hillsey/ Helsey, Joseph	Private	Fourth, Forman	Dec 1777-March 1778; April 1778-sick present; May-June 1778-sick in hospital.
Hinds, Dennis	Private/ Sergeant	Fourth, Kinsey	Dec 1777-Jan 1778; Feb 17, 1778-promoted to sergeant; Feb-June 1778.
Hinds, Jarmieh	Private	Fourth, Kinsey	March 1778-deserted.
Hinds/Hines, John	Private	Fourth, Kinsey	Oct 1777-deserted; April 1778-on command; May 1778.
Hinkle, Jacob	Private	Second, Luse	May 6, 1778-enlisted; June 1778.
Hite/Hoyte, Christopher	Private	Spencer's, Wilkins/ Edsall	Dec 1777-June 1778. In May he transferred to Edsall's Co.
Hixon, Amos	Sergeant	Fourth, Forman	Dec 1777-Jan 1778; Feb 1778-discharged.
Hixon/ Hickson, James	Private	Third, Ballard	May 28, 1778-enlisted; May-June 1778.
Hixon/ Hickson, John	Private	Third, Ballard	May 28, 1778-enlisted; May-June 1778.
Hixon/ Hickson, Joseph	Private	Third, Ballard	May 28, 1778-enlisted; May-June 1778.
Hoagland, Abraham	Private	First, Angel	May 31, 1778-joined; May 1778-on command; June 1778.
Hoagland/ Hogland, John	Private	First, Angel	May 31, 1778-joined; May 1778; June 1778-on command.
Hoagland/ Hougland, John	Private	First, Flahavan	May-June 1778.

Name	Rank	Company	Service
Hobble, George	Private	Fourth, Forman	Dec 1777-Feb 1778; March 1778-on command; April-May 1778; June 1778-on guard.
Hobbs, Elisha	Private	Third, Hennion	March 17, 1778-enlisted; April 1778; May 1778-on command; June 1778-on guard.
Hockingbury, John	Private	Third, Ballard	June 6, 1778-enlisted; June 1778.
Hofman, John	Private	Spencer's, Lyon	Jan 25, 1778-died.
Hogancamp/Hovencamp, John	Private	Spencer's, Brittin	Dec 1777-March 1778-sick hospital; April 1, 1778-died.
Holcomb/Oakham, Elijah	Sergeant	Fourth, Anderson	May 25, 1778-joined; May-June 1778.
Holden, Benjamin	Private	Third, Ross	May 1778-joined; May-June 1778.
Holdin, Benjamin	Private	Second, Phillips	May 22, 1778-enlisted; June 1, 1778-joined; June 1778.
Holdron, Henry	Private	Second, Helms	May 17, 1778-enlisted; June 14, 1778-joined; June 1778.
Holiday/Holyday, James	Private	Spencer's, Brittin	Dec 1777-Jan 1778; Feb 1778-sick present; March-June 1778.
Holland, Jeremiah	Private	Second, Sparks	Dec 1777-April 1778; May 1778-wagoner; June 1778-on command.
Holland, Thomas	Private	Third, Ross	Dec 1777; Jan 1778-sick in Huts; Feb 1778; March-April 1778; on guard; May 1778-on furlough; June 1778-on guard.
Hollinshead, John	Captain	Second, Hollingshead	Dec 1777-June 1778.
Holmes, James	Sergeant	First, Piatt	Dec 1777-Feb 1778; March 1778-sick in camp; April-June 1778.
Holmes, James	Captain	Fourth, Holmes	Dec 1777-Feb 1778; March 17, 1778-resigned. March 1778 payroll shows he resigned on March 18.
Holmes, John	1st. Lt.	First, Polhemus	Dec 1777-on command to the Jerseys; Jan-June 1778.
Holmes/Homes, William	Private	Second, Reading	May 1, 1778-enlisted and joined; May-June 1778; July 10, 1778-deserted.
Holt, Daniel	Corporal	Second, Helms	May 12, 1778-enlisted; June 7, 1778-joined; June 1778.
Hood, William	Sergeant	Third, Anderson	Dec 1777-June 1778.
Hooey/Hosey, John	Private	Second, Luse	Dec 1777-sick at hospital; Jan 1778-sick absent; Feb-June 1778.

Name	Rank	Company	Service
Hoping/Hopping, Abraham	Private	Spencer's, Lyon	Dec 1777-sick in Country; Jan-April 1778; May 1778-on guard; June 1778.
Hopkins, John	Private	First, Morrison	Dec 1777; Jan 1778-sick in hospital; Feb 1778-sick absent; March 1778-sick in Jersey; April 1778-deserted.
Hopper, Henry	Private	Third, Gifford	December 1777-wounded absent; Jan 4, 1778-died.
Hopsaker/Hopsiker, Powlis	Private	First, Polhemus	Dec 1777-Feb 1778; March-April 1778-on command; May-June 1778.
Hopson, Jordan	Corporal/Sergeant	Second, Helms	Dec 1777-May 1778; June 1, 1778-promoted to sergeant; June 1778.
Horine, Solomon	Drummer	First, Polhemus	Dec 1777-prisoner in Philadelphia.
Horkingbury, John	Private	Fourth, Ballard	June 6, 1778-enlisted; June 1778.
Horn/Horne, Benjamin	2nd. Lt.	Fourth, Mitchell	Dec 1777-on furlough; Jan-June 1778. Oath at Valley Forge on May 11, 1778.
Horn, Benjamin	Private	Second, Reading	Jan-June 1778.
Horn/Horne, James	Private	Third, Gifford	Dec 1777-Jan 1778; Feb 1778-on furlough; March-June 1778.
Horn/Horne, Moses	Private	First, Angel	March-April 1778; May 1778-on command; June 1778-on guard.
Horn, Ralph	Private	Fourth, Anderson	Dec 1777; Jan 1778-on command.
Horn, Thomas	Private	First, Piatt	March 14, 1778-enlisted; April 19, 1778-deserted.
Hornbaker, Phillip	Private	First, Helms	May 9, 1778-enlisted; June 26, 1778-joined; June 1778.
Hornblower/Horenblower, Joseph	Private	First, Mead	Jan 26, 1778-enlisted and joined; Jan-March 1778; April 1778-sick present; May 1778-sick in Pennsylvania; June 1778.
Horneford/Hornaford, Andrew	Private	Fourth, Martin	Dec 1777-March 1778-sick absent; April 1778-on furlough; April 30, 1778-deserted; May 1778-on guard; June 1778-sick hospital.
Hortwick, Barnabas	Private/Fifer	Second, Bowman	Dec 1777-Feb 1778; March 1, 1778-promoted to fifer; March-April 1778; May 1778-sick absent; June 1778.
Hortwick, Mathias	Private	Second, Bowman	Dec 1777-April 1778; May 1778-sick absent; June 1778.
Hoskins, John	Drummer	Forman's, Wikoff	Dec 1777-June 1778.
Hottman/Hotman, George	Private	Third, Anderson	Dec 1777-June 1778.

Name	Rank	Company	Notes
Hough, John	Private	Second, Hollingshead	March 5, 1778-enlisted; April 1778; May-June 1778-sick in the hospital.
Houseman, Matthew	Private	First, Morrison	Dec 1777; Jan 1778-discharged.
Howard, Benjamin	Corporal	Spencer's, Ward	Dec 1777-Jan 1778; Feb-May 1778-on furlough; June 1, 1778-deserted.
Howard, Elihu	Private	Third, Cox	June 5, 1778-joined, June 1778.
Howard, Ephraim	Drummer	Fourth, Forman	Dec 1777-March 1778; April 1778-on command; May-June 1778.
Howard, Ephraim	Private	Fourth, Forman	June 5, 1778-joined; June 1778.
Howard, Ezekiel	Private	First, Flahavan	Dec 1777-Feb 1778; March 1778-command; April 1778; May 1778-on guard; June 1778-on guard.
Howard, John	Private	Third, Ross	Dec 1777; Jan-March 1778-sick absent; April 1778-sick in Jersey; May-June 1778-sick absent; July 30, 1778-deserted.
Howard, Joseph	Private	First, Baldwin	Dec 1777-April 1778; May 1778-sick present; June 1778.
Howard, Joseph	Corporal/ Sergeant	Fourth, Forman	Dec 1777-sick in hospital; Jan-March 1778; Feb 1778 muster roll shows he was promoted to sergeant on Feb 19; March 1778 muster roll shows he was promoted on March 1; April 1778-on guard; May 1778; June 1778-on guard.
Howe/How, John	Sergeant Major	Third	Dec 1777-Feb 1778; March 1778-on furlough; April 1778; May-June 1778-sick absent.
Howell/ Howard, Benjamin	Private	First, Morrison	May 27, 1778-joined; May 1778; June 1778-picket.
Howell/ Howel, Edward	Corporal	Third, Ross	Dec 1777-March 1778; April-June 1778-"prisoner with ye enemy." However payroll for April 1778 shows him as "since returned."
Howell/ Howel, John	1st. Lt.	First, Mead	Dec 1777-Feb 1778; March 1778-on command; April 1778; May 1778-on command; June 1778.
Howell, Jonathan	Private	First, Morrison	Dec 1777.
Howell/ Howel, Jonathan	Private	Third, Paterson	Dec 1777; Jan 1778-on command; Feb-April 1778; May-June 1778-sick absent.
Howell, Lewis	Surgeon	Second	Dec 1777-May 1778. June 1778 muster roll shows he died on June 5, but July payroll shows he died on July 5.

Name	Rank	Regiment	Notes
Howell, Richard	Major	Second	Dec 1777-May 1778; June 1778-sick absent. He was grandfather of Jefferson Davis's wife Varina.
Howell/Howel, Thomas	Private	Third, Ross	May 25, 1778-joined; May-June 1778.
Howel/Howall, William	Private	Fourth, Kinsey	March 1, 1778-enlisted; March 31, 1778-joined; March-May 1778; June 1778-sick hospital.
Hubble/Hubbil, John	Private	First, Piatt	Dec 1777-Jan 1778; Feb 1778-on command in Jersey; March-May 1778; June 1778-prisoner.
Hubbs, David	Private	First, Longstreet	June 4, 1778-joined; June 1778.
Hubs, Jonathan	Private	First, Mead	June 5, 1778-joined; June 1778-picket.
Huch/Hutch, John	Private	Fourth, Lyon	December 1777-sick absent. Jan 1778 muster roll and payroll show he deserted on January 25; Feb 1778 muster roll shows he deserted on January 21; March 28, 1778-joined; April 1778; May 1778-sick Yellow Springs; June 1778.
Hudson, Abraham/Abram	Sergeant	Fourth, Mitchell	Dec 1777-Feb 1778; March 1778-on furlough; April 1778-sick at Morristown; May-June 1778.
Hueston, John	Private	Second, Cummings	May 20, 1778-enlisted; June 1778.
Huffman/Hoopman, Huah	Private	Spencer's, Lyon	Dec 1777. Jan 1778 muster roll shows he died on Jan 29, but the Jan payroll shows he died on Jan 23.
Hughs, Dominick/Dom	Private	Fourth, Mitchell	Dec 1777-Feb 1778; March 1778-waiter at the Surgeon General's; April 1778-at the Surgeon General's; May-June 1778.
Hulett, Charles	Drummer	First, Morrison	May 27, 1778-joined; May-June 1778.
Hull, Benjamin	Corporal	Fourth, Forman	Dec 1777-March 1778; April 12, 1778-deserted.
Hull, Isaac	Private	Second, Luse	May 10, 1778-enlisted; June 1778-sick absent.
Hull, Johiel	Drummer	Spencer's, Brittin	Dec 1777-on furlough; Jan 1778-sick absent; Feb 1778; March 1778-sick present; April 1778; May 1, 1778-taken as a substitute Jersey Brigade. The man listed below is probably the same individual.
Hull, Johial/Johiel	Drummer	Third, Paterson	May-June 1778.

64

Hull, John	Private	Spencer's, Edsall		Dec 1, 1777-discharged.
Hull, Stille	Sergeant	Spencer's, Edsall		Dec 1777-Feb 1778; March 1778-sick present; April 5, 1778-died.
Humphreys/ Humphries, Joseph	Private	Fourth, Anderson		Dec 1777-May 1778; June 1778-on guard.
Hunt, James	Private	Second, Luse		Dec 1777; Jan 1778-sick absent; Feb-June 1778.
Hunt, Josiah	Private	Spencer's, Brittin		Dec 1777-sick hospital; Jan 1778-on furlough; Feb-May 1778; June 1778-on furlough.
Hunter, Andrew (Rev.)	Chaplain	Fourth		Dec 1777; Jan 1778-on furlough; Feb 1778-April 1778; May 1778-on furlough. Oath at Valley Forge on May 11, 1778.
Hunter, Herman	Private	Fourth, Anderson		Dec 1777; Jan-Feb 1778-absent without leave; March 1778-deserted; April 1778-sick in camp; May 1778-sick absent; June 1778.
Hunter, Joseph	Private	Third, Ross		Dec 1777; Jan 29, 1778-dead.
Huntingdon, Gilbert	Private	Third, Cox		June 1, 1778 enlisted; June 5, 1778-joined; June 1778.
Huston/ Houston, James	Private	Spencer's, Edsall		Dec 1777-Jan 1778; Feb 1778-sick present; March 1778-sick in the country; April 1778-in Ephrata Hospital; May-1778-Ephrata Hospital; June 1778-[ ].
Hutchins/ Hutchin, John	2nd. Lt./ 1st. Lt.	Second, Bowman/ Sparks		Dec 1777 in Bowman's Co. Jan 1, 1778-promoted to 1st. Lt. and moved to Sparks' Co.; Jan 1778-on furlough; Feb-March 1778; April 5, 1778-taken prisoner.
Hutchings, Gabriel	Private	Fourth, Mitchell		Jan 12, 1777-deserted; April 1778; May 1778-sick Yellow Springs; June 1778.
Hutchison, William	Private	Fourth, Anderson		May 28, 1778-enlisted; May 1778.
Hyler, Henry	Private	Spencer's, Weatherby		Jan 1778-waiter; Feb-April 1778-on command; May 22, 1778-deserted.
Hynds/Hinds, Peter	Drummer	Fourth, Martin		Dec 1777-March 1778; April 1778-sick present; May-June 1778.
Hyner, Frederick	Private	First, Baldwin		June 1778.
Hynoll, Thomas	Private	Forman's, Combs		Dec 1777-June 1778.
Imlay, Gilbert	1st. Lt./ Paymaster	Forman's, Burowes		Dec 1777-May 1778; June 1778-promoted to paymaster.

Name	Rank	Regiment/Company	Service
Incell/Insell, Daniel	Private	Fourth, Holmes	Dec 1777-Feb 1778-hospital; March 1778-sick in hospital; April 1778-deserted.
Ink, John	Private	Third, Cox	Dec 1777; Jan 1778-on command; Feb 1778; March 1778-deserted.
Innis, Robert	Private	Fourth, Anderson	May 28, 1778-enlisted; May-June 1778.
Insell, John	Private	Second, Cummings	Dec 1777-April 1778; May 1778-on command; June 1778.
Ireland, John	Sergeant	Second, Cummings	Dec 1777-April 1778; May 1778-on furlough; June 1778.
Ireland, Joseph	Private	Second, Hollingshead	Dec 1777-April 1778; May 1778-on furlough; June 1, 1778-deserted.
Ireland, Thomas	Corporal/Sergeant	Third, Gifford	Dec 1777-June 1778; July 1, 1778 promoted to sergeant.
Irwin, James	Private	Second, Phillips	May 22, 1778-enlisted; May 28, 1778-joined; May 1778; June 1778-on command.
Irwin/Irwen, William	Private	Fourth, Kinsey	May 1778.
Isalington, Jonathan	Private	First, Longstreet	June 4, 1778-joined; June 1778.
Jackes/Jacks, Thomas	Sergeant	Spencer's, Lyon	Dec 1777-Jan 1778; Feb 1778-sick camp; March-May 1778; June 1778-on furlough.
Jackson, Daniel	Private	Second, Cummings	Dec 1777; Jan 1778-sick absent; Feb 7, 1778-dead.
Jackson, George	Ensign	Forman's, Combs	Dec 1777; Jan 7, 1778-resigned.
Jackson, Richard	Private	First, Angel	Dec 1777-on furlough. Jan-April 1778; May 1778-sick at Princeton; June 1778-sick absent.
Jacobson/Jacobeson, Henry	Private	First, Morrison	May-June 1778.
James, David	Private	Second, Cummings	Dec 1777-June 1778.
Jameson, Andrew	Private	First, Polhemus	June 4, 1778-joined; June 27, 1778-deserted.
Jay, Joseph	2nd. Lt.	First, Baldwin	Dec 1777 and Feb 1778-absent without leave. On June 1778 payroll he is paid for two months and 28 days, beginning on March 1.
Jeffrey, Humphrey	Private	Forman's, Burowes	Dec 1777-April 1778; May 1778-on command; June 1778.
Jenkins, Ezekiel	Private	First, Piatt	June 1778.

Jenkins, Nathaniel	2nd. Lt./ 1st. Lt.	Second, Cummings	Dec 1777; Jan 1778-promoted to 1st. Lt.; Jan 1778 on furlough; Feb-June 1778.
Jennings, John	Private	First, Mead	June 1778.
Jennings/ Ginnengs, William	Corporal	Spencer's, Brittin	Dec 1777-Jan 1778-on furlough; Feb-March 1778-sick absent; April 1778-sick [ ]; May-June 1778-sick Newark.
Jesper, Richard	Private	First, Flahavan	May 25, 1778-joined; May 1778; June 1778-prisoner.
Jewell, Samuel	Private	Third, Paterson	May 27, 1778-joined; May-June 1778.
Jewell/Jewel, Seth	Private	Spencer's, Brittin	Dec 1777-Jan 1778; Feb-April 1778-on furlough; May 1778; June 1778-on guard.
Jewett, Phenix	Private	First, Piatt	Jan-Feb 1778-with Col. Biddle; March-May 1778-command at Col. Biddle's; June 1778-with Col. Biddle.
Jibs - see Gibs			
Jobes, Ezekiel	Corporal	Second, Phillips	Dec 1777-April 1778; May 1778-on command; June 1778.
Jobes, John	Private	Second, Phillips	Dec 1777-April 1778; May 1778-sick present; June 1778.
Jobes, Samuel	Private	Second, Phillips	Dec 1777-June 1778.
Jobes, William	Corporal	Second, Phillips	Dec 1777-March 1778; April 5, 1778-taken prisoner.
Jobs/Jobes, Richard	Drum Major	Fourth	Dec 1777-March 1778; April-May 1778-sick Middlesex; June 1778.
Johnson, Abner	Private	First, Baldwin	May-June 1778.
Johnson, Benjamin	Private	First, Morrison	May 27, 1778-joined; May-June 1778.
Johnson/ Jonson, Benjamin	Private	Fourth, Lyon	Dec 1777-Jan 1778; Feb 1778-inoculated smallpox; March 1778; April 1778-sick present; May 1778; June 1778-sick hospital.
Johnson/ Jonson, Cato	Private	Spencer's, Lyon	Dec 1777-June 1778.
Johnson, Erick	Private	Spencer's, Maxwell	Dec 1777-May 1778; June 16, 1778-died.
Johnson, Henry	Private	Forman's, Burowes	Dec 1777-April 1778; May 1778-on guard; June 1778.
Johnson/ Johnston, James	Private	First, Morrison	Dec 1777-Jan 1778; Feb 1778-sick in hospital; March 1778-sick in camp; April 1778-sick present; May-June 1778.

Johnson/ Johnston, John	Private	First, Angel	Dec 1777-May 1778. June 1778 muster roll shows him on command, but the payroll shows him sick absent.
Johnson/ Jonson, John	Private	First, Angel	May 31, 1778-joined; May-June 1778.
Johnson, John	Fifer	First, Polhemus	Dec 25, 1777-deserted.
Johnson, John	Private	Third, Ballard	May 21, 1778-enlisted; May 1778; June 1778-on guard.
Johnson/ Johnston, John	Sergeant	Second, Helms	Dec 1777-June 1778.
Johnson/ Johnston, John	Private	Spencer's, Pierson	Dec 1777; Jan 1778-on command; Feb 1778; March 1778-on furlough; April 1778-on command; May 1778-sick camp; June 1778-wagons.
Johnson/ Johnston, Joseph	Private	Third, Ross	Dec 1777; Jan 1778-on command with armorer; Feb 1778; March 1778-on command armorer; April 1778-on command with armorer; May 1778-armoring; June 1778-on command.
Johnson, Levi	Private	Third, Ross	Dec 1777-Feb 1778; March 1778-on command; March 19, 1778-transferred to Commander-in-Chief's Guard.
Johnson/ Johnston, Lewis	Private	Spencer's, Weatherby	Dec 1777-June 1778.
Johnson, Matthew	Private	Spencer's, Maxwell	Dec 1777-Feb 1778; March-April 1778-on command; May 1778-butcher for Commissary; June 1778-butcher.
Johnson, Samuel	Corporal	Third, Ross	Dec 1777-Feb 1778; March 1778-on furlough; April 1778; May 1778-on command; June 1778-on guard.
Johnson/ Johnston, Samuel	Private	Fourth, Martin	August 5, 1777-deserted; Jan 21, 1778-joined; Jan-June 1778.
Johnson/ Johnston, Seth	1st. Lt.	Fourth, Martin	Dec 1777; Jan 1778-on furlough; Feb 1778; March 1778-on command; April-June 1778. Oath at Valley Forge on May 11, 1778.
Johnson, Thomas	Private	Fourth, Kinsey	October 4, 1777-missing; March 31, 1778-returned; March-May 1778.
Johnson, Thomas	Corporal	Spencer's, Ward	Dec 1777-Feb 1778-wounded hospital; March-April 1778-wounded absent; May 1778-Morristown Hospital; June 1778-wounded Morris County.
Johnson/ Johnston, William	Private	First, Morrison	Feb 19, 1778-enlisted; March 1778, April 1778-command; May 1778-on command; June 1778; July [2], 1778-deserted.

Name	Rank	Company	Service
Johnson/Johnston, William	Private/Sergeant/Private	First, Longstreet	Jan 1, 1778-enlisted; Jan 12, 1778-joined; Jan-March 1778; March 1778-promoted to sergeant; April 1778-reduced to private; April 1778; May 1778-deserted.
Johnson, William	Private	Spencer's, Maxwell	Dec 1777-Feb 1778; March 26, 1778-died.
Johnston/Johnson, Andrew	Private	Spencer's, Weatherby	Dec 1777-June 1778.
Johnston, George	Private	Third, Cox	Dec 1777-June 1778.
Johnston, Isaac	Corporal	Second, Cummings	Dec 1777-April 1778; May 1778-on guard; June 1778.
Johnston, James	Private	Second, Bowman	Dec 1777-April 1778; May 1778-on command; June 1778.
Johnston/Johnson, John	Sergeant	First, Polhemus	Dec 1777-Jan 1778; Feb 11, 1778-died.
Johnston, John	Fifer	First, Polhemus	Dec 24, 1777-deserted.
Johnston, John	Quartermaster Sergeant	Fourth	Dec 1777-Feb 1778; March 1778-sick present; April-June 1778.
Johnston, Martin	Sergeant	Fourth, Anderson	Dec 1777-May 1778; June 1778-sick in hospital.
Johnston, Peter	Private	First, Mead	June 5, 1778-enlisted; June 1778.
Johnston/Johnson, Robert	Private	Third, Hennion	Dec 1777-March 1778-sick absent; April-June 1778.
Johnston/Jonston, Thomas	Private	Fourth, Kinsey	October 4, 1777-taken prisoner; March-May 1778; June 1778-deserted.
Johnston/Johnson, William	Private	Third, Anderson	Dec 1777-April 1778; May 1778-on guard; June 1778.
Jonas, John	Private	Fourth, Forman	Dec 1777-March 1778; April 1778-on command; May-June 1778.
Jones, Abraham	Private	Spencer's, Brittin	Dec 1777-Jan 1778; Feb-April 1778-on furlough; May-June 1778-sick Kakiat.
Jones/Johnes, Alexander	Private	Third, Mott	Dec 1777-June 1778.
Jones, Ambrose	Private	Fourth, Mitchell	Dec 1777; Jan 1778-on command; Feb 1778; March 1778-on command; April 1778; May-June 1778-sick Yellow Springs.

Name	Rank	Company	Service
Jones, Armstrong	Private	Third, Ballard	Dec 1777-Feb 1778; March 1778-on command; April 1778-sick present; May 1778-sick in Yellow Springs; June 1778-sick Valley Forge.
Jones, Asey	Private	Second, Luse	Dec 1777-May 1778.
Jones, Daniel	Private	First, Flahavan	May 25, 1778-joined; May-June 1778.
Jones, David	Private	Spencer's, Brittin	Dec 1777; Jan-Feb 1778-sick present; March 30, 1778-died.
Jones, Ebenezer	Private	Fourth, Forman	Dec 1777-May 1778; June 1778-on guard.
Jones, Gershom	Private	Spencer's, Edsall	Dec 1777-Jan 1778; Feb-March 1778-sick present; April 2, 1778-died.
Jones, Isaac	Sergeant	Third, Gifford	Dec 1777-Jan 1778; Feb 1778-on furlough; March-May 1778; June 1778-on furlough.
Jones, Isaac	Private	Second, Helms	May 23, 1778-enlisted; June 14, 1778-joined; June 1778.
Jones, James	Private	Fourth, Lyon	June 15, 1778-joined; June 1778-on command.
Jones/Jons, John	Private	Fourth, Kinsey	Dec 1777-Feb 1778; March 24, 1778-dead.
Jones, Joseph	Private	Second, Bowman	Dec 1777; Jan 1778-on command; Feb-March 1778; April 5, 1778-taken by Enemy; July 17, 1778-exchanged.
Jones, Joseph	Private	Spencer's, Brittin	Dec 1777-Feb 1778-on furlough; March 1778-sick absent; April-May 1778-sick Kakiat; June 1778.
Jones, Joshua	Private	Fourth, Anderson	May 28, 1778-enlisted; May-June 1778.
Jones, Meredith	Private	First, Piatt	Dec 2, 1777-deserted; March 1778-sick in Jersey.
Jones, Michael	Private	First, Baldwin	Dec 1777-Feb 1778; March 1778-on command; April 1778-on command at the lines; May 1778-on the lines in Jersey; June 1778.
Jones, Samuel	Private	First, Piatt	May 26, 1778-joined; May 1778; June 1778-on command.
Jones, Samuel	Private	Second, Hollingshead	Dec 1777-April 1778; May-June 1778-on command.
Jones, Thomas	Private	First, Piatt	Jan-March 1778-sick in Jersey.
Jones, William	Private	First, Angel	Jan 28, 1778-joined; Jan-March 1778; April 1778-drunk present; May 1778-on command; June 1778-on guard.
Jones, William	Private	First, Piatt	Dec 1777-June 1778.

Name	Rank	Company	Notes
Jones, William	Private	Third, Gifford	Dec 1777-Feb 1778; March-April 1778-sick present; May 5, 1778-died.
Jordan, Felix	Private	Second, Phillips	May 8, 1778-enlisted; May 28, 1778-joined; May-June 1778.
Jorden, James	Private	Second, Luse	May 6, 1778-enlisted; June 1778.
Joy/Jay, James	Private	Third, Ballard	Dec 1777-June 1778.
Justice, Jesse	Private	Second, Bowman	April 22, 1778-enlisted; April-June 1778.
Kain, Edward	Private	Fourth, Mitchell	June 1778.
Kaits/Kaites, Philip	Private	Second, Hollingshead	Dec 1777-April 1778; May 1778-on command; June 1778.
Kane, John	Private	First, Baldwin	May 1778; June 1778-on command.
Karrel/Kirl, William	Private	Fourth, Kinsey	Dec 1777-June 1778.
Keen, Jacob	Private	Second, Reading	Dec 1777-June 1778.
Keesby - see Caseby			
Kellehen - see Callehen			
Kelly/Kelley, Bartholomy	Private	Fourth, Martin	Dec 1777-Feb 1778; March-April 1778-on command; May-June 1778.
Kelly, Edward	Private	Forman's, Combs	Dec 1777-June 1778.
Kelly, James	Private	First, Morrison	Dec 29, 1777-joined; Dec 1777-April 1778; May 1778-on command at camp; June 1778-left sick at Valley Forge.
Kelly, John	Private	Second, Sparks	May 10, 1778-enlisted; June 1778.
Kelly, John	Private	Spencer', Combs	Dec 1777-June 1778.
Kelly, Patt	Private	Fourth, Mitchell	June 1778.
Kelly, Peter	Private	First, Polhemus	Feb 20, 1778-enlisted; Feb 23, 1778-deserted.
Kelsey/Kilsay, John	Private	Second, Cummings	May 20, 1778-enlisted; May 27, 1778-joined; May-June 1778.
Kelso, Robert	Quartermaster	First	Dec 1777-Jan 1778-sick absent; Feb-March 1778.
Keltey, Michael	Private	Third, Anderson	June 7, 1778-enlisted; June 1778-on guard.
Keltey, William	Private	Third, Anderson	June 7, 1778-enlisted; June 1778.

Kemble/ Kimble, Nathan	Private	Third, Mott	Dec 1777; Jan 1778-on command; Feb-June 1778.
Kendra, Christopher	Private	Second, Luse	Dec 1777-June 1778.
Kennedy/ Kenedy, Charles	Corporal	Second, Bowman	Dec 1777-June 1778.
Kennedy/ Cannady, William	Private	Fourth, Martin	Dec 1777-sick in hospital; Jan 1778-sick absent; Feb-March 1778-sick in hospital; April 1778; May 1778-on command; June 1778.
Kennon/ Henion, Peter	Private	First, Longstreet	May 24, 1778-joined; May-June 1778.
Kent, Jacob	Corporal/ Sergeant	Third, Ballard	Dec 1777-Feb 1778; Feb 21, 1778-promoted to sergeant; March 1778-on command; April 1778; May 1778-on guard; June 1778.
Kent, Jonas	Private	First, Flahavan	Dec 1777-April 1778; May 1778-sick at Princeton Hospital; June 1778-on guard.
Kent, Simeon	Private	First, Baldwin	Dec 1777-deserted; Jan 1778-sick present; Feb 1778-sick in Jerseys; March 1778-in Jersey; April 1778-deserted.
Kenworthy, William	Sergeant	Second, Luse	Dec 1777; Jan 3, 1778-deserted.
Kerr - see Carr			
Kersey, William	2nd. Lt.	Third, Ross	Dec 1777-Jan 1778; Feb 1778-on command; March-June 1778. Oath at Valley Forge on May 11, 1778.
Ketchem/ Ketcham Daniel	Private	Second, Cummings	Dec 1777-April 1778; May 1, 1778-deserted.
Ketcher/ Hecher, John	Private	Spencer's, Lyon	Dec 1777-May 1778; June 1778-detached Artillery.
Keys/Kays, Richard	Private	Second, Luse	Dec 1777-Feb 1778; March 19, 1778-deserted.
Kibbe/Kibby, Ephraim	Private	Fourth, Martin	Dec 1777-June 1778.
Kibler, George	Private	First, Piatt	June 1778.
Kilborn/ Kilbourn, Moses	Sergeant	First, Morrison	Dec 1777; Jan-Feb 1778-on command; March 1778-on command in Jersey; April 1778-command; May 1778 roll shows he deserted on April 10.

Kilpatrick, Henry/Samuel	Private	First, Mead	June 5, 1778-enlisted; June 1778-on command. June muster roll shows him as Henry. The June payroll and later rolls show him as Samuel.
Kilsey, George	Private	Second, Cummings	June 1778.
Kimble/ Kemble, Caleb	Private	Second, Helms	May 10, 1778-enlisted; June 14, 1778-joined, June 1778-on guard.
Kimble/ Kemble, Jacob	Private	Spencer's, Brodrick	Dec 1777-sick in hospital; Jan 1, 1778-deserted.
King, Anthony	Private	Third, Gifford	Dec 1777-Feb 1778; March-April 1778-sick present; May 1778-sick at the Yellow Springs Hospital; June 1778.
King, Anthony	Private	Fourth, Forman	Dec 1777-April 1778; May 1778-on command; June 1778.
King, John	Private	First, Flahavan	Dec 1777-Feb 1778, March 1778-deserted.
King, Joseph	Adjutant	Fourth	Dec 1777-March 1778-prisoner; April 1778-sick Morristown; May 1778-sick Morris County; June 1778-sick Morristown.
King, Joseph	Private	First, Flahavan	Dec 1777; Jan 1778-sick in hospital; Feb 1778-in hospital; March 1778-sick in hospital; April 1778-Princeton; May-June 1778.
King, Joseph	Private	Fourth, Mitchell	May 1778-sick Yellow Springs; June 1778-sick hospital.
Kingsland, Isaac	Private	Third, Gifford	Dec 1777-Feb 1778; March-April 1778-sick present; May 1778-sick at the Yellow Springs Hospital; June 1778.
Kinnard/ Kennard, John	Corporal	Second, Reading	Dec 1777; Jan 1778-sick absent; Feb-June 1778.
Kenneybrook/ Kinnebrough, James	Private	Third, Paterson	June 1778-on furlough.
Kinney, John	2nd. Lt./ 1st. Lt.	Third, Paterson	Dec 1777; Jan 6, 1778-promoted to 1st. Lt.; Jan-March 1778; April 1778-on furlough; May-June 1778.
Kinsey, James	Private	Fourth, Kinsey	Dec 1777-Jan 1778; Feb 1778-on furlough; March-April 1778-sick present; May-June 1778.
Kinsey, Jonathan	Captain	Fourth, Kinsey	Kinsey died in Nov 1777. Lt. Bateman Lloyd assumed command, but the company continued to be called Kinsey's.
Kinsey, Shadrack	Private	Second, Cummings	March 1778; April 5, 1778-taken prisoner.

Name	Rank	Company	Notes
Kirkpatrick, James	Private	Third, Paterson	June 1778-on guard.
Kitchen, Henry	Private	Third, Ballard	Dec 1777-Feb 1778; March 1778-sick absent; April 1778-sick in Jersey; May-June 1778.
Knapp/Knap, David	Private	Fourth, Lyon	June 15, 1778-joined; June 1778.
Knapp/Knap, Richard	Private	Fourth, Lyon	Joined June 15, 1778; June 1778.
Knapp/Knap, Thomas	Sergeant	First, Morrison	Dec 1777-April 1778; May 1778-on command: June 1778.
Knowland - see Nowland			
Kullemon/ Culleman, John	Private	Spencer's, Maxwell	Dec 1777-April 1778; May 1778-on command at the lines; June 16, 1778-died.
Kuyser - see Cuysor			
Labor/Laber, George	Private	Third, Cox	Dec 1, 1777-joined; Dec 1777-March 1778; April-June 1778-sick absent in Pennsylvania.
Lacey/Lacy, Joseph	Private	Fourth, Forman	Dec 1777-Feb 1778; March-April 1778-on command; May 1778; June 1778-sick in hospital.
Lacy/Lacey, Samuel	Private	Spencer's, Brittin	Dec 1777-Jan 1778-sick absent; Feb-May 1778; June 1778-sick absent.
Lahey/Lakey, William	Private	First, Piatt	Dec 1777-June 1778.
Lahy, John	Sergeant	Fourth, Anderson	Dec 1777; Jan 1778-dead.
Lambard, Samuel	Private	First, Morrison	June 1778.
Lambert, David	Private	Third, Ballard	May 30, 1778-enlisted; May 1778; June 1778-on guard.
Lambert, Joseph	Private	First, Morrison	May 27, 1778-joined; May-June 1778.
Lambert, Lancelot	Private	Second, Cummings	Dec 1777; Jan 1778-sick absent; Feb-June 1778.
Lambert, Lott	Private	Fourth, Martin	Dec 1777-wounded in Battle of Germantown; Jan 1778-Princeton; Feb 1778-sick absent, wounded in battle; March 1778-sick absent; April 30-deserted; May 1778-sick present; June 1778-sick hospital.
Lambert, Samuel	Private	First, Morrison	May 27, 1778-joined; May 1778; June 1778-picket.
Lambert, William	Private	Fourth, Lyon	Dec 1777; Jan 1778-on command; Feb-June 1778.

Name	Rank	Company	Service
Land, James	Private	Spencer's, Weatherby	Dec 1777-Jan 1778-sick hospital; Feb 1778-deserted from hospital.
Land, Joseph	Private	Second, Hollingshead	Dec 1777; Jan 1778-sick in hospital; Feb-April 1778; May-June 1778-on command.
Landon, Benjamin	Private/ Corporal	Second, Luse	Dec 1777-Jan 1778; Feb 1, 1778-promoted to corporal; Feb-June 1778.
Landon, James	Private	Second, Luse	May 10, 1778 enlisted; June 1778.
Landon, Laben	Private	Malcolm's/ Second Tom's/ Luse	Dec 1777-Jan 1778 in Malcolm's Regiment; Feb 1, 1778 transferred to Second New Jersey; Feb 1778; March 19, 1778-transferred to Commander-in-Chief's Guard.
Landon, Samuel	Sergeant	Second, Luse	Dec 1777-June 1778.
Landsgrove, John	Private	Second, Cummings	Dec 1777-March 1778; April 15, 1778-dead.
Lane, Aaron	1st. Lt.	Second, Bowman	Dec 1777; Jan 1778-on command; Feb 1778; March-April 1778-recruiting; May-June 1778-on command.
Lane, Derick	2nd. Lt./ 1st. Lt.	Second, Hollingshead /Luse	Dec 1777; Jan 1, 1778-promoted to 1st. Lt. and transferred to Luse's company; Jan-June 1778.
Lane, James	Private	Second, Reading	Jan 1778. Appears as dead on composite muster roll dated June 12, 1778. Last appears on payroll of Feb 1778.
Lane, John	Private	Spencer's, Ward	Dec 1777-Jan 1778; Feb-March 1778-on furlough; April 1778; May 1778-on duty; June 1778.
Lane, Michael	Private/ Corporal	First, Polhemus	Dec 1777; Jan-Feb 1778-command; March-April 1778; May 1778-promoted to corporal; May-June 1778.
Lane, William	Private	Fourth, Forman	May 20, 1778-joined; May 1778; June 1778-on guard.
Langley, Elnathan/ Elliathen	Private	Third, Mott	Dec 1777; Jan-March 1778-sick absent; April-June 1778.
Langley, Jasper	Private	Third, Ballard	Dec 1777-Feb 1778; March 1778-on his Excellency's Guard; transferred to Commander-in-Chief's Guard.
Langley, John	Private	Third, Hennion	Dec 1777-May 1778; June 1778-on command.
Lawrance/ Lawrence, Jack	Private	Spencer's, Lyon	Dec 1777-June 1778.
Lawrence, Adam	Sergeant	Fourth, Holmes	Dec 1, 1777-deserted.

Name	Rank	Regiment/Company	Notes
Lawrence/ Laurence, Benjamin	1st. Lt.	Fourth, Anderson	Dec 29, 1777-resigned.
Lawson, James	Private	Spencer's, Edsall	Dec 1777-sick at hospital; Jan 1778 sick in hospital; Feb 1778-sick absent; March 28, 1778-deserted.
Lawson, John	Private	Second, Helms	May 12, 1778-enlisted; June 7, 1778-joined; June 1778.
Leadbetter/ Leadbeater, George	Private	Third, Ross	Jan, Feb and April 1778-"prisoner with ye enemy." May payroll states: "Taken prison^r. 11th of Sepr 1777 made his escape 30th. April 78. Enlisted 11th. March 77 omitted thro a mistake in former rolls." June 1778-sick absent.
Leak, Spencer	Private	Second, Luse	May 10, 1778-enlisted; June 1778-sick absent,
Leanard, Joshua	Private	First, Baldwin	June 1778.
Lee, David	Private	First, Mead	Dec 1777-Feb 1778; March 1778-on furlough; April 1778; May 1778-on guard; June 1778.
Lee, David	Private	Spencer's, Maxwell	Dec 1777-April 1778-absent wounded; May-June 1778-wounded Morristown.
Lee, John	Private	First, Longstreet	June 4, 1778-joined; June 1778-on command.
Lee, Owen	Private	Forman's, Forman	Dec 1777-June 1778.
Lee, Thomas	Private	First, Flahavan	May 25, 1778-joined; May-June 1778.
Lefever/ Lefevour, Mindert	Private	First, Longstreet	May 26, 1778-joined; May 1778; June 1778-on command.
LeFord, Vincent	Private	Second, Phillips	May 14, 1778-enlisted; May 28, 1778-joined; May-June 1778.
Lemon/ Leamon, George	Private	Fourth, Holmes	Dec 1777-April 1778; May 1778-on command; June 1778-on guard.
Lennington, Henry	Private	Fourth, Kinsey	Sept 1777-deserted; April 1778-sick present; May-June 1778-sick in hospital.
Leonard, Elijah	Private	Third, Cox	June 1, 1778-enlisted; June 5, 1778-joined; June 1778.
Leonard, Enoch	Private	First, Piatt	Dec 1777-March 1778; April 1778-on Commissary Guard; May-June 1778.
Leonard, Nathaniel	1st Lt.	Third, Mott	Dec 1777-Feb 1778; March 1778-on furlough; April-May 1778; June 1778-on command.
Leonard, Samuel	Private	Third, Paterson	June 1778.

Name	Rank	Company	Service
Leonard, Stephen	Private	Third, Cox	June 1, 1778-enlisted; June 5, 1778-joined; June 1778-on guard.
Leonard/Lenord, Stephen	Private	Fourth, Mitchell	March 1778-at Chatham; April 1778-sick in camp; May 1778-sick in Princeton.
Leonard/Leanard, William	Private	First, Angel	May 31, 1778-joined; May 1778-on guard; June 1778.
Leonard, Zephaniah	Private	Third, Anderson	Dec 1777-March 1778; April 1778-sick absent in New Jersey; May-June 1778.
Letts, John	Private	First, Longstreet	June 4, 1778-joined; June 1778.
Levy/Levey, Asher	Private/Cadet	First, Flahavan	Feb 1778; March 1778-on furlough; April 1778-promoted to cadet; April 1778; May 1778-on command; June 1778.
Lewis, Benjamin	Private	First, Mead	Dec 1777-Jan 1778; Feb 1778-wagoner; March-April 1778; May 1778-sick at Princeton; June 1778.
Lewis, David	Private	Forman's, Forman	Dec 1777-June 1778.
Lewis, James	Private	Spencer's, Weatherby	Dec 1777-March 1778; April 1778-sick present; May 1778-fatigue; June 1778-sick Elizabethtown.
Lewis, Richard	Private	First, Morrison	May-June 1778.
Lewis, William	Private	Fourth, Kinsey	December 1777-dead.
Lewis, William	Private/Corporal	Spencer's, Brodrick	June 6, 1777-deserted; April 23, 1778-joined; May 1, 1778 promoted to corporal; May 1778-command lines; June 1778-on command Clove.
Licitt/Luitt, Patrick	Private	First, Baldwin	Jan 27, 1778-enlisted; Feb 1778; March-April 1778-on command; May-June 1778.
Liddle/Little, Robert	Sergeant/Private/Corporal/Sergeant	First, Flahavan	Dec 1777-March; Jan 1778-reduced to private; Feb 1778-promoted to corporal; March 1778-promoted to sergeant; April-June 1778.
Lightning, John	Drummer	Spencer's, Maxwell	Dec 1777-Jan 1778; Feb-March 1778-on furlough; April 1778-in Elizabethtown Goal; May 1778-command at the Lines; June 1778-Elizabethtown Goal.
Likens/Lykins, Andrew	Sergeant	Second, Bowman	Dec 1777-Feb 1778; March-April 1778-recruiting; May-June 1778.
Likens/Licens, Jacob	Private	Third, Ross	Dec 1777-April 1778; May 1778-on command; June 1778.

Name	Rank	Company	Notes
Lindsey, James	Private	First, Polhemus	Dec 1777-sick absent; Jan-June 1778.
Lindsley, Eliazer	Lt. Col.	Spencer's	Dec 1777; Jan 1778-on command; Feb-March 1778; April-May 1778-on furlough; June 1778-sick Morristown.
Linwood, John	Private	First, Piatt	Dec 1777-April 1778; May-June 1778-sick absent.
Lippencut, John	Private	Second, Cummings	June 5, 1778-enlisted and deserted; August 15, 1778-rejoined.
Lisk, Benjamin	Private	First, Baldwin	Dec 1777-Feb 1778-sick at Bethlehem; March 1778-in Jersey; April 1778-deserted; May-June 1778.
Lisk/Lish, John	Private	First, Piatt	Dec 1777-June 1778.
Lites/Lipes, John	Private	Fourth, Lyon	Dec 1777-Jan 1778; Feb 1778-inoc small pox; March-April 1778; May 1778-sick Princeton; June 1778.
Little, Eliakim	1st. Lt.	First, Angel	Dec 1777-Jan 1778-on command; Feb 1778-on command in Jersey; March 1778; April 1778-on command in Jersey; May-June 1778.
Little, Jacob	Private	Second, Helms	Dec 1777-April 1778; May 1778-on command; June 1778.
Little, Robert	Sergeant	Spencer's, Maxwell	June 1778-on furlough.
Littler, Phillip	Private	Second, Helms	May 9, 1778-enlisted; June 26, 1778-joined; June 1778.
Lloyd, Bateman	1st. Lt.	Fourth, Kinsey	Captain Jonathan Kinsey died in Nov 1777. Lloyd assumed command, but the company continued to be called Kinsey's. Dec 1777-Feb 1778; March 1778-on command; April 1778-taken prisoner in March; June 1778.
Lloyd, David	Private	First, Morrison	Dec 1777-June 1778.
Lloyd/Loyd, John	Fifer	First, Morrison	Dec 1777-Feb 1778; March 1778-sick in camp; April-June 1778.
Lloyd/Loyd, John	Private	Second, Sparks	Dec 1777-sick hospital; Jan 1778-sick absent; Feb-April 1778; May 1778-sick absent; June 1778-on command making clothes.
Lloyd, Joseph	Fifer	Third, Ballard	January 9, 1778-enlisted; Feb-June 1778.
Lock, Philip	Private	Second, Cummings	Dec 1777-June 1778.
Locker, John	Private	First, Baldwin	May-June 1778.
Lockwood, Silas	Private	First, Angel	Dec 1777-absent since Germantown battle; Jan 1778-deserted.

Name	Rank	Company	Service
Loden, Reuben	Private	Second, Hollingshead	May 30, 1778-enlisted; May-June 1778-on furlough.
Loder, Zenos	Private	Second, Hollingshead	May 8, 1778-enlisted; June 1778.
Lodwick, Simon	Private	Third, Cox	March 4, 1778-enlisted; March-April 1778-sick present; May-June 1778-sick at Yellow Springs.
Logan, Robert	Sergeant	Fourth, Mitchell	Dec 1777-April 1778; May 1778-on command; June 1778.
Logan, William	Private	Third, Ballard	Dec 1777-Feb 1778; March 1778-on command; April-June 1778.
Long, John	Private	Third, Cox	Dec 1777-Jan 1778; Feb 5, 1778-died.
Long, Joseph	Sergeant	First, Mead	Dec 1777-sick; Jan-June 1778.
Long, Richard	Private	Second, Cummings	Dec 1777-March 1778; April 5, 1778-prisoner.
Longhose, Jacob	Sergeant	Third, Gifford	Dec 1777-March 1778; April-May 1778-on command; June 1778.
Longstreet, Elias	Captain	First, Longstreet	Dec 1777-Feb 1778-prisoner on parole; March 1778-on parole; April 1778-prisoner on parole; May 1778-prisoner of war; June 1778-prisoner on parole.
Loper, Abraham	Sergeant	Second, Cummings	Dec 1777-April 1778; May 1778-furlough; June 1778.
Lopes/Lopas, Isaac	Private	Spencer's, Brodrick	Dec 1777-sick absent; Jan-May 1778; June 1778-sick.
Loring/Loree, Ephraim	Surgeon's Mate	Third	Dec 1777-April 1778; May 1778-on furlough; June 1778. Oath at Valley Forge on May 11, 1778.
Lorvey/Lurvey, Vincent	Private	Second, Reading	Dec 1777-June 1778.
Losey/Locey, Abram/Abraham	Private	Fourth, Mitchell	Dec 1777; Jan-March 1778-sick present; April-June 1778.
Losey/Locey, Benjamin	Private	Fourth, Mitchell	Dec 1777; Jan-Feb 1778-sick present; March 1778-sick hospital; April 1, 1778-died in Allentown.
Lott, Peter	2nd. Lt.	First, Polhemus	Dec 1777-Jan 1778; Feb 1778-on command to Jersey; March-April 1778; May 1778-on command; June 1778-sick at B. Brook.
Lounsbery/Lounsburry, Walkar	Private	Fourth, Kinsey	March 1, 1778-enlisted; March 31, 1778-joined; March 1778; April 1778-sick present; May-June 1778.
Love, Alexander	Corporal	Third, Anderson	Dec 1777-June 1778.

Name	Rank	Company	Service
Love, James	Sergeant	Second, Cummings	Dec 1777; Jan 1, 1778-deserted.
Love, William	Quartermaster Sergeant	Third	Dec 1777-March 1778; April 1778; May 1778-sick in Jersey; June 1778.
Lovelett/Lovlit, Lott	Private	Fourth, Anderson	Dec 1777-March 1778; April 1778-on command at the lines; May 1778.
Loveless, Gersham	Private	Second, Phillips	March 30, 1778-enlisted; April 1778; May 1778-on command; June 1778-on furlough.
Loyhead, James	Private	Fourth, Anderson	June 1778-joined, June 1778-sick absent.
Loyer, James	Private	Second, Luse	May 10, 1778-enlisted; June 1778-sick absent.
Loyle/Loyl, Thomas	Private	First, Piatt	Dec 1777-June 1778.
Loyon, Solomon	Private	First, Flahavan	May 25, 1778-joined; May 1778.
Lubin/Lubten, John	Private	Second, Cummings	May 21, 1778-enlisted; May 24, 1778-joined; May-June 1778.
Ludlow, Abraham	Private	Third, Ballard	Dec 1777-June 1778.
Ludlow, Daniel	Sergeant	First, Piatt	Dec 1777; Jan-Feb 1778-on furlough; March 1778; April 1778-sick present.
Ludlow, Watts	Private	First, Angel	Dec 1777-sick near Newark; Jan 1778-sick at Newark.
Luir, Thomas	Private	Fourth, Lyon	May 31, 1778-joined; May-June 1778.
Luse, Francis	Volunteer	Second, Luse	Appears as a volunteer on the muster rolls for Dec 1777-June 1778. On the payrolls for the period he receives private's pay.
Luse, Henry	Captain	Second, Luse	Dec 1777-June 1778.
Lye, William	Private	Second, Cummings	Dec 1777-March 1778; April 5, 1778-prisoner.
Lynch/Linch, Dennis	Private	Second, Sparks	Dec 1777; Jan 1778-on command; Feb-April 1778; May 1778-on guard; June 1778.
Lynch, William	Private	Second, Helms	Dec 1777-June 1778.
Lyon, Abraham	Captain	Fourth, Lyon	Dec 1777; Jan 1778-on furlough; Feb-May 1778; June 1778-on command. Oath at Valley Forge on May 11, 1778.
Lyon, David	Captain	Spencer's, Lyon	Dec 1777; Jan 1778-on furlough; Feb-March 1778; April 10, 1778-resigned.
Lyon/Lion, Enos/Enoch	Private	First, Morrison	May-June 1778.

Lyon, Henry	Corporal	First, Morrison	July 24, 1777-enlisted; Jan 1778-joined; Jan-March 1778; April 1778-sick present; May 1778-sick at camp; June 1778.
Lyon, Henry	Private	Second, Luse	May 6, 1778-enlisted; June 1778.
Lyon, Jedediah	Private Corporal	Spencer's, Ward	Dec 1777-Feb 1778; March 1, 1778-promoted to corporal; March-June 1778.
Lyon, Nathaniel	Private	Fourth, Lyon	May 31, 1778-joined; May-June 1778.
Lyon, Patrick	Private	First, Morrison	Feb 28, 1778-enlisted; March 1778-sick in Pennsylvania; April 1778-sick Pennsylvania; May 1778-sick at Princeton; June 1778.
Lyons/Lions, Elias	Private	Fourth, Anderson	Dec 1777-March 1778; April 1778-sick in camp. See Sallisbury, Nathaniel.
Lyons/Loyns, John	Private	Second, Phillips	Dec 1777-March 1778; April 5, 1778-taken prisoner.
Lyons/Lines, Surring/Suring	Private	First, Mead	April 25, 1778-enlisted, May 1778-June 1778.
Lyons, William	Private	Third, Ross	Dec 1777-March 1778; April 1778-on picket; May 1778-on command; June 1778.
McAfferty, Joseph	Private	Third, Ross	May 25, 1778-joined; May-June 1778-on command.
McAllister, William	Private	Fourth, Kinsey	Dec 24, 1777-deserted.
McAnelly/McAnalle, Patrick	Private	Fourth, Anderson	April 15, 1777-taken prisoner; May 1778; June 1778-on furlough.
McAuliff, John	Drummer	Forman's, Forman	Dec 1777-June 1778.
McBee, James	Private	First, Longstreet	June 4, 1778-joined; June 1778.
McBurney, James	Private	First, Polhemus	Dec 1777-Jan 1778; Feb 1778-command Jerseys; March 1778-command; April-June 1778.
McCabe, Henry	Private	Third, Gifford	Dec 1777-Feb 1778-sick absent; March 1778; April 1778-on command; May-June 1778.
McCall/McCaul, William	Private	Spencer's, Edsall	Dec 1777-Feb 1778; March 29, 1778-died.
McCall/McCaul, William	2nd. Lt.	Spencer's, Wilkins	Dec 1777-Feb 1778-on furlough; March 3, 1778-resigned.

Name	Rank	Company	Service
McCallister, William	Private	Fourth, Kinsey	December 24, 1777-deserted.
McCann/ McCan, Henry	Private	First, Baldwin	Dec 1777-"taken 22 August Staten Island, omitted from payroll being prisoner." June 1778.
McCann, John	Private	Second, Phillips	May 14, 1778-enlisted; May 28, 1778-joined; May 1778; June 1778-on command.
McCarrhan, John	Private	Second, Helms	May 15, 1778-enlisted; June 10, 1778-joined; June 1778.
McCarty, David	Private	Third, Anderson	Dec 1777; Jan 6, 1778-deserted.
McCarty, Hugh	Private	Third, Ballard	May 26, 1778-enlisted; May 1778; June 1778-on guard.
McCarty, John	Private	Second, Helms	April 27, 1778-enlisted; May-June 1778.
McCawley, Alexander	Private	Second, Reading	Jan-April 1778; May 1778-on command; June 1778.
McClain/ McClane, David	Private	Third, Paterson	Dec 1777; Jan 6, 1778 deserted.
McClain/ McClean, Hugh	Private/ Corporal	Second, Phillips	Dec 1777-April 1778; May 1, 1778; promoted to corporal; May-June 1778-on furlough.
McClary/ McClarey, Daniel	Private	First, Piatt	May 1778-on guard; June 1778-sick absent.
McCleny/ McClony, Hugh	Private	Spencer's, Lyon	Dec 1777-Jan 1778; Feb 1778-on duty; March 1778-sick camp; April-May 1778. June 1778 muster roll shows he was discharged on June 1, 1778, but the July 1778 muster roll and payroll shows him discharged on July 10.
McClure/ McCuir, Andrew	Sergeant	Fourth, Forman	Dec 1777-May 1778; June 1778-sick absent.
McClure/ McLure, James	Private	Fourth, Anderson	July 10, 1777-deserted; Feb-April 1778; May 1778-"in dispute Col Stuarts Reg." June 1778-"in dispute absent."
McCollam/ McColm, John	Private	Second, Luse	Dec 1777-June 1778.
McConnell/ McConnel, Hugh	Private	Spencer's, Maxwell	Dec 1777-May 1778; June 1778-Commissary's guard.
McCormick, Dennis	Private	Fourth, Anderson	Dec 1777-April 1778; May 1778-sick Princeton Hospital; June 1778.
McCormick, Stephen	Private	Forman's, Burowes	Dec 1777-April 1778; May 1778-guard; June 1778.

Name	Rank	Company	Service
McCowen, Constantine	Private	Second, Cummings	Dec 1777-April 1778; May 1778-on command; June 1778.
McCoy, Daniel	Private	Third, Paterson	Jan-Feb 1778; March 1, 1778-deserted.
McCoy, James	Private	Second, Phillips	May 14, 1778-enlisted; June 1, 1778-joined; June 1778.
McCoy, Joseph	Private	Fourth, Lyon	Dec 1777-March 1778-sick absent; April 1778-sick Trenton; May 20, 1778-discharged.
McCrackin/McCraken, Philip	Private	Spencer's, Weatherby	Dec 1777-April 1778; May 1778-on guard; June 1778.
McCray/McCrae, Philip	Corporal/Sergeant	First, Piatt	Dec 1777-Jan 1778; Feb 1778-promoted to sergeant; Feb-May 1778; June 1778-sick absent.
McCulley, John/James	Private	Second, Bowman	March 1, 1778-joined; March-June 1778.
McCully/McCulley, John	Private	Third, Ross	Dec 1777-Jan 1778; Feb 1778-on furlough, March 1778-on command; April-May 1778; June 1778-on guard.
McDade/McDadd, William	Private	Fourth, Kinsey	Dec 1777-March 1778-sick in hospital; April 1778; May 1778-on guard; June 1778.
McDaniel/McDonald, Daniel	Drummer	Third, Hennion	Dec 1777-Feb 1778; March 1778-on command; April-June 1778.
McDaniel/McDonnel, John/Joseph	Private	Third, Paterson	Dec 11, 1777-enlisted; Dec 1777-Feb 1778-sick in Jersey; March-April 1778-sick absent; June 1778-deserted.
McDaniel/McDannell, John	Private	Spencer's, Maxwell	Dec 1777-March 1778; April 1778-on command; May-June 1778.
McDonald, Benjamin	Private	First, Polhemus	Jan 17, 1778-joined; Jan-April 1778; May 1778-at the lines; June 1778-on command.
McDonald/McDonal, Benjamin	Private	Fourth, Forman	Dec 1777-April 1778; May 1778-on command; June 1778.
McDonald, Cornelious	Private	First, Longstreet	June 4, 1778-joined; June 1778-on command.
McDonald, George	Quartermaster Sergeant	Second	Dec 1777-June 1778.
McDonald, James	Private	Second, Reading	Feb 5, 1778-enlisted; March-May 1778; June 1778-sick present.
McDonough/McDonaugh, Dennis	Private	Second, Reading	Jan-April 1778; May 1778-on command; June 1778.

Name	Rank	Company	Notes
McDuffy, Randle	Private	Fourth, Holmes	Dec 1777-furlough; Jan-Feb 1778; March 1778-on command; April 1778; May-June 1778-on command.
McElrath, Andrew	Private	Second, Luse	May 6, 1778-enlisted; June 1778.
McEvony, Patrick	Private	Spencer's, Ward	Dec 1777-discharged.
McFaden/McFadin, Conoly	Private	First, Longstreet	May 24, 1778-joined; May-June 1778.
McFaddin, John	Private	Third, Anderson	June 7, 1778-enlisted; June 1778.
McGee, Abraham	Private	Second, Hollingshead	May 4, 1778-enlisted; June 1778.
McGee, James	Private	First, Polhemus	June 1778.
McGee, William	Sergeant/ Private	Second, Hollingshead	Dec 1777-Jan 1778; Feb 14, 1778-reduced to private; Feb-June 1778.
McGill, James	Private	First, Piatt	May 21, 1778-joined; May-June 1778.
McGill, John	Private	First, Piatt	May 1778-on command; June 1778.
McGill, William	Sergeant	Spencer's, Wilkins/ Edsall	Dec 1777-Jan 1778; Feb-March 1778-on furlough; April 1778; May 1778-transferred to Edsall's Co.; sick in camp; June 1778-sick absent.
McGinte/ McGinta, John	Private	Third, Cox	Sept 17, 1777-deserted; May 1, 1778-joined; May-June 1778.
McGlockin/ McLaughlin, Hugh	Corporal	Fourth, Martin	Dec 1777; Jan 1778-on command; Feb-June 1778.
McGlocklin/ McGloghlin, Charles	Private	First, Piatt	March 23, 1778-enlisted; April 1778; May 1778-with baggage; June 1778.
McGonagle/ McGonegle, George	Private	Fourth, Holmes	Dec 1777-Feb 1778-hospital; March 1778-sick in hospital; April 1778-sick Schaefers Hospital; May 1778-sick absent; June 1778-on command.
McGuire, John	Private	First, Mead	Jan 28, 1778-enlisted; Jan-March 1778; April 1778 prisoner in Conway's [Battalion.]
McGuire, Thomas	Private	Second, Luse	Dec 1777-March 1778; April 1, 1778-deserted.
McHugo, Edward	Corporal	Third, Paterson	Dec 1777-June 1778.
McHugo/ McCugo, Thomas	Private	Third, Ballard	Dec 1777-April 1778; May-June 1778-sick Valley Forge.

Name	Rank	Company	Service
McIntire/ McKintire, Joseph	Private	Third, Paterson	Dec 1777-May 1778; June 1778-wagoner.
McKendrick/ McKindrick, Robert	Private	Third, Ballard	Dec 1777-Feb 1778; March 1778-on command; April 1778-sick present; May 8, 1778-died.
McKenny, Joseph	Private	First, Piatt	May 21, 1778-joined; May-June 1778.
McKenny, William	Private	First, Piatt	Dec 1777-wounded in Jersey; Jan 1778-on furlough; Feb 1778-sick in Jersey; March 1778; April 1778-unfit for service; May 1778; June 1778-sick absent.
McKinney, Timothy	Private	Third, Anderson	Dec 1777-June 1778.
McKinsey/ McKensey, John	Private	Spencer's, Brittin	Dec 1777-June 1778.
McLafferty/ McLiferty, Henry	Private	Third, Ballard	May 21, 1778-enlisted; May 1778; June 1778-on guard.
McLane, John	Private	Second, Helms	May 12, 1778-enlisted; June 7, 1778-joined; June 1778.
McLure - see McClure			
McLaughlin/ McLaughlon, John	Private	Fourth, Mitchell	Dec 1777-at hospital sick; Jan 1778-on command; Feb-March 1778; April 1778-sick in camp; May-June 1778.
McMahon/ McMiken, Jeremiah	Private	Second, Sparks	Dec 1777-sick in hospital; Jan 1778-sick absent; Feb-April 1778; May 1778-on furlough; June 1778-on command "making clothes."
McMannis/ McManus Christopher	Corporal	First, Angel	Dec 1777-Jan 1778; Feb 1778-on command; March 1778; April 1778-on command at "Buxcounty." May-June 1778.
McManus/ McManis, William	Private	First, Piatt	Dec 1777-sick in hospital; Jan-April 1778-sick in Jersey; May-June 1778-sick absent.
McMillan, Charles	Sergeant	Second, Cummings	Dec 1777-April 1778; May 1778-on guard; June 1778.
McMillin/ McMillen, John	Private	Fourth, Martin	Dec 1777-May 1778; June 1778-on guard.
McMullen/ McMullin, William	Private	First, Piatt	March-June 1778.

Name	Rank	Company	Service
McNeal, Hector	Sergeant	Spencer's, Weatherby	Dec 1777-Jan 1778; Feb-April 1778-on furlough; May-June 1778.
McNier/ McNear, Robert	Private	First, Baldwin	Dec 1777-June 1778.
McPharron/ McPherron, Zachariah	Private	Second, Bowman	March 25, 1778-enlisted; May 1778-not joined.
McPharson, Joseph	Private	Spencer's, Weatherby	Dec 1777-Jan 1778; Feb-March 1778-on command; April 1778-sick present; May 1778-command lines; June 1778-sick Elizabethtown.
McQuay, John	Private	Second, Cummings	Feb 1, 1778-enlisted; April 1778.
McQuillen, Alexander	Private	Second, Luse	March 27, 1778-joined; March 1778; April 15, 1778-deserted.
McQuinn, Philip	Private	First, Mead	April 1778.
McSherry, Matthew	Private	Fourth, Anderson	Dec 1777-Jan 1778.
Macondon/ Maucindon, John	Private	First, Morrison	Dec 1777; Jan-Feb 1778-left sick in Jersey.
Magee/Mage, Robert	Private	Fourth, Kinsey	Dec 1777-sick hospital; Jan 1778; Feb 25, 1778-died.
Mahone, Daniel	Private	Third, Anderson	Dec 1777-April 1778; May 1778-on command; June 1778.
Maines, Michael	Private	Third, Mott	March-April 1778; May 19, 1778-deserted.
Malatt/Mallot, Abraham	Private	First, Baldwin	Dec 1777-sick present; Jan 1778-absent without leave; Feb-June 1778.
Malcolm, John	Private	Second, Phillips	May 8, 1778-enlisted; May 25, 1778-joined; May-June 1778.
Mall, Uriah	Private	Third, Mott	Dec 1777-Feb 1778; March 1778-on furlough; April-May 1778; June 1778-artillerymen.
Mallebe/ Malleby, Thomas	Private	Fourth, Anderson	May 28, 1778-joined; May-June 1778.
Man, Abraham	Private	Spencer's, Pierson	Dec 1777-died hospital.
Mann, Richard	Corporal	Forman's, Forman	Dec 1777-June 1778.
Manning, Thomas	Private/ Corporal	Third, Ballard	Dec 1777-Jan 1778; Feb 21, 1778-promoted to corporal; Feb-March 1778; April 1778-sick present; May 1778-sick at Princetown; June 1778.
Mapes, William	Private	Third, Cox	June 1, 1778-enlisted; June 5, 1778-joined; June 1778.

Mapps, Frederick	Corporal	Forman's, Burowes	Dec 1777-June 1778.
March/ Martch, Philip	Private	Second, Reading	Dec 1777-June 1778.
Marling/ Marlin, Baunt	Private	Spencer's, Lyon	Dec 1777-March 1778; April 1778-sick present; May-June 1778.
Marlin, Robert	Private	Third, Gifford	Dec 1777-sick absent; Jan 1, 1778-died.
Marr, Edmond	Private	First, Piatt	March 14, 1778-enlisted; April 19, 1778-deserted.
Marsh, George	Private	First, Mead	June 5, 1778-enlisted; June 1778-guard.
Marsh, Samuel	Private	First, Mead	June 5, 1778-enlisted; June 1778.
Marshall/ Marshel, James	Private	Spencer's, Brittin	Dec 1777-March 1778-on furlough; April 1778-sick Elizabethtown; May 1778-sick camp; June 1778-sick Yellow Springs.
Marshell/ Mashell, Street	Sergeant	Third, Gifford	Dec 1777-Feb 1778-wounded absent; March 1778-sick absent; April 1778-sick at Reading; May-June 1778-sick present.
Martin, Absalom	Paymaster	Fourth	Dec 1777-April 1778; May 1778-Barnards Town on furlough; June 1778-at Princeton. Oath at Valley Forge on May 11, 1778.
Martin/ Martain, Daniel	Private	First, Angel	March 1778; April 1778-sick present; May 1778-picket guard; June 1778.
Martin, David	Corporal	Third, Gifford	Dec 1777-April 1778; May 1778-on command; June 1778.
Martin, Ephraim	Colonel	Fourth	Dec 1777-March 1778-sick absent; April-May 1778; June 1778-at Princeton on command. Oath at Valley Forge on May 11, 1778.
Martin, Jacob	Captain	Fourth, Martin	December 23, 1777-resigned. Lt. Seth Johnson assumed command of this company, but it continued to be called Martin's.
Martin, James	Private	Fourth, Lyon	Dec 1777-May 1778; June 1778-on command.
Martin, Nicholas	Private	Second, Reading	Jan 1778-sick absent; Feb-April 1778; May 1778-sick Yellow Springs; June 1, 1778 died.
Martin/ Marten, Thomas	Private	Third, Ballard	Dec 1777-Feb 1778; March 1778-on command; April-May 1778-on command at the lines; June 1778-on weeks command.

Name	Rank	Company	Notes
Martin, Thomas	Private	Fourth, Forman	Dec 1777-sick absent; Jan-March 1778-sick in hospital; April 1778-sick absent; May 1778-hospital Reading; June 1778-sick absent.
Martin, William	Private	Fourth, Lyon	Dec 1777-March 1778; April 1778-on guard; May-June 1778-sick hospital.
Martin, William	Private	Fourth, Martin	Dec 1777-Feb 1778; March 1778-unfit for service.
Mason, Andrew	Corporal	Second, Hollingshead	Dec 1777-April 1778; May 1778-on command; June 1778.
Massey, Benjamin	Private	Third, Gifford	May 27, 1778-joined; May-June 1778.
Masters, Stephen	Private	Second, Helms	Dec 1777-April 1778; May 1778-on command; June 1778.
Matchet, William	Private	First, Longstreet	Dec 1777-sick in Pennsylvania hospital; Jan 1778; Feb 1778-sick in Pennsylvania hospital; March 1778-sick absent; April 1778-sick absent not known where; May 1778-sick absent; June 1778.
Mathews, John	Private	Second, Phillips	March 4, 1778-enlisted; March 1778; April 2, 1778-deserted.
Matson, Aaron	Private	Fourth, Mitchell	June 1778.
Mattison, Jacob	Private	First, Piatt	June 1778-on command.
Maxwell, James	Captain	Second, Helms	December 1, 1777-resigned. Captain William Helms assumes command of the company in January 1778.
Maxwell, John	Captain	Spencer's, Maxwell	Dec 1777-Jan 1778; Feb 1778-on furlough; March 1778; April 11, 1778-resigned.
Maxwell/Maxfell, Nathaniel	Private	Spencer's, Pierson	Dec 1777-March 1778; April 1778-sick present; May 7, 1778-died.
Maxwell, William	Brigadier General		Oath at Valley Forge on May 22, 1778, witnessed by Washington.
May, Andrew	Private	First, Baldwin	Dec 1777; Jan 1778-command lines; Feb 1778-sick in Jersey; March 1778-sick present; April-May 1778; June 1778-on command.
Maybee, Edward	Private	Second, Sparks	Dec 1777-sick in hospital; Jan 1778-sick absent; Feb-April 1778; May 1778-sick absent.
Mayburrey/Maybury, Joseph	Corporal	Third, Anderson	Dec 1777; Jan 28, 1778-died.
Mays, Edward	Private	Second, Luse	May 10, 1778-enlisted; June 1778-sick absent.

Name	Rank	Company	Service
Mays/Mase, Samuel	Private	Second, Hollingshead	Dec 1777-June 1778.
Mead/Meads, James	Private	First, Baldwin	Dec 1777-June 1778.
Mead/Meed, Yelles	Captain	First, Mead	Dec 1777-sick absent; Jan-April 1778; May 1778-on command; June 1778.
Meads/Meeds, Daniel	Corporal	Third, Cox	Dec 1777-Jan 1778; Feb 1778-on furlough; March 1778-sick absent; April-June 1778-sick absent in Jersey.
Medagh, Emanuel	Private	Second, Helms	May 10, 1778-enlisted; June 14, 1778-joined; June 1778-on guard.
Medagh, Moses	Corporal	Second, Helms	May 10, 1778-enlisted; June 12, 1778-joined; June 1778.
Meeker/Meecher, John	Private	First, Flahavan	June 1778-on command.
Meeker, Michael	Private	Third, Anderson	May 27, 1778-joined; May-June 1778.
Meeker, Robert	Private	First, Morrison	May 27, 1778-joined; May 1778; June 1778-General's Guard.
Meeker, Uzal/Uzial	2nd. Lt.	Spencer's, Maxwell	Dec 1777-sick present; Jan 1778-furlough; Feb-June 1778; Oath at Valley Forge on May 11, 1778.
Mer - see Dimer			
Meramley/Moraniley, John	Private	Spencer's, Wilkins/Edsall	Dec 1777; Feb 1778; March 26, 1778-deserted; May 1778-duty camp; June 1778. In May he transferred to Edsall's Co.
Mercer, John	1st. Lt.	First, Morrison	March-April 1778-prisoner with the enemy; May 1778; June 1778-prisoner of war.
Merrick/Merick, John	Private	Fourth, Forman	Dec 1777-March 1778-sick in hospital; April 1778-sick absent; May 1778-hospital Reading; June muster roll shows he was discharged on July 14, 1778.
Merron/Marron, Joseph	Private	Fourth, Kinsey	Dec 1777-May 1778; June 1778-sick hospital.
Meurheid, John	Private	Third, Ballard	June 3, 1778-enlisted; June 1778.
Micker, Michael	Private	Third, Paterson	May 27, 1778 joined; May 1778; June 1778-prisoner.
Micker/Mecker, Michael	Private	Spencer's, Pierson	Dec 1777-sick absent; Jan-April 1778; May 1778-sick camp; June 1778-Yellow Springs sick.
Middleton, Thomas	Private	Second, Sparks	Dec 1777-June 1778.

88

Middleton/ Miedleton, Joseph	Private	Third, Cox	June 1, 1778 enlisted; June 28, 1778-joined; June 1778.
Milburne/ Milbourn, John	Private	Fourth, Mitchell	Dec 1777-Jan 1778-at hospital sick; Feb 1778; March 1778-on command; April 1778; May 1778-on command; June 1778.
Miles, Thomas	Private	Third, Cox	Dec 1777-Feb 1778; March 1778-deserted.
Miller, Benjamin	Private	Third, Mott	June 1778.
Miller, Frederick	Private	Fourth, Kinsey	Oct 4, 1777-missing; July 16, 1778-exchanged.
Miller, John	Sergeant	Third, Mott	Dec 1777; Jan-Feb 1778-sick absent; April 1, 1778-reported for duty; April-May 1778; June 1778-on command.
Miller, Joseph	Private	Fourth, Kinsey	Dec 1777; Jan-March 1778-on furlough; April 1778-deserted.
Miller, Noah	Private	First, Morrison	May 27, 1778-joined; May-June 1778.
Miller, William	Private	Second, Cummings	March 1, 1778-joined; March-May 1778; June 1, 1778-deserted
Mills, Cornelius	Private	First, Morrison	Dec 1777; Jan-Feb 1778-sick hospital; March 1778-sick in Jersey; April-May 1778; June 1778-picket.
Mills, Israel	Private	First, Longstreet	April 23, 1777-deserted; April 19, 1778-joined; April 1778; May 1778-on command; June 1778.
Mills, Reuben	Private	Second, Sparks	Dec 1777-sick in hospital; Jan 1778-on command; Feb-April 1778; May 1778-on guard; June 1778-on command.
Mills, Richard	Private	Second, Bowman	March 13, 1778-enlisted; April 8, 1778-joined; April-June 1778.
Millsom/ Milsom, James	Private	Spencer's, Pierson	Dec 1777 payroll-"wounded the 4th." Dec 1777-on furlough; Jan 1778-wounded; Feb-May 1778-on furlough; June 1778.
Mimnough/ Nimmough, Neal	Private	Second, Reading	Jan-June 1778.
Minnis, Robert	Private	Fourth, Mitchell	Dec 1777-April 1778. May 1778 muster roll shows he died on May 24, 1778, but May payroll has May 21 as date of death.
Minthorn, John	Sergeant	First, Baldwin	Nov 19, 1777-appointed; April 15, 1778-joined; April 1778; May 1778-on guard; June 1778 on furlough.

Name	Rank	Company	Notes
Minthorn, Philip	Corporal	Fourth, Mitchell	Dec 1777-June 1778.
Minthorn, Samuel	Private	First, Baldwin	June 5, 1778-joined; June 1778.
Minthorn, William	Private	Fourth, Mitchell	Dec 1777-Feb 1778; March 1778-sick present; April 1778-sick in camp; May-June 1778.
Mires, John	Private	Second, Luse	Composite muster roll dated June 12, 1778 shows him as deserted, no other information.
Mirick, John	Private	First, Angel	May 31, 1778-joined; May 1778; June 1778-on furlough.
Miscoe, Conrad	Private	First, Piatt	May 21, 1778-joined; May-June 1778.
Mitchell, Alexander	Captain	Fourth, Mitchell	Dec 1777-April 1778; May 1778-on command; June 1778. Oath at Valley Forge on May 11, 1778.
Mitchell, John	Private	Fourth, Holmes	Dec 1777; Jan 3, 1778-deserted.
Mitchell, Joseph	Private	Fourth, Cox	March 1778-sick absent; April 1778-sick absent in Jersey; May 10, 1778-deserted.
Mitchell/ Mitchel, Richard	Private	Forman's, Burowes	Dec 1777-April 1778. May 1778 muster roll shows he deserted on May 20. The June 1778 payroll shows he deserted on June 3 and rejoined on June 18 "making 15 days for which he requires pay."
Mitchell, William	Drummer	Fourth, Anderson	July 9, 1777-deserted; Feb-April 1778; May 1778-"in dispute Col Stuart's Regt."
Mitop/Mitops, Gabriel	Private	Third, Hennion	Dec 1777-Feb 1778; March-May 1778-on furlough, June 1778-sick absent.
Mitop, James	Private	Third, Ross	Dec 1777; January 28, 1778-died.
Molatt, Peter	Private	Second, Luse	May 5, 1778-enlisted; June 1778.
Molholand/ Molholen, Patrick	Private	Spencer's, Edsall	May 1778-command lines; June 1778.
Monford, Isaac	Private	Second, Luse	May 5, 1778-enlisted; June 1778.
Monson/ Munson, Solomon	Private	Third, Ballard	Dec 1777-Feb 1778; March 1778-on command; April-June 1778.
Montgomery/ M^{t}Gomery, William	Private	Spencer's, Maxwell	Dec 1777-Feb 1778-sick absent; March-May 1778; June 1778-supposed to be deserted.

Name	Rank	Company	Service
Mooney/Moony, Barny	Private	Spencer's, Lyon	Dec 1777-sick in Country; Jan 1778; Feb 1778-command; March-April 1778; May 1778-on fatigue; June 1778.
Mooney/Moony, John	Private	Fourth, Forman	Dec 1777-May 1778; June 1778-on guard.
Moor, Matthias	Private	First, Longstreet	June 4, 1778-joined; June 1778.
Moore/More, James	Private	Fourth, Kinsey	Dec 17, 1777-deserted.
Moore/More, John	Private	First, Polhemus	Dec 1777-Jan 1778; Feb 1778-on command; March-April 1778; May 1778-guard; June 1778.
Moore/Moor, Jonathan	Private	Third, Paterson	Dec 1777; January-1778-on command; Feb 1778; March 1778-in his Excellency's Guard.
Moore/Moor, Joseph	Private	Third, Paterson	Dec 1777; Jan 1778-on command; Feb 1778; March 1778-on command; April-May 1778; June 1778-on command.
Moore, Judiah	Private	Fourth, Forman	Dec 1777-Jan 1778; Feb 1778-discharged.
Moore/More, William	Private	First, Morrison	Dec 29, 1777-joined; Dec 1777-April 1778; May 1778-sick Princeton; June 1778-left sick at Valley Forge.
Moore, William	Private	Third, Paterson	May 1778-joined; May 1778; June 1778-on guard. See More, William.
Moore/More, William	Private	Fourth, Kinsey	Dec 1777-Jan 1778 Feb-March 1778-sick hospital; April 1778-sick present; June 1, 1778-died.
More/Moar, William	Private	Spencer's, Brodrick	Dec 1777-April 1778; May 1778-"being a substitute [ ] in the Jersey Reg^t. May 11." This may be the William Moore in Paterson's Co. of the Third New Jersey.
Moorhouse/Moorhouse, Jacob	Private	Third, Paterson	Dec 1777-Jan 1778-sick absent; Feb 1778-sick in Jersey; March 1778; April 1778-on guard; May 1778; June 1778-on command.
Moorhouse, Simon	Private	Third, Paterson	May 27, 1778-joined; May-June 1778.
Morgan/Moyan, Charles	Private	Third, Gifford	Dec 1777-Feb 1778; March-April 1778-on command; May 1778; June 1778-on furlough.
Morgan, Samuel	Private	Spencer's, Weatherby	Dec 1777-April 1778; May 1778-command driving wagon camp; June 1778.
Morgan, William	Private	Third, Anderson	December 15, 1777-discharged.

Name	Rank	Company	Service
Morgan/ Morgin, William	Private	Fourth, Kinsey	March 1, 1778-enlisted; March 31, 1778-joined; March 1778; April 1778-sick present; May 1778; June 1778-sick hospital.
Morrell, William	Private	Spencer's, Brodrick	Dec 1777-March 1778-absent wounded.
Morris, Benjamin	Private	First, Flahavan	Dec 1777-March 1778-sick in Jersey; April 1778-deserted.
Morris, David	Private	Fourth, Lyon	Dec 1777-Feb 1778; March 1778-on furlough; April-June 1778.
Morris/ Morrison, James	Private	Third, Ross	Dec 1777; Jan 1778-on command; Feb 1778; March 1778-on guard; April-June 1778.
Morris, Joseph	Major	First	Dec 1777-with Col. Morgan's Regiment. He was mortally wounded at White Marsh, Pa. on Dec 5. He died on Jan 4, 1778.
Morris, Thomas	Private	Third, Ross	Dec 1777-Jan 1778; Feb-March 1778-sick absent; April-June 1778.
Morris, Timothy	Private	Third, Ballard	June 5, 1778-enlisted; June 1778.
Morrison, Isaac	Captain	First, Morrison	Dec 1777-wounded; Jan 1778-recruiting; Feb 1778; March 1778-absent with leave; April-June 1778.
Morrison, James	Private	Second, Luse	Dec 1777; Jan 1778-sick absent; Feb-June 1778.
Morrison, John	Private	Second, Helms	Dec 1777-March 1778; April 5, 1778-killed.
Mosely, Miles	Private	First, Mead	April-June 1778.
Moslander, Sheron	Private	Second, Hollingshead	May 4, 1778-enlisted; June 1778; July 9, 1778-deserted.
Moss, Philip	Private	Spencer's, Brodrick	Dec 1777-April 1778; May 1778-on command at Radnor; June 1778.
Mott, David	Private/ Corporal	Fourth, Mitchell	Dec 1777-Jan 1778-on command; Feb 1778; March 1778-on command; April 1778; May 1778-promoted to corporal, May 1778 sick present; June 1778.
Mott, John	Captain	Third, Mott	Dec 1777; Jan-Feb 1778-on furlough; March-April 1778; May-June 1778-sick absent. Oath at Valley Forge on May 11, 1778.
Mount, George	Private	Forman's, Burowes	Dec 1777-June 1778.
Mounteer/ Mounteare, John	Private	Third, Ross	Dec 1777; Jan-March 1778-sick absent; April 1778; May 1778-on guard; June 1778-sick absent.
Muirheid/ Meurheid, John	Private	Third, Ballard	June 3, 1778-enlisted; June 1778.

Mulford/ Mulferd, Furman	Private	First, Baldwin	May 1778-on furlough; June 1778.
Mulford, Joseph	Private	Spencer's, Weatherby	Dec 1777-Feb 1778; March [2]4, 1778-died.
Mullett, George	Private	Forman's, Combs	Dec 1777-June 1778.
Mullicki/ Malachy, Abraham	Private	Second, Cummings	Dec 1777; Jan 1778-sick absent; Feb 1, 1778-died.
Mullin, John	Private	First, Polhemus	June 4, 1778-joined; June 1778.
Mullock, William	Sergeant	Fourth, Forman	Dec 1, 1777-appointed; Dec 1777-March 1778; April 12, 1778-deserted.
Mumford, David	Private	Fourth, Mitchell	Dec 1777-March 1778; April 12, 1778-deserted.
Murdock, John	Sergeant	Fourth, Kinsey	Dec 15, 1777-deserted.
Murdock, William Thompson	Sergeant	First, Polhemus	Dec 1777-June 1778.
Murfey/ Murfee, James	Private	Second, Luse	Dec 1777-Feb 1778; March 19, 1778-deserted.
Murphy, Daniel	Private	Third, Gifford	June 7, 1778-joined; June 1778.
Murphy, David	Private	Third, Paterson	March 1778-joined; March 1778; April 30, 1778-deserted.
Murphy/ Murphey, John	Private	Third, Anderson	Dec 1777-June 1778.
Murphy/ Murfey, Philip	Private	Second, Helms	Dec 1777-March 1778; April 5, 1778-killed.
Murphy, Thomas	Corporal	Spencer's, Wilkins	Dec 1777-Jan 1778; Feb 15, 1778-deserted.
Murray, James	Private	Second, Helms	May 23, 1778-enlisted; June 14, 1778-joined; June 1778-on guard.
Murray, James	Private	Third, Ross	June 1, 1778-joined; June 1778-on guard.
Murray, William	Private	Second, Helms	May 23, 1778-enlisted; June 14, 1778-joined; June 1778.
Murrey, John	Private	First, Mead	Jan 21, 1778-enlisted; Feb 1778-deserted.
Murtice/ Murtis, Stephen	Private	Third, Anderson	Dec 1777-June 1778.
Musbrook/ Mushbroke, John	Private	Second, Sparks	Dec 1777-sick in hospital: Jan 1778-on command; Feb-April 1778; May 1778-tending sick; June 1778-on command.
Myers, Martin	Private	Forman's, Burowes	Dec 1777-April 1778; May 1778-sick at Princeton; June 1778.

Name	Rank	Company	Service
Nafey/Nafies, Garret	Private	First, Longstreet	May 24, 1778-joined; May-June 1778.
Naglee/Naglie, Samuel	1st. Lt.	Second, Helms	Dec 1777-June 1778.
Neal, Thomas	Private	Second, Hollingshead	Dec 1777-April 1778; May 1778-on command; June 1778.
Neavs/Neaves, Thomas	Private	Second, Hollingshead	May 27, 1778-enlisted; June 1778.
Nestler, John	Private	Third, Gifford	June 8, 1778-joined; June 1778-sick absent.
Nester/Nestor, John	Private	Third, Paterson	May 27, 1778-joined; May-June 1778.
Newman/Numan, Elijah	Fifer	Spencer's, Wilkins	Dec 1777-Feb 1778; March 26, 1778-deserted.
Newton, Silas	Sergeant	Fourth, Anderson	Dec 1777-June 1778.
Newton, Thomas	Private	First, Polhemus	Dec 1777-March 1778; April 1778-Jersey; May 1778-at the lines; June 1778.
Nichols/Nicholds, Isaiah	Private	Second, Bowman	Dec 1777-Feb 1778; March 1778-recruiting; April-June 1778.
Nichols/Nickles, Rice	Corporal	Spencer's, Pierson	Dec 1777-Jan 1778; Feb-April 1778-on furlough; May 1778; June 1778-[guard] Elizabethtown.
Nichols/Nicholason, Thomas	Private	Second, Hollingshead	May 27, 1778-enlisted; June 1778.
Nicklas, Jonathan	Sergeant	Third, Mott	April 1778 payroll-"Deduct-not mustered", May-June 1778.
Nickson, George	Private	Second, Cummings	May 20, 1778-enlisted; June 1778.
Nickson, Robert	Private	Second, Cummings	May 20, 1778-enlisted; June 1778.
Nicolls, Jonathan	Sergeant	Spencer's, Maxwell	Dec 1777; Jan 1778-on furlough; Feb-April 1778; May 1778-"taken 21st May to Jersey."
Nie, James	Private	Third, Cox	Dec 1777-Feb 1778-sick at Morristown; March 1778-sick absent; April-May 1778-sick absent in Pennsylvania; June 1778-sick in Pennsylvania.
Nimmough - see Mimnough			
Nixon/Nickson, Isaac	Private	Second, Cummings	May 24, 1778-joined; May-June 1778.
Nixon, Richard	Private	First, Longstreet	May 24, 1778-joined; May 1778; June 1778-on command.

Nixon, William	Private	Spencer's, Brittin	Dec 1777-Jan 1778-sick absent; Feb-March 1778-sick present.
Noblet, John	Private	Spencer's, Brittin	Dec 1777-on furlough; Jan 1778-wounded absent; Feb 1778-wounded; March 1778-wounded absent; April 1778-deserted L. Island.
Noe, James	Private	Third, Anderson	June 5, 1778-enlisted; June 1778.
Noe/Nowes, Luis/Lewis	Private	Fourth, Martin	Dec 1778; Jan-March 1778-on command; April-May 1778; June 1778-waiter.
Nolt, Philip	Private	Second, Hollingshead	Dec 1777; Jan 1778-on command baking; Feb-June 1778.
Norcross/ Norcros, Benjamin	Drummer	Third, Ross	Dec 1777-June 1778.
Norris/Norres, Peter	Private	Spencer's, Ward	Dec 1777-April 1778-on furlough; May-June 1778-Morris County sick.
Norris, Thomas	Private	Forman's, Burowes	Dec 1777-April 1778; May 1778-on command; June 1778.
North, John	Private	Forman's, Burowes	Dec 1777-April 1778; May 1778-sick at [ ]; June 1778.
Nowy, Samuel	Private	Spencer's, Maxwell	Dec 1777-Jan 1778; Feb 1778-on guard; March 1778-on Lord Stirling's guard; April 1778-on command; May-June 1778.
Nowland/ Knowland, John	Private/ Sergeant	First, Mead	Dec 1777-in Jersey Jan-Feb 1778; March 1778-promoted to sergeant; March-June 1778.
Nunn/Nun, Ephraim	Private	Fourth, Forman	Jan 1778 muster roll notes "In place of Robt Stephens." Feb 1778; March 1778-on command; April 1778; May 1778 muster roll notes "taken by prior enlistm^t 15 May." May 1778 payroll shows the date taken as May 20.
Oakham/ Okham - see Holcomb			
Oar/Ore, James	Private	First, Angel	Feb-April 1778; May-June 1778-on command.
Obert, George	Private	First, Longstreet	May 24, 1778-joined; May-June 1778.
Obert, John	Private	First, Longstreet	May 24, 1778-joined; May-June 1778.
O'Brien/ Obrine, John	Private	Spencer's, Pierson	Dec 1777-May 1778; June 10, 1778-"Returned to Jersey Regt." This is probably the same man shown below.
Obrion, John	Private	Fourth, Martin	May 1778-on command; June 1778.

Name	Rank	Company	Notes
O'Bryan - see Bryan			
Ockerman/Ocerman, John	Private	First, Longstreet	June 1778-on command.
Ockerman/Ocerman, Garlin	Private	First, Longstreet	May 24, 1778-joined; May 1778-on command; June 1778-sick absent.
O'Flaherty, John	Private	Second, Phillips	May 26, 1778-enlisted & joined; May 1778; June 1778-on command.
Ogden, Aaron	Paymaster	First	Dec 1777-March 1778; April 1, 1778-resigned.
Odgen, Barne	1st. Lt.	Spencer's, Ward	Dec 1777-on furlough; Jan-May 1778; June 1778-acting as adjutant. Oath at Valley Forge on May 11, 1778.
Ogden/Ogdon, Eliakim	Private	Third, Paterson	May 27, 1778-joined; May-June 1778.
Ogden, Elikem	Private	Spencer's, Brittin	Dec 1777-March 1778-sick absent; April 1778-on furlough; May 1, 1778-discharged.
Ogden, Ludlow	Private	Spencer's, Pierson	Dec 1777-Jan 1778; Feb-March 1778-on command; April 1778-sick present; May 1778-sick camp; June 1778-Turkey sick.
Ogden, Mathias	Colonel	First	Dec 1777-absent; Jan 1778-on command; Feb-March 1778; April 1778-on command; May-June 1778.
Ogden, Moses	Sergeant	Spencer's, Brittin	Dec 1777-Jan 1778-on furlough; Feb 1778-on guard; March-May 1778; June 1778-on furlough.
Ogden, Nathaniel	Quartermaster	Spencer's	Dec 1777-Jan 1778; Feb 1778-on furlough; March-June 1778. Oath at Valley Forge on May 11, 1778.
Ogden/Ogdon, Noah	Drummer	Second, Helms	Dec 1777-June 1778.
O'Hara/Oharah, Joseph	Private	Spencer's, Wilkins/Edsall	Dec 1777-March 1778; April 1778-on guard; May 1778-transferred to Edsall's Co., sick in camp; June 1778-sick absent.
Okely/Ocly, John	Private	Third, Paterson	May 27, 1778-joined; May-June 1778.
Olden, Thomas	Private	Second, Phillips	May 14, 1778-enlisted; May 28, 1778-joined; May 1778; June 1778-on command.
Oliver, David	Private	First, Baldwin	May-June 1778.
Oliver, Joseph	Private	First, Baldwin	May 1778; June 1778-on command.

Name	Rank	Regiment/Company	Service
Oman/ Omman, Charles	Drummer	Third, Cox	March 13, 1778-enlisted; March-June 1778.
Omock/ Omack/ Omuck, Thomas	Private	Third, Gifford	Dec 1777-Jan 1778; Feb-June 1778-on furlough.
O'Neal/ O'Neale, Arthur	Private	Fourth, Forman	Dec 1777-March 1778-sick in hospital; April-June 1778.
O'Neal, Henry	Private	Second, Hollingshead	Dec 1777-April 1778; May 1778-on command; June 1778-on furlough.
O'Neal/ O'Neil, Henry	Private	Fourth, Forman	Dec 1777-Jan 1778-sick in hospital; Feb-May 1778-sick absent; June 1778.
O'Neal/ O'Neil, John	Corporal	First, Piatt	Dec 1777-sick in Jersey; Jan-Feb 1778; March 1778-on furlough; April-May 1778; June 1778-under guard.
O'Neal, John	Private	Second, Luse	Dec 1777-June 1778.
O'Neal, Neal	Private	Fourth, Kinsey	Dec 1777; Jan 1778-on command; Feb 1778; March 1778-on command; April-June 1778.
O'Neill, John	Private	Forman's, Burowes	Dec 1777-June 1778.
Organ, John	Corporal	Spencer's, Wilkins/ Edsall	Dec 1777-March 1778; April-May 1778-sick in camp; June 1778. In May he transferred to Edsall's Co.
Organ, Mathew	Private	Spencer's, Wilkins/ Edsall	Dec 1777-April 1778; May 1778-sick camp; June 1778. In May he transferred to Edsall's Co.
Orr/Ore, John	Private	Fourth, Forman	Dec 1777-June 1778.
Orr, John	2nd. Lt.	Spencer's, Weatherby	Dec 1777-April 1778; May 1778-on duty; June 1778. Oath at Valley Forge on May 11, 1778.
Osborn/ Osburn, Absalom	Private	Second, Cummings	Dec 1777-Jan 1778; Feb 17, 1778-dead.
Osborn, David	Private	First, Morrison	May-June 1778.
Osborn/ Osbourn, Jedediah	Private	First, Flahavan	Dec 1777-Jan 1778-sick in Jersey; Feb-March 1778; April 1778-Yellow Springs Hospital; May 1778-sick Yellow Springs; June 1778-sick in hospital.
Osborn/ Osburn, John	Private	Third, Mott	Dec. 1777; Jan-March 1778-wagoner.
Osborn, Joel	Private	First, Morrison	June 1778-command.

Name	Rank	Company	Notes
Osborn/ Osborne, Nathaniel	Private	First, Piatt	Dec 1777-Jan 1778-on command; Feb 1778-with sick at Reading; March 1778-command on the lines; April 1778-on picket guard; May-June 1778.
Osborn/ Osbourn, Stephen	Private/ Drummer/ Private	First, Flahavan	Dec 1777-June 1778. In March 1778 he is listed as drummer, all other months as a private.
Osburn, Jesse	Private	Fourth, Lyon	May 31, 1778-joined; May 1778; June 1778-sick hospital.
Osburn, Joseph	Private	Fourth, Anderson	Dec 1777-Feb 1778; March 1778-on command; April 1778-on command driving cattle; May 1778; June 1778-on command.
Osburn, Luke	Private	Fourth, Forman	Dec 1777-Feb 1778; March 1778-on command; April 1778; May 1778-sick present; June 1778-sick absent. June payroll shows he returned from the hospital.
Osman, John	Private	Fourth, Anderson	Dec 1777-Jan 1778; Feb 1778-missing on the lines; March 1778-on command; April 1778-sick at Yellow Springs; May 1778; June 1778-on command.
Osmon, Benjamin	Corporal	First, Longstreet	March 18, 1778-enlisted; April-June 1778.
Osmun, Benajah	Quarter-master	Second	Dec 1777-June 1778.
Otway/ Ottway, David	Private	Second, Sparks	Dec 1777-sick in hospital; Jan 1778-sick absent; Feb-April 1778.
Outgalt, Simon	Private	First, Longstreet	May 24, 1778-joined; May 1778; June 1778-on command.
Owen, Stephen	Private	Fourth, Kinsey	Dec 1777-Jan 1778-sick hospital; Feb 1778; March 1778-sick hospital; April 1778-deserted.
Owens, Hiram	Sergeant	Second, Helms	Dec 1777-April 1778; May 1778-on command; June 21, 1778-deserted.
Owens, James	Private	Spencer's, Wilkins/ Edsall	Dec 1777-April 1778; May 1778-sick in camp; June 1778-sick absent. In May he transferred to Edsall's Co.
Packer, Jacob	Private	First, Longstreet	May 26, 1778-joined; May 1778; June 1778-on command.
Palmer, Philip	Private	Second, Phillips	May 2, 1778-enlisted; June 1, 1778-joined; June 1778.
Palmer/ Pallmer, Richard	Private	Second, Luse	Dec 1777-March 1778; April 5, 1778-taken prisoner.
Pangborn/ Pangman, Joseph	Private	First, Morrison	Dec 1777; Jan-Feb 1778-sick in hospital; March 1778-sick in Jersey; April 1778-sick Princeton; May 1778-on furlough; June 1778-sick Newark.

Name	Rank	Company	Service
Parker, Daniel	Private	Spencer's, Brittin	Dec 1777-Jan 1778; Feb-April 1778-on furlough.
Parker, Gershom	Private	Third, Paterson	March-May 1778-on command.
Parker, Jonathan	Sergeant	Forman's, Burowes	Dec 1777-Feb 1778; March 23, 1778-deserted.
Parker, Nathaniel	Private	Third, Cox	Dec 1777-April 1778; May 8, 1778-deserted.
Parkison/ Parkenson, Daniel	Private	Spencer's, Edsall	May-June 1778.
Parks, John	Private	Second, Luse	Dec 15, 1777-dead.
Parks, Zebulon	Corporal	Third, Paterson	Dec 1777-April 1778; May 1778-on command; June 1778.
Parquist/ Parcrest, John	Sergeant	Fourth, Martin	Dec 1777-March 1778-sick in hospital; April 1778; May 1, 1778-deserted.
Parr, Benjamin	Private	Second, Luse	May 6, 1778-enlisted; June 1778.
Parr, John	Private	Second, Luse	June 1, 1778-joined; June 1778.
Parr, William	Private	First, Polhemus	Dec 1777-sick absent; Jan 1778; Feb-March 1778-sick Jersey; April 1778-dead.
Parrot, Adaniran	Private	Third, Ballard	Dec 1777-on furlough; Jan-March 1778; April 1778-sick present; May 1778.
Parrot, William	1st. Lt.	Second, Reading	Jan 1778-resigned.
Parrott/Parret, Silas	2nd. Lt.	First, Angel/ Piatt	Dec 1777-sick absent, Jan 1778; March-May 1778; June 1778-on furlough. For March and April he appears on the rolls of Piatt's Co. and on those of Angel's Co. for the other months.
Parsel/Parcel, Swain	Fifer	Third, Paterson	Dec 1777-sick absent; Jan-May 1778; June 1778-on furlough.
Parsell/Parcel, Antony	Fifer	Spencer's, Ward	Dec 1777-June 1778.
Parsells, Thomas	Private	First, Morrison	May-June 1778.
Pase, Michael	Private	Second, Luse	May 6, 1778-enlisted; June 1778.
Paterson, Thomasd	Captain	Third, Paterson	Dec 1777-Feb 1778; March 1778-on furlough; April-June 1778.
Paterson, Edward	1st. Lt.	Third, Paterson	Dec 1777-on command; Jan 6, 1778-resigned.
Patterson, Andrew	Private	Forman's, Combs	Dec 1777-Jan 1778; Feb 12, 1778-deserted.

Name	Rank	Company	Notes
Patterson/ Paterson, John	Corporal	Second, Sparks	Dec 1777-sick hospital; Jan 1778-sick absent; Feb-April 1778; May 1778-on command; June 1778.
Patterson, John	Sergeant	Fourth, Holmes	Oct 11, 1777-deserted. No other record until Feb 1778 muster roll which shows him as deserted.
Paul, After	Private	Spencer's, Brittin	Dec 1777-June 1778.
Paul, Benjamin	Quartermaster Sergeant	Spencer's	Dec 1777-June 1778.
Paul/Pall, James	Corporal/ Sergeant	Spencer's, Brittin	Dec 1777; Jan 1, 1778-promoted to sergeant; Jan-Feb 1778; March 1778-on command.
Paul, Joseph	Private	Second, Cummings	Dec 1777; Jan 1778-on furlough; Feb 1778-deserted.
Paull/Paul, James	2nd. Lt.	Second, Helms	Dec 1777-April 1778; May 1778-on command; June 1778.
Paull, Josiah	Private	Second, Luse	Dec 1777-April 1778; May 1778-on command; June 1778.
Pawling, Albert	Major	Spencer's	Dec 1777-June 1778.
Peache/ Peachhe, Benjamin	Private	Second, Cummings	May 21, 1778-enlisted; May 24, 1778-joined; May-June 1778.
Pearson/ Parson, John	Private	Second, Reading	May 14, 1778-enlisted; June 1778 muster roll shows he joined on May 1, but the June 1778 payroll shows his pay beginning on May 14; June 1778.
Pearson/ Pierson, Nicholas	Private	Fourth, Mitchell	Sept 11, 1777-taken by the enemy; April-June 1778. In the May 1778 payroll he was paid back to Sept 11, 1777.
Pease, Jonathan	Private	First, Longstreet	June 4, 1778-joined; June 1778.
Peck, John	Paymaster	Second	Jan-June 1778.
Peck, Moses	Private	First, Morrison	Aug 1, 1777-enlisted; Jan 1778-April 1778. On the Jan 1778 payroll he received pay back to Aug 1, 1777.
Peddle, Joseph	Private	Second, Hollingshead	Dec 1777; Jan 1778-sick in hospital; Feb-April 1778; May 1, 1778-discharged.
Pedley/Pedly, Thomas	Private	Third, Paterson	Dec 16, 1777-enlisted; Dec 1777-May 1778; June 1778-on furlough.
Peirson/ Person, David	Corporal	Spencer's, Brittin	Dec 1777-sick hospital; Jan 1778-sick present; Feb 1778-sick in camp; March 1778-sick present; April 1778-on furlough; May-June 1778-sick Elizabethtown.

Name	Rank	Company	Service
Peirson/ Person, Mathias	Private	Spencer's, Brittin	Dec 1777-Jan 1778; Feb-March 1778-on command; April 1778-prisoner. Roll dated Sept 11, 1778 shows him returned to duty.
Peirson/ Pearson, Samuel	Private	Spencer's, Brittin	Dec 1777; Jan 1778-sick present; Feb-May 1778; June 1778-on furlough.
Pemberton, Robert	2nd. Lt./ Adjutant	Forman's, Forman	Dec 1777-April 1778; May 1, 1778-promoted to adjutant; May-June 1778.
Pendergrass, Thomas	Private	First, Baldwin	Dec 1777-sick Pennsylvania; Jan-March 1778-sick at Reading; April 1778-sick at Lancaster; May-June 1778.
Pennington, Nathaniel	Private	First, Morrison	May-June 1778.
Penton, James	Corporal	Fourth, Holmes	Dec 1777-Jan 1778; Feb 1778-sick present; March-April 1778; May 1778-on command; June 1778-on guard.
Pepper/ Peppard, William	Private	Fourth, Forman	Dec 1777-March 1778; April 1778-on guard; May 1778.
Percy/Percey, Adam	Private	Second, Cummings	May 20, 1778-enlisted; June 1778.
Perdon/ Pardon, James	Drummer	First, Piatt	Dec 1777-Feb 1778; March 1778-sick in camp; April-June 1778.
Periam/ Peream, Joseph	Quarter-master	Third	Dec 1777; Jan 1778-on command; Feb-June 1778.
Perkins, Eleazer	Private	Third, Cox	June 1, 1778-enlisted; June 5, 1778-joined, June 1778-on guard.
Perkins/ Pirkins, Eleazer	Private	Fourth, Mitchell	Dec 1777-Jan 1778; Feb-March 1778-on furlough; April 1778; May 30, 1778-deserted.
Perry/Pery, Henry	Private	Third, Cox	Oct 4, 1777-missing; March 1, 1778-enlisted; April 1778; May 1778-sick at Princetown Hospital; June 1778-on command. This may be two men with the same name.
Perry, John	Private	Second, Luse	Dec 1777-April 1778; May 1778-on command; June 1778.
Perry, Jotham/ Jothum	Private	First, Morrison	May 27, 1778-joined; May 1778-on command; June 1778.
Perry/Perrey, Thomas	Private	Fourth, Mitchell	Dec 1777-Feb 1778; March 1778-on picket; April-June 1778.
Person, John	Private	Second, Cummings	May 20, 1778-enlisted; May 24, 1778-joined; May-June 1778.
Peters, Levi	Private	Third, Mott	March 15, 1778-enlisted; March-June 1778.
Peters, Phillip	Private	Second, Hollingshead	May 27, 1778-enlisted; June 1778.

Peterson, Abraham	Private	Second, Hollingshead		May 4, 1778-enlisted; June 1778.
Peterson, Abraham	Private	Third, Ross		Dec 1777; Jan 1778-sick absent; Feb-March 1778; April 1778-sick present; May-June 1778-sick absent.
Peterson, Henry	Private	Second, Hollingshead		May 4, 1778-enlisted; June 1778.
Peterson, Jacob	Private	Second, Cummings		May 20, 1778-enlisted; June 1778.
Peterson, Peter	Private	Forman's, Wikoff		Dec 1777-June 1778.
Peterson, Samuel	Private	Second, Luse		May 10, 1778-enlisted; June 1778-sick absent.
Peterson, Zac	Private	Second, Helms		May 9, 1778-enlisted; June 26, 1778-joined; June 1778.
Pew/Peu, Reuben	Private	First, Mead		Jan 1, 1778-enlisted; Jan-March 1778; April 1778-on guard; May-June 1778.
Pharis/Faris, Amarriah	Private	First, Longstreet		May 24, 1778-joined; May 1778; June 1778-sick absent.
Phillips, Francis	Private	Second, Phillips		Dec 1777-April 1778; May 21, 1778-taken prisoner.
Phillips, Jacob	Private	First, Piatt		Dec 18, 1777-deserted.
Phillips, Jonathan	Captain	Second, Phillips		Dec 1, 1777-promoted to captain; Dec 1777; Jan 1778-on command; Feb-April 1778; May-June 1778-on command.
Phips/Fipps, John	Private	First, Baldwin		Dec 1777-Jan 1778-sick Morristown; Feb-March 1778-sick in Jersey; April 1778-deserted.
Piatt, Daniel	Captain	First, Piatt		Dec 1777; Jan 1778-sick; Feb 1778-on furlough; March-June 1778.
Piatt, Jacob	Adjutant	First		Dec 1777; Jan 1778-on furlough; Feb-May 1778; June 1778-sick absent.
Piatt, William	1st. Lt.	First, Piatt		Dec 1777-Jan 1778; Feb 1778-recruiting; March 1778-on command in Jersey; April-June 1778.
Pickett, George	Private	Second, Luse		May 10, 1778-enlisted; June 1778-sick absent.
Pickett, Robert	Private	Fourth, Anderson		Dec 1777-Feb 1778-sick in hospital; March-June 1778.
Picking/Pikings, Alexander	Private	Fourth, Forman		May 31, 1778-joined; May-June 1778.
Pierce, John	Private	First, Polhemus		Dec 1777-sick absent; Jan 1778; Feb 1778-sick present; March 1778-sick Jersey; April 1778-Jersey; May 1778-at the lines; June 1778-on guard.
Pierce, William	Private	First, Polhemus		June 4, 1778-enlisted; June 1778.

Name	Rank	Regiment/Company	Service
Pierson/Person, Calib	Private	Fourth, Martin	Dec 1777-March 1778-sick absent; April 30, 1778-deserted.
Pierson, Daniel	1st. Lt.	Fourth, Forman	Dec 1777; Jan 1778-on furlough; Feb 1778; March 1778-sick absent; April 1778; May 1778-sick absent; June 1778.
Pierson, Jonathan	Captain	Spencer's, Pierson	Dec 1777; Jan 1778-sick absent; Feb-April 1778-on furlough; May 1778-on furlough wounded at German Town; June 1778-wounded Elizabethtown.
Pilor/Piler, George	Sergeant	Second, Sparks	Dec 1777-April 1778; May 1778-on command; June 1778.
Pinkney/Pikney, William	Private	Fourth, Lyon	May 30, 1778-joined; May-June 1778.
Pipes, Joseph	Private	Fourth, Mitchell	Dec 1777-absent without leave; Jan-Feb 1778-sick Rockaway; March 1778-deserted.
Pitts, Thomas	Drummer	Second, Bowman	Dec 1777; Jan 1778-on furlough; Feb 1778-deserted to Enemy.
Plough, Jacob	Private	Second, Helms	May 10, 1778-enlisted; June 14, 1778-joined; June 1778.
Plumb/Plum, Stephen	Private	First, Flahavan	Dec 1777-Jan 1778; Feb 1778-on furlough; March 1778; April 1778-on guard; May 1778; June 1778-on guard.
Plumer, John	Private	Third, Gifford	June 7, 1778-joined; June 1778.
Plummer, James	Private	Second, Cummings	May 21, 1778-enlisted; May 27, 1778-joined; May 1778-on command; June 1778.
Polen, John	Sergeant	Second, Luse	March 22, 1778-enlisted; April-June 1778.
Polhemus/Polhamus, John	Captain/Major/Captain	First, Polhemus	Dec 1777-Jan 1778; Feb 1778-promoted to major; April 1778-reverted to captain, April 1778-on command; May 1778; June 1778-on command.
Polk, Job	Private	Fourth, Mitchell	June 1778-sick hospital.
Pollard, John Barton	Sergeant	First, Angel	Dec 1777-May 1778; June 1778-sick Princeton.
Pollard/Pollars, Thomas	Private	Second, Helms	Dec 1777-June 1778.
Pool/Poole, John	Private	Second, Luse	Dec 1777; Jan 1778-sick absent; Feb-June 1778.
Poole, Lewis	Private	Forman's, Burowes	Dec 1777-April 1778; May 1778-sick at Princeton; June 1778.

Name	Rank	Company	Service
Porteus/ Portius, Samuel	Private	Second, Phillips	March 17, 1778-enlisted; March-April 1778; May 1778-confined in guard house; June 1778.
Potter, John	Private	Fourth, Mitchell	Dec 1777-March 1778; April 1778-sick in camp; May 1778-sick Princeton Hospital; June 1778.
Potter, Samuel	Sergeant	Third, Mott	Dec 1777-March 1778; April 1778-sick in Jersey; May-June 1778-sick absent.
Potter, Thomas	Corporal/ Sergeant	Second, Kinsey	Dec 1777-sick hospital; Jan-April 1778; May 1778-promoted to sergeant; May-June 1778.
Potts, Jasper	Private	Third, Ross	Dec 1777-March 1778; April 1778-on furlough; May-June 1778.
Pounder, William	Private	Second, Hollingshead	May 8, 1778-enlisted; June 1778.
Powell, John	Private	Second, Luse	Dec 3, 1777-deserted.
Powell/Powel, Thomas	Drum Major	First	Dec 1777-Feb 1778-absent in Jersey; March 1778.
Powers, George	Private	Fourth, Anderson	Dec 1777-April 1778; May 1778-on command; June 1778.
Powers - see Bowers			
Powers/ Power, Thomas	Corporal	Fourth, Forman	Dec 1777-March 1778; April 1778-on guard; May 1778; June 1778-returned from hospital.
Price, Benjamin/ Bennam	Private	Fourth, Anderson	Dec 1777-Jan 1778-sick present; Feb-June 1778.
Price, John	Private	Third, Ballard	Dec 1777-Feb 1778; March 1778-on command; April 1778-on weeks command; May 1778-on guard; June 1778.
Price, John	Private	Fourth, Lyon	Dec 1777-Jan 1778; Feb-April 1778-sick present; May-June 1778.
Price, Rice	Private	Fourth, Lyon	June 15, 1778-joined; June 1778.
Price, Stephen	Private	Third, Ballard	Dec 1777-Feb 1778; March 1778-on command; April 1778; May-June 1778-sick in Princetown.
Price, Thomas	Private	Spencer's, Weatherby	Dec 1777-Jan 1778-sick hospital; Feb 1778-deserted from hospital; May 29, 1778-joined; May 1778; June 1778-supposed to be deserted; Sept 9, 1778-returned.
Price, William	Private	Second, Phillips	Feb 14, 1778-enlisted; March 1778; April 5, 1778-taken prisoner.

Name	Rank	Company	Notes
Pricket/ Prichet, John	Private	First, Longstreet	May 24, 1778-joined; May 1778; June 1778-sick present.
Prickett, John	Private	Fourth, Forman	May 1778.
Pridmore/ Prigmire John	Private	First, Angel	May 31, 1778-joined; May-June 1778.
Prince, Thomas	Private	Fourth, Kinsey	June 1778.
Printey, William	Private	Second, Phillips	Dec 1777; Jan 1778-on command; Feb-April 1778; May-June 1778-on command.
Prior, Thomas	Private	First, Piatt	June 15, 1778-deserted.
Proctor/ Procter, Robert	Private	Fourth, Kinsey	March 10, 1778-enlisted; March 31, 1778-joined; March 1778; April 1778-sick present; May-June 1778-sick hospital.
Prout, James	Private	Third, Cox	May 1, 1778-joined; May 1778; June 1778-on command. This James Prout and the one listed below are probably the same individual.
Prout, James	Private	Spencer's, Ward	Dec 1777-March 1778; April 1778-sick present; May 1778-"being a substitute and transf^d to the Jersey Brigade 10 May."
Pruden, Adaniran	Private	Third, Ballard	Dec 1777-Feb 1778; March 1778-on command; April 1778-on weeks command; May 1778-on command at lines; June 1778-on furlough.
Quackenbush, Isaac	Private	First, Longstreet	May 26, 1778-joined; May 1778; June 1778-on command.
Quick, Moses	Private	First, Piatt	Feb 20, 1778-enlisted; March 1778; April 1778-on the lines; May 1778-sick present; June 1778-sick absent.
Quick, William	Private	Fourth, Anderson	May 28, 1778-joined; May-June 1778.
Quigley, David	Private	Fourth, Anderson	Dec 1777-June 1778.
Quimby/ Quimbey, John	Private	First, Piatt	Jan 1778-on furlough in Jersey; Feb-April 1778-sick in Jersey; May-June 1778-sick absent.
Race, Andrew	Private	Fourth, Anderson	May 28, 1778-enlisted; June 1778.
Ralph, Richard	Private	Fourth, Forman	June 15, 1778-joined; June 1778.
Randle/ Randal, Rufus	Private	First, Baldwin	Dec 1777-Jan 1778-sick Bethlehem; Feb 1778-sick in Jersey; March 1778; April 1778-on fatigue; May-June 1778.

Name	Rank	Company	Service
Rankins, James	Private	Second, Luse	Dec 1777-June 1778.
Rarity, John	Private	First, Mead	June 5, 1778-enlisted; June 1778.
Ray/Rhea, James	Private	Third, Mott	Dec 1777; Jan 1778-sick absent; Feb 1778; March 1778-on guard; April-June 1778.
Raymond/Ramond, James	Private	Fourth, Lyon	Dec 1777-Feb 1778; March 1778-sick present; April-June 1778.
Raynolds/Reanolds, Thomas	Private	Spencer's, Ward	Dec 1777-April 1778; May 1778-command lines; June 1778.
Read, William	Private	First, Mead	June 5, 1778-joined; June 1778.
Reading, John	1st. Lt.	Third, Cox	Dec 1777-Jan 1778; Feb-March 1778-on command; April-June 1778. Oath at Valley Forge on May 11, 1778.
Reading, Samuel	Captain	Second, Reading	Jan 1778-on command; Feb-June 1778.
Ready, James	Private	First, Baldwin	Dec 1777-deserted.
Redding/Reddinger, Samuel	Sergeant	Forman's, Wikoff	Dec 1777-April 1778; May 1778-command; June 1778.
Redman, John	Private	Fourth, Forman	Dec 1777-Feb 1778; March 1778-on command; April-June 1778.
Read, George	Private	Third, Ballard	May 28, 1778-enlisted; May-June 1778.
Reece/Reese, Thomas	Private	First, Morrison	Dec 29, 1777-enlisted; Jan-Feb 1778; March 1778-on command; April 1778; May 1778-on command; June 1778-sick Princeton
Reed, Clawson	Sergeant/Private	Second, Phillips	Dec 1777; Jan 1778-on command; Feb-April 1778; May 15, 1778-reduced to private; May 1778; June 1778-sick absent.
Reed/Read, Ephraim	Private	First, Polhemus	May 1778 muster roll shows he joined on May 25, but the payroll shows he joined on May 29. May-June 1778.
Reed, George	Private	First, Flahavan	Dec 1777-April 1778; May 1778-command; June 1778.
Reed/Read, Giles	Private	Third, Paterson	Dec 1777-Jan 1778-sick absent; Feb 1778-sick in Jersey; March-June 1778.
Reed, Isaiah	Private	Third, Anderson	Dec 1777-June 1778.
Reed/Read, John	Private	Second, Reading	Jan 1778-on command; Feb-June 1778.

Name	Rank	Company	Service
Reed, John	2nd. Lt.	Fourth, Martin	Dec 1777-Jan 1778; Feb-March 1778-on furlough; April 1778; May 1778-on command; June 1778.
Reed/Read, John	Private	Fourth, Holmes	Dec 1777-sick present; Jan-May 1778; June 1778-on command.
Reed, John	Sergeant	Spencer's, Wilkins	Dec 1777-June 1778.
Reed, Lewis	Private	Spencer's, Ward	Dec 1777-Feb 1778; March 24, 1778-discharged.
Reed, Thomas	Private	Second, Phillips	Dec 1777-April 1778; May 1778-on guard; June 1778.
Reed, William	Private	First, Morrison	June 13, 1778-joined; June 1778. On June 1778 payroll he was paid back to Dec 29, 1777.
Reed, William	Private	Spencer's, Wilkins/ Edsall	Dec 1777-Jan 1778-sick absent; Feb-March 1778-on furlough; May 1778-tending sick; June 1778-sick absent. Transferred to Edsall's Co. in May.
Reese, David	Private	Third, Gifford	Dec 1777-Feb 1778; March-April 1778-on guard; May-June 1778.
Renock/ Renok, Jacob	Private	Third, Paterson	May 27, 1778-joined; May-June 1778.
Reeves, James	Private	Spencer's, Wilkins	Dec 30, 1777-died.
Reeves, John	Private	Fourth, Forman	May 30, 1778-joined; May-June 1778.
Reubart, John	Private	First, Piatt	May 26, 1778-joined; May-June 1778.
Reynolds, George	1st. Lt.	Second, Sparks	Dec 1777; Jan 3, 1778-resigned.
Reynolds, James	Private	Third, Ballard	May 26, 1778-enlisted; May-June 1778.
Reynolds, John	Private	Second, Hollingshead	May 26, 1778-enlisted; June 1778.
Reynolds/ Raynolds, Thomas	Private	Spencer's, Brodrick	Dec 1777-March 1778; April 1778-on guard; May 1778-tending sick; June 1778.
Rhea, David	Lt. Col.	Second	Jan-June 1778.
Rhea, Jonathan	Ensign	Second, Bowman/ Reading	March-April 1778; May 1778-on command; June 1778-transferred to Reading's Co.
Ribbets/ Ribbits, William	Private	Fourth, Forman	Dec 1777-Feb 1778; March 1778-on command; April 1778; May 1778-on command; June 1778.
Rice, James	Corporal	First, Polhemus	Dec 1777; Jan-Feb 1778-on command; March-April 1778; May 1778-at lines; June 1778-sick at Princeton.
Rice, Thaddeus	Private	Fourth, Mitchell	Dec 1777-April 1778; May 1778-sick Princeton Hospital; June 1778.

Name	Rank	Company	Service
Richard, Carter - see Carter, Richard			
Richardson, John	Private	Fourth, Forman	Dec 1777-Jan 1778; Feb 25, 1778-died.
Richardson, Joseph	Private	First, Longstreet	May 26, 1778-joined; May-June 1778.
Richman, John	Volunteer	First, Polhemus	March 1778.
Rickey, Cornelius	Private	Third, Ballard	May 21, 1778-enlisted; May 1778; June 1778-on guard.
Rider, Seth	Private	First, Piatt	Dec 1777-Jan 1778-sick in Reading; Feb 15, 1778-dead.
Riggar/Ryger, Peter	Private	Second, Cummings	Dec 1777-April 1778; May 1778-on command; June 1778.
Riker/Ricker, John J.	Private	First, Morrison	May 27, 1778-joined; May-June 1778.
Riker, John Berian	Surgeon	Fourth	Dec 1777-April 1778; May 1778-Hunterdon Co. sick; June 1778-sick. Oath at Valley Forge on May 11, 1778.
Riley/Reyley, Jacob	Private	Spencer's, Weatherby	Dec 1777-Jan 1778-sick hospital; Feb 1778-sick absent; March 1778-sick hospital; April 1778-deserted.
Riley/Ryley, James	Corporal	Third, Anderson	Dec 1777-June 1778.
Riley/Reley, Thomas	Private	Forman's, Combs	May-June 1778.
Rinearson, Isaac	Private	First, Angel	May 31, 1778-joined; May 1778-on command; June 1778.
Rinehart/Reneheart, Matthias	Private	First, Angel	Jan-Feb 1778; March 17, 1778-dead.
Rinehart/Rhinehart, Philip	Private	Third, Anderson	Dec 1777-Feb 1778.
Riorden, John	Private	Third, Anderson	June 7, 1778-enlisted; June 1778.
Risner, Adam	Private	Fourth, Anderson	June 1778-on command.
Roads/Rodes, Matthew	Drummer/ Private/ Drummer/ Private	First, Angel	Dec 1777-Jan 1778; Jan 1778-reduced to private; Feb 1778; March-April 1778-on command; April 15, 1778-promoted to drummer; May 1778-reduced to private; May 1778; June 1778-dead
Roberson, James	Private	Third, Ballard	June 5, 1778-enlisted; June 1778-on guard.
Roberts, John	Drummer	Fourth, Forman	April 1, 1778-joined; April-June 1778.

Name	Rank	Company	Service
Roberts, Stephen	Private	Fourth, Lyon	Dec 1777-March 1778-sick absent; April-June 1778-sick Chatham.
Roberts/ Robert, Thomas	Sergeant Major	Forman's	Dec 1777-May 1778; June 1778-on furlough.
Robertson/ Robinson, Cornelius	Fifer	Third, Hennion	Dec 1777-June 1778; June 30, 1778-reduced to private.
Robertson/ Robeson, Isaac	Private	Third, Hennion	Dec 1777-Feb 1778; March 1778-on furlough; April 1778; May 1778-sick Yellow Springs; June 1778.
Robertson, Isaac	Private	Fourth, Lyon	June 15, 1778-joined; June 1778-sick present.
Robertson, Jacob	Private	Second, Cummings	April 1778; May 1778-sick absent.
Robins, Thomas	Private	Second, Phillips	May 22, 1778-enlisted; May 28, 1778-joined; May-June 1778.
Robins, Thomas	Private	Spencer's, Weatherby	Dec 1777-Feb 1778; March 1778-sick present; April-May 1778; June 1778-on guard.
Robins, William	Private	Forman's, Burowes	Dec 1777-June 1778.
Robinson, Edmund	Private	Forman's, Burowes	Dec 1777-June 1778.
Robinson, James	Private	Second, Helms	May 12, 1778-enlisted; June 7, 1778-joined; June 1778.
Robinson, John	Corporal	Second, Hollingshead	Dec 1777-March 1778; April 5, 1778-taken prisoner at Cooper's Ferry; July 17, 1778-exchanged.
Robinson/ Robertson, Robert	1st. Lt.	First, Baldwin	Dec 1777-wounded; Jan-Feb 1778; March-April 1778-on command Bethlehem; May-June 1778.
Robinson/ Robison, William	Private	Spencer's, Wilkins	Dec 1777-March 1778-sick absent; April 1778-sick Bethlehem.
Rockhill, William	Private	Fourth, Holmes	Dec 1777-Feb 1778-hospital; March 1778-sick in hospital; April 1778-sick Princeton; May 1778-sick absent.
Rockley, George	Private	Second, Luse	Dec 1777-June 1778.
Rodgers/ Rogers, David	Drummer	Fourth, Lyon	Dec 1777-May 1778; June 1778-on command.
Rodgers, James	Private	First, Mead	June 1778.
Rodgers/ Rogers, James	Sergeant Major	Fourth	Dec 1777-June 1778.
Roff, Adam	Private	Spencer's, Maxwell	Dec 1777-April 1778-sick absent; May 1778-sick absent Trenton; June 1778.

Name	Rank	Unit	Service
Rogers, William	Private	Forman's, Combs	Dec 1777-June 1778.
Roller/Roler, Philip	Private	First, Polhemus	June 4, 1778-joined; June 1778.
Rolph, Jonathan	Private	Fourth, Forman	May 26, 1778-joined; May-June 1778.
Rose/Ross, John	Corporal	First, Longstreet	Dec 1777-April 1778; May 1778-sick absent; June 1778.
Rose/Ross, John	Corporal	Fourth, Forman	Dec 1777-March 1778; April 12, 1778-deserted.
Rose, Joseph	Private	Third, Ballard	Dec 1777-Feb 1778; March 1778-sick present; April-June 1778.
Rose, Thomas	Drum Major	First	Dec 1777-April 1778-absent in Jersey; May-June 1778.
Rose, William	Private	Second, Cummings	Dec 1777; Jan 1778-on command; Feb-April 1778; May 1778-on command; June 1778.
Roseburgh/Roseburg, John	Private	Fourth, Forman	Dec 1777-March 1778; April 1778-on guard; May 1778-on command; June 1778.
Rosegrants/Rosegrane, Peter	Private	Spencer's, Edsall	Dec 1777-March 1778; April 1778-sick present; May 1778-sick in camp; June 1778.
Rosely, Richard	Private	Third, Ballard	June 15, 1778-enlisted; June 1778-sick present.
Ross, George	2nd. Lt.	Second, Helms	Dec 18, 1777-resigned.
Ross, John	Corporal	First, Morrison	May-June 1778.
Ross, John	Captain	Third, Ross	Dec 1777-Jan 1778; Feb-June 1778-on command.
Ross, William	Private	First, Angel	May 31, 1778-joined; May-June 1778.
Ross, William	Sergeant	Third, Anderson	Dec 1777-March 1778; April 1778-sick absent; May 1778-sick in Sussex; June 1778-sick absent; July 1, 1778-deserted.
Rounsaville, John	Private	Third, Anderson	May 1778 payroll shows he was taken prisoner on Staten Island in August 1777, and exchanged on July 14, 1778; July 1778 muster roll shows he was exchanged on July 14.
Rouse, John	Private	Second, Reading	March 17, 1778-enlisted; March 27, 1778-deserted.
Roy, Patrick	Private	First, Baldwin	June 1778.
Royal, David	Fifer	Third, Gifford	Dec 1777-June 1778.
Royal, John	Private	Third, Gifford	Dec 1777-June 1778.

Name	Rank	Company	Service
Rucastle/Ruecastle, John	2nd. Lt./ 1st. Lt.	Third, Paterson	Dec 1777; Jan 7, 1778 promoted to 1st. Lt.; Jan-Feb 1778; March 1778-on command; April-June 1778.
Ruckman/ Rutman, Samuel	Private	First, Angel	May 31, 1778-joined; May-June 1778.
Ruker, Jacob	Private	First, Mead	Jan 25, 1778-joined; Jan-March 1778; April 1778-on command; May-June 1778.
Ruker, John	Private	Fourth, Forman	Dec 1777-Feb 1778-wagoner; March 1778-on command; April-June 1778-wagoner.
Runyon/ Runyan, Conrad	Private	Third, Ballard	Dec 1777; Jan 1778-driving wagon; Feb 1778; March 1778-driving wagon; April 1778-sick present; May 1778; June 1778-on guard.
Rush, John	Private	First, Piatt	Dec 1777-March 1778; April 1778-sick present; May 1778-sick absent; June 1778.
Russel, William	Private	Forman's, Burowes	Dec 1777; Jan 1, 1778-deserted.
Russell/ Russle, Casper	Private	Second, Helms	May 10, 1778-enlisted; June 14, 1778-joined; June 1778-on guard.
Russell/ Russel, Edward	Corporal/ Private	Third, Mott	Dec 1777-March 1778; April 1778-sick absent; May 1778-reduced to private; June 1778-batman.
Russell, Thaddeus	Private	First, Morrison	May-June 1778.
Russell/ Russle, William	Sergeant	Fourth, Martin	Dec 1777-March 1778; April 1778-sick present; May-June 1778.
Ruterick, Joseph	Private	Second, Hollingshead	Dec 1777; Jan 25, 1778-deserted.
Ruth/Routh, James	Private/ Corporal	Spencer's, Pierson	Dec 1777-sick absent; Jan 1778-promoted to corporal; Jan-March 1778; April-May 1778-on furlough; June 1778-[deserted].
Rutherford, Thomas	Private	Forman's, Combs	Dec 1777-June 1778.
Ryan, John	Private	Fourth, Anderson	May 28, 1778-enlisted; June 1778.
Ryan, Patrick	Private	Third, Ross	Dec 1777-Feb 1778; March 1778-on guard; April 1778; May 1778-on command; June 1778-sick present.
Ryley/Riley, Edward	Private	Second, Cummings	March 1, 1778-joined; March-April 1778; May 1778-on command; June 1, 1778-[deserted].
Ryley, Joseph	Private	Third, Gifford	May 27, 1778-joined; May-June 1778.

Name	Rank	Company	Notes
Sahmant, Barnard	Private	First, Morrison	Dec 1777; Jan 1, 1778-deserted.
Sallisbury, Nathaniel	Private	Fourth, Anderson	May 1778 payroll-"in Elias Lyon's place." June 1778.
Sambo, Negro/ Stephenson, Samuel/ Simson, Samuel	Private	Fourth, Anderson	May 20, 1778-joined. The May 1778 payroll shows "Sam[1] Stephenson Negro" paid for eleven days service, but does not list Sambo. Neither Stephenson nor Sambo are on the June muster or payrolls but "Samuel Simson" appears for the first time on both. These appear to be the same man; May-June 1778.
Sampson/ Samson, Jacob	Private	Fourth, Holmes	Dec 1777-Feb 1778-hospital; March 1778-sick in hospital; April 1778-deserted.
Sandall/ Sandal, George	Drummer/ Private	Fourth, Anderson	Dec 1777-Feb 1778; Feb 1778-reduced to private; March 1778-sick present; April-May 1778-on command; June 1778.
Sanders, John	Private	First, Longstreet	May 24, 1778-joined, May 1778-sick present; June 1778.
Sanders, Thomas	Private	First, Longstreet	May 26, 1778-joined; May 1778; June 1778-on command.
Sanders, Timothy	Private	First, Piatt	May 21, 1778-joined; May 1778; June 1778-sick absent.
Sargeant, David	Private	First, Flahavan	May 25, 1778-enlisted; May-June 1778.
Saree/Sere, Lawrence	Private	Third, Hennion	Dec 1777-June 1778.
Saterly, Samuel	Private	Second, Helms	May 10, 1778-enlisted; June 14, 1778-joined; June 1778.
Satler, Charles	Private	Second, Cummings	Dec 1777; Jan 1778-dead.
Saunders/ Sanders, John	Private	Third, Paterson	Dec 1777-April 1778; May 1778-on guard; June 1778.
Saxon/Sexton, Timothy	Sergeant	Third, Holmes	Dec 1777-sick absent; Jan-Feb 1778; March 1778-on furlough; April 1778-on guard; May 1778; June 1778-on guard.
Saxton, Jessey	Private	Second, Luse	March 3, 1778-enlisted; April-June 1778.
Say, John	Private	Second, Phillips	March 30, 1778-enlisted; April-June 1778.
Sayres/Sears, Ichabod	Private	First, Flahavan	Dec 1777-March 1778-sick in Jersey; April 1778-deserted. April payroll states he was "returned deserted in Muster Rolls but since found to be a mistake." May-June 1778.

113

Name	Rank	Company	Notes
Schenck/Schenk, William	Ensign	Forman's, Wikoff	Dec 1777-June 1778.
Schooley, John	Private	Second, Luse	May 5, 1778-enlisted; June 1778.
Scithin/Sithin, John	Fifer	Second, Cummings	Dec 1777-June 1778.
Scobey, James	2nd. Lt.	Third, Anderson	December 15, 1777-resigned.
Scobey/Scoby, John	Sergeant	Spencer's, Weatherby	Dec 1777-sick hospital; Jan-March 1778; April 1778-on guard; May 1778-on duty; June 1778-on guard.
Scofield/Schofield, John	Sergeant	Spencer's, Edsall	May 1778-on furlough; June 1778.
Scott, Andrew	Private	Second, Cummings	Dec 1777; Jan 1, 1778-deserted.
Scott, Michael	Private	Second, Helms	May 10, 1778-enlisted; June 14, 1778-joined; June 1778.
Scudder, Abijah	Private	First, Piatt	Dec 1777-Feb 1778; March 1778-on command on the lines; April 1778-sick present; May 1778-sick absent; June 1778-sick present.
Scudder/Scuder, David	Private	Spencer's, Pierson	Dec 1777-Jan 1778; Feb-March 1778-on furlough; April-June 1778.
Scull, Daniel	Private	Second, Cummings	May 20, 1778-enlisted; May 27, 1778-joined; May 1778-on command; June 1778.
Scull/Scul, Daniel	Private	Fourth, Holmes	Dec 1777-Feb 1778-hospital; March 1778-sick in hospital; April-May 1778; June 20, 1778-deserted.
Scull/Schull, David	Private	First, Angel	Dec 1777-Feb 1778; March 1778-sick present; April 1778; May-June 1778-furlough.
Seaburn, Richard	Private	Second, Helms	May 9, 1778-enlisted; June 26, 1778-joined; June 1778-on guard.
Seagar, John	Private	Forman's, Forman	Dec 1777-June 1778.
Sealy/Seely, Samuel	2nd. Lt.	First, Mead	Dec 1777-Jan 1778; Feb 1778-on command; March 1778; April 1778-on command in Jersey; May 1778-on command; June 1778-sick at Chatham.
Search/Sarck, James	Private	Fourth, Anderson	May 28, 1778-enlisted; May-June 1778.
Sears/Seers, David	Private	Spencer's, Weatherby	Dec 1777-March 1778-on furlough; April 1778-deserted.
Sears/Seers, Samuel	Private	Fourth, Forman	May 20, 1778-joined; May-June 1778.
Sears, William	Private	First, Mead	June 5, 1778-enlisted; June 1778.

Name	Rank	Company	Notes
Seeds, William	Corporal	Fourth, Holmes	October 11, 1777-deserted; Feb 1778-deserted.
Seeley, John	Sergeant	Second, Sparks	May 10, 1778-enlisted; June 1778.
Seely/Cealey, John	Private	Fourth, Holmes	Dec 1777-Feb 1778; March 1778-on command; May-June 1778.
Seely, David	Private	Third, Paterson	May 1778; June 1778-on command.
Selnave/Salnave, Peter	Private	First, Angel	Dec 1777-Jan 1778-sick at Elizabethtown; Feb 1778-sick at Springfield; March 1778-sick at Elizabethtown; April 1, 1778-deserted; June 1778-main guard.
Sennet, Richard	Private	Third, Gifford	Dec 1777-June 1778.
Sewart, Samuel	Private	First, Mead	June 5, 1778-joined, June 1778-missing at Monmouth.
Sezar - see Cezar			
Shaddock/Shadick Levi	Private	Fourth, Mitchell	Dec 1777-June 1778.
Shafer, John	Private	Third, Ballard	Dec 11, 1777-died.
Shafer/Sheafer, Theophilus.	Private	Third, Mott	March 1778; April 1778-on guard; May-June 1778.
Shannon, Daniel	Private	Third, Cox	Dec 1, 1777-enlisted; Dec 1777; Jan 23, 1778-deserted.
Sharon, John	Private	First, Morrison	Dec 29, 1777-enlisted; Jan 1, 1778-deserted.
Sharp, Henry	Private	Spencer's, Weatherby	Dec 1777-Jan 1778-sick hospital; Feb 1778-deserted.
Sharp, Hugh	Private	Second, Luse	Feb 1, 1778-joined; Feb-April 1778; May 1, 1778-deserted.
Shavaral/Chiverall, George	Private	Spencer's, Wilkins/Edsall	Dec 1777-April 1778-sick absent; May 1778-tending sick; June 1778-sick absent. Transferred to Edsall's Co. in May.
Shaver, Jacob	Private	Second, Luse	Dec 1777-April 1778; May 1778-on command; June 1778.
Shaver, Joseph	Private	Second, Luse	Feb 21, 1778-enlisted; March-April 1778; May 1778-on guard; June 1778.
Shaw, Daniel	Private	Spencer's, Pierson	Dec 1777-sick absent.
Shaw, David	Private	First, Piatt	May 26, 1778-joined; May 1778; June 1778-on guard.
Shaw, Emanuel	Private	Forman's, Combs	Dec 1777-June 1778.

Name	Rank	Company	Notes
Shaw, John	Private	First, Morrison	Dec 1777; Jan 1778-sick in hospital; Feb 1778-sick absent; March 1778-sick in Jersey; April 1778-deserted; June 1778-sick at Newark.
Shaw, John	Private	Second, Hollingshead	May 8, 1778-enlisted; May 1778-sick hospital; June 1778-command.
Shaw, John, Jr.	Private	Second, Hollingshead	March 30, 1778-enlisted; April-May 1778; June 1, 1778-deserted.
Shaw, John	Private	Spencer's, Pierson	Dec 1777-Jan 1778-sick absent; Feb-April 1778-sick in country.
Shay/Shea, James	Sergeant	Third, Ross	Dec 1777; Jan 1778-on command; Feb-May 1778; June 1778-on guard.
Shearman, John	Private	Third, Gifford	Dec 1777-March 1778; April 1778-on guard; May-June 1778.
Shears/Shoers, Jonathan	Private	Third, Ross	May 20, 1778-enlisted; June 1778.
Shelock, John William	Private	Second, Hollingshead	Dec 1777-June 1778.
Shepherd, Nathan	Private	Second, Cummings	Dec 1777-June 1778.
Sheridan/Sherridan, John	Private	Fourth, Forman	May 31, 1778-joined; May-June 1778.
Sherrard/Shirrid, James	Private	First, Angel	Jan 16, 1778-joined; Jan-April 1778; May-June 1778-on command.
Shipman, John	Private	Spencer's, Lyon	Dec 1777-Jan 1778-sick Chatham; Feb 1778.
Shipman, Joseph	Private	First, Flahavan	Dec 1777-Feb 1778; March 1778-on His Excellency's Guard.
Shippard/Sheppard, Samuel	Adjutant	Third	Dec 1777-June 1778. Oath at Valley Forge on May 11, 1778.
Shires/Shiers, Richard	Drummer	First, Mead	Dec 1777-May 1778; June 1778-sick hospital.
Shirts, Mathias	Corporal	Fourth, Martins	Dec 1777-June 1778.
Shoemaker, William	Private	Second, Bowman	Dec 1777-June 1778.
Shores/Shords, Joseph	Private	Fourth, Anderson	Dec 1777; Jan 1778-wagoner; Feb-March 1778; April 1778-sick in camp; May 10, 1778-died.
Showers, Adam	Private	Fourth, Mitchell	Dec 1777-April 1778; May-June 1778-sick in Princeton Hospital.
Shreve, Israel	Colonel	Second	Jan-May 1778; June 1778-sick absent.
Shreve, John	2nd. Lt.	Second, Luse	Dec 1777-June 1778.
Shrigley, Azariah	Private	Second, Phillips	March 1, 1778 enlisted; March-April 1778; May-June 1778-on command.

Name	Rank	Company	Notes
Shubart/ Shubach, John	Private	First, Longstreet	May 24, 1778-joined; May-June 1778.
Shumard/ Chumard, Thomas	Private	Fourth, Lyon	Dec 1777-April 1778; May-June 1778-on command.
Shurmer, Benjamin	Private	Third, Holmes	Feb 20, 1778-enlisted; March 30, 1778-deceased.
Shute, Samuel Moore	Ensign/ 2nd. Lt.	Second, Cummings	Dec 13, 1777-promoted to 2nd. Lt.; Dec 1777; Jan 1778-on furlough; Feb-April 1778; May 1778-on command; June 1778.
Sickle, Jacob	Corporal	Third, Anderson	Dec 1777-April 1778; May 1778-on command; June 1778.
Sigler/Segler, John Phillip	Private	Second, Hollingshead	May 28, 1778-enlisted; June 23, 1778-deserted.
Silvester, Peter	Private	First, Polhemus	May 1778; June 1778-sick Princeton.
Simmons/ Simons, James	Private	Fourth, Forman	Dec 1777-Feb 1778; March 1778-on command; April 1778; May 1778-on command; June 1778-deserted.
Simpson/ Simson, Abraham	Private	First, Polhemus	Dec 1777-sick absent; Jan 1778; Feb-March 1778-sick Jerseys; April 1778-Jersey; May-June 1778-sick Princeton.
Simpson, Thomas	Private	First, Mead	May 1778; June 1778-at Chatham.
Simson, Samuel - see Sambo, Negro			
Sinclair/ Sinclear, George	Private	Second, Reading	May 26, 1778-enlisted; June 1778 muster roll shows he joined on May 1 but the June 1778 payroll shows his pay beginning on May 14; June 1778.
Sitcher, William	1st. Lt.	Spencer's, Brittin	June 1778.
Skilman/ Skillman, Thomas	Private	First, Angel	Dec 1777-April 1778; May-June 1778-on command.
Skilton, Thomas	Private	Second, Cummings	June 1778.
Slater, John	Private	Fourth, Kinsey	May 1778; June 1778-sick hospital.
Slingland, Henry	Private	First, Longstreet	June 4, 1778-joined; June 1778-sick present.
Sloan, James	Private	First, Piatt	May-June 1778-with the artillery.
Small, William	Private	Fourth, Martin	May 30, 1778-joined; May-June 1778.
Smallwood, John	Private	Second, Hollingshead	May 27, 1778-enlisted; June 1778.

Name	Rank	Company	Notes
Smith, Charles	Private	First, Angel	Dec 25, 1777-joined; Dec 1777-Jan 1778; Feb 1778-deserted.
Smith, Daniel	Private	Spencer's, Wilkins/ Edsall	Dec 1777-April 1778; May 1778-sick in camp; June 1778-sick absent.
Smith, Hosea	Private	Second, Cummings	Dec 1777; Jan 1778-on command; Feb-June 1778.
Smith, James	Sergeant/ Private	Forman's, Combs	Dec 1777-Jan 1778; Jan 12, 1778-reduced to the ranks; Feb 15, 1778-deserted.
Smith, James	Private	Forman's, Burowes	Dec 1777-June 1778.
Smith, Jesse see Smith, Joseph	Private	First, Angel	Dec 1777-Feb 1778-sick absent; April 1778-dead.
Smith, John	Private	First, Longstreet	May 24, 1778-joined; May-June 1778.
Smith, John	Private	First, Morrison	Feb 19, 1778-enlisted; March 1778; April 1778-sick present; May 1778-on picket: June muster roll shows he deserted on May 8.
Smith, John	Private	First, Morrison	Feb 19, 1778-enlisted; Feb-April 1778; May 8, 1778-deserted; June 1778.
Smith, John	Corporal/ Private	First, Piatt	Dec 1777; Jan-Feb 1778-blind; March 1778; April 1778-reduced to private, unfit for service. A John Smith appears on the May 1778 payroll, beginning on May 21, and is on the rolls for July, but is not on the June rolls. See below.
Smith, John	Private	First, Piatt	May 21, 1778-enlisted. See above.
Smith, John	Corporal	Second, Bowman	Dec 1777; Jan 3, 1778-deserted; June 15, 1778-joined.
Smith, John	Private	Second, Luse	May 10, 1778-enlisted; June 1778.
Smith, John	Private	Fourth, Kinsey	Dec 1777-March 1778-sick hospital; April 1778-deserted.
Smith, John	Private	Fourth, Martin	Dec 1777; Jan 1778-sick absent; Feb-March 1778; April 1778-sick present; May 1778-sick Pennsylvania; June 1778.
Smith, Joseph see Smith, Jesse	Private	First, Angel	March 1778-sick at Lancaster. This is the only mention of Joseph Smith and is probably the same individual as Jesse Smith, who does not appear on the roll of Angel's Co. for March 1778.
Smith, Matthew	Private	Forman's, Burowes	Dec 1777-June 1778.

Smith, Michael	Private	First, Mead	Dec 1777-March 1778; April 1778-sick present; May-June 1778.
Smith/Smyth, Michael/ Mikel	Private	Spencer's, Brittin	Dec 1777; Jan 1778-missing since Jan 1, 1778.
Smith, Nathaniel	Private	Second, Cummings	May 26, 1778; enlisted; June 5, 1778-joined; June 1778.
Smith, Peter	Corporal	Third, Ballard	Dec 1777-Feb 1778; March 1778-on furlough; April-June 1778.
Smith, Peter	Private	Third, Cox	Dec 1777-Feb 1778-sick in hospital; March 1778-sick absent; April 1778; May 1778-at Yellow Springs Hospital; June 1778-sick at Yellow Springs.
Smith, Samuel	Private	Fourth, Mitchell	May 1778-sick Princeton Hospital; June 1778.
Smith, Samuel	Private	Forman's, Burowes	Dec 1777-June 1778.
Smith, Terence	Private	Fourth, Forman	Dec 1777-March 1778-sick in hospital; April 1778; May 1778-on command; June 1778-sick absent. June 1778 payroll notes he returned from the hospital.
Smith, Thomas	Private	Fourth, Lyon	Dec 1777-Feb 1778; March 1778-sick present; April 27, 1778-died.
Smith, Thomas	Private	Forman's, Combs	Dec 1777-June 1778.
Smith, Thomas	Private	Forman's, Burowes	Dec 1777-April 1778; May 1778-sick at Princeton; June 1778.
Smith, William	Private	First, Longstreet	June 4, 1778-joined; June 1778-sick absent.
Smith, William	Private	Third, Ross	Sept 11, 1777-taken prisoner; Jan-March 1778-prisoner with ye enemy.
Smith, William	Private	Fourth, Martin	Dec 1777-March 1778; April 1778-sick present; May 1778-sick Yellow Springs; June 1778-Yellow Springs.
Smith, William	Private	Spencer's, Pierson	Dec 1777-March 1778-on furlough; April 1778-deserted.
Smith, Zenos	Private	Second, Hollingshead	May 26, 1778-enlisted; June 1778.
Smock/ Smook, Josiah	Private	First, Angel	May 31, 1778-joined; May 1778-on command; June 1778.
Snell, Richard	Private	Second, Hollingshead	Dec 1777-June 1778.
Snowden, Jonathan	2nd. Lt.	First, Morrison	Dec 1777-furlough; Jan-June 1778.
Snyder, Christian	Private	Third, Cox	Dec 1777-March 1778; April 1778-sick absent in Pennsylvania; May-June 1778-sick in Pennsylvania.

Name	Rank	Company	Notes
Snyder, Elias	Private	Third, Cox	Dec 1777-Feb 1778-sick at Morristown; March 1778-sick absent; April-May 1778-sick absent in Pennsylvania; June 1778-sick in Pennsylvania.
Snyder/Snider, Henry	Private	Spencer's, Maxwell	Dec 1777-Feb 1778; March 1778-on command; April-June 1778.
Snyder, Martin	Private	Third, Cox	Dec 1777-April 1778; May 1, 1778-deserted.
Snyder, Peter	Private	Third, Cox	Dec 1777-Feb 1778; March 1778-deserted.
Sodan/Soden, Joshua	Private	First, Anderson	Dec 1777-Feb 1778; March 1778-sick present; April-June 1778.
Solley, Nathaniel	Private	Third, Gifford	June 26, 1778-joined, June 1778-on command.
Sollomon, John	Private	Third, Paterson	June 1778.
Solm/Sollom, John	Private	First, Longstreet	May 24, 1778-joined; May 1778-on command; June 1778.
Soper/Soapert, Joseph	Private	First, Mead	Dec 1777-March 1778; April 1778-on command; May 1778-sick at Princeton; June 1778-on command.
Soper/Soppor, Thomas	Private	Fourth, Martin	Dec 1777; Jan 1778-on command; Feb-March 1778; April 1778-sick present; May 1778-sick Yellow Springs; June 1778 Yellow Springs.
Sork/Sorke, Michael	Private	Fourth, Martin	Dec 1777; Jan 1778-on command; Feb-April 1778; May 1778-sick Princeton; June 1778.
Southerland/Southerlen, James	Private	Spencer's, Lyon	Dec 1777-Jan 1778-sick Kakiat; March 1, 1778-deserted; June 1778.
Southward/Suthard, Abraham	Private	Third, Mott	Jan-June 1778-sick absent.
Space, John	Private	Second, Luse	March 15, 1778-joined; March-April 1778; May 15, 1778-deserted.
Sparks, John	1st. Lt./Captain	Second, Sparks	Dec 1777; Jan 1, 1778-promoted to captain; Jan-May 1778; June 1778-on furlough.
Spear, Abraham	Private	First, Morrison	May-June 1778.
Spear/Speer, David	Private	Spencer's, Wilkins/Edsall	Dec 1777-Feb 1778-sick absent; March-April 1778; May 1778-sick camp; June 1778-sick absent. In May he transferred to Edsall's Co.
Spencer, Oliver	Colonel	Spencer's	Dec 1777-on furlough; Jan-Feb 1778; March 1778-on furlough; April-June 1778. Oath at Valley Forge on May 11, 1778.

Name	Rank	Company	Service
Spencer, Robert	Paymaster	Spencer's	Dec 1777-April 1778; May 1778-on furlough; June 1778.
Spicer, John	Private	Fourth, Martin	Dec 1777-Feb 1778; March 1778-on command; April 1778; May 1778-on guard; June 1778-Yellow Springs.
Spinnage/Spinage Isaac	Private	First, Baldwin	May-June 1778.
Springer, Levi/Levea	Private	Fourth, Holmes	Dec 1777-April 1778; May 1778-on guard; June 1778.
Sprouls/Sprowls, Moses	Private	Third, Paterson	Dec 1777; Jan 1778-sick absent; Feb-April 1778; May 1778-on command; June 1778.
Squire/Squir, Joseph	Private	Spencer's, Pierson	Dec 1777-March 1778; April 1778-sick present; May-June 1778.
Stackhouse, Amos	Private	First, Baldwin	Dec 1777-Feb 1778; March-April 1778-on command; May 1778-on guard; June 1778.
Stackhouse, John	Private	First, Baldwin	May-June 1778.
Stacks/Stakes, Daniel	Private	Second, Cummings	May 20, 1778-enlisted; May 24, 1778-joined; May-June 1778.
Staples/Steeples, Thomas	Private	Second, Sparks	Dec 1777-June 1778.
Starkey, William	Private	First, Longstreet	June 4, 1778-joined; June 1778.
Stephens, Andrew	Private	Spencer's, Ward	Dec 1777-April 1778; May 1778-"Being a substitute transf^d to the Jersey Brigade 10 May."
Stephens, Charles	Private	Fourth, Kinsey	Dec 1777-sick present; Jan-April 1778; May 1778-on command; June 1778.
Stephens/Stevens, Ebenezer	Private	Spencer's, Brodrick	Dec 1777-sick in hospital; Jan 1778; Feb 1778-sick absent; March 1778-sick in hospital; April 1778; May-June 1778-Trenton Hospital.
Stephens/Stevens, Henry	Private	First, Morrison	Dec 1777-Jan 1778; Feb 1778-sick in hospital; March 1778-sick in Jersey; April 1778-deserted.
Stephens/Steaphines, Isaac	Private	Third, Anderson	July 16, 1777-deserted. Apparently returned as he appears on the April 1778 rolls but on April 24, 1778, deserted again.
Stephens, Robert	Private	Fourth, Forman	Dec 1777-sick in hospital. See Nunn, Ephraim.
Stephens, Stephen	Private	Second, Cummings	May 21, 1778-enlisted; May 27, 1778-joined; May-June 1778.

Name	Rank	Company	Notes
Stephenson, Cornelius	Private	Second, Sparks	May 1778 payroll shows he enlisted on May 2; the May muster shows he enlisted on May 10; June 1778-joined; June 1778
Stephenson/ Stevenson, James	Corporal	First, Longstreet	May 24, 1778-joined, May 1778-on guard; June 1778.
Stephenson, Matthew	Sergeant Major	First	Dec 1777-absent with leave.
Stephenson, Samuel			See Sambo, Negro.
Stephenson/ Steveson, William	Private	First, Angel	May 31, 1778-joined; May 1778; June 1778-"joynd" artillery.
Stevens/ Stephens, Daniel	Private	Fourth, Forman	May 20, 1778-joined; May 1778; June 28, 1778-missing.
Stevens, Nicholas	Private	Forman's, Burowes	Dec 1777-June 1778.
Stevens, William	Private	Second, Helms	May 10, 1778-enlisted; June 14, 1778-joined; June 1778.
Stewart, Alexander	Private	Second, Reading	May 14, 1778-enlisted. The June 1778 muster roll shows he joined on May 1, but the June payroll shows his pay beginning on May 14; June 1778.
Stewart/ Steward, Alexander	Private	Fourth, Kinsey	Dec 1777-sick hospital; Jan-Feb 1778-waiter at hospital; March 1778 payroll shows he enlisted on March 1 and the March 1778 muster roll shows he joined on March 31. March-May 1778.
Stewart/ Steward, John	Private	First, Piatt	May 21, 1778-joined; May-June 1778.
Stewart, John	Ensign	Fourth, Kinsey	December 30, 1777-resigned.
Stewart/ Stuart, Jonathan	Private	First, Morrison	Dec 1777; Jan 1778-left [ ] in Jersey; Feb 1778-sick absent in Jersey; March 1778-sick in Jersey; April 1778-deserted; May 1778-sick at home Newark; June 1778-sick at Newark.
Stewart, Robert	Private	Fourth, Kinsey	Nov 1777-wounded; Dec 1777-dead.
Stewart, Thomas	Private	First, Mead	June 5, 1778-enlisted; June 1778-guard.
Stewart, William	Private	First, Mead	June 1778 payroll shows him as "Prisoner Joind from N York."
Stiff, John	Sergeant	Second, Helms	May 10, 1778-enlisted; June 14, 1778-joined; June 1778.

Stiles, Aaron	Private	Spencer's, Ward	Dec 1777-Jan 1778-wounded; Feb 1778-wounded hospital; March 1778-wounded absent; April-May 1778; June 1778-on furlough.
Stiles, Job	Private	First, Morrison	Dec 1777; Jan 1778-sick hospital; Feb 1778-sick hospital; March 1778-sick in Jersey; April 1778-sick Jersey; May-June 1778.
Stillinger/ Stelinger, Thomas	Fifer	Second, Sparks	Dec 1777-June 1778.
Stillwell/ Stilwell, Ezekiel	Private	Fourth, Lyon	Dec 1777-June 1778.
Stillwell/ Stilwel, William	Private	First, Longstreet	May 1778-on command; June 1778.
Stineman/ Stinman, John	Private	Third, Ballard	Dec 1777-Jan 1778; Feb 1778-driving wagon; March 1778-sick present; April 1778; May 17, 1778-died.
Stirling, Lord - see Alexander, William			
Stivens, John	Private	Third, Cox	June 21, 1778-enlisted; June 26, 1778-joined; June 1778.
Stivers/Stives, Samuel	Private	Third, Cox	Dec 1777-Jan 1778-attending sick at hospital; Feb 1778-attending sick in hospital; March 1778-attending sick in ye hospital; April-June 1778.
Stives/ Stevens, William	Fifer	Third, Cox	March-June 1778.
Stone, Philip	Private	Fourth, Martin	Dec 11, 1777-deserted.
Stonebaugh/ Stonabaugh, Philip	Private	Second, Helms	May 9, 1778-enlisted; June 26, 1778-joined; June 1778.
Storm, Abraham	Private	First, Flahavan	Dec 1777-Jan 1778; Feb 1778-on command; March 1778-on furlough; April 1778-deserted. April payroll states he was "returned deserted in Muster Rolls but since found to be a mistake." May-June 1778.
Storm, John	Private	First, Piatt	May 21, 1778-joined; May-June 1778.
Story/Storey, William	Private	First, Angel	May 31, 1778-joined; May-June 1778.

Name	Rank	Company	Notes
Stout, Abraham	2nd. Lt./ 1st. Lt.	Second, Reading	Jan 1778-promoted to 1st. Lt.; Jan-March 1778; April 5, 1778-taken prisoner.
Stout, Elisha	Private	Forman's, Burowes	Dec 7, 1777-deserted.
Stout, James	Sergeant	First, Polhemus	June 1778-on command.
Stout, James	Private	Second, Phillips	Dec 1777; Jan 1778-sick absent; Feb-April 1778; May 1778-on guard; June 1778.
Stout, Joseph	Private	First, Piatt	Dec 1777-Feb 1778; March-April 1778-sick in Jersey; May 1778-sick absent; June 1778.
Stout, Wessel T.	2nd. Lt.	Fourth, Lyon	Dec 1777-Jan 1778; Feb 1778-on furlough; March 1778-on command; April-June 1778. Oath at Valley Forge on May 11, 1778.
Strattin, Annanias	Private	Second, Cummings	Dec 1777-April 1778; May 1778-on command; June 1778.
Striker, Abraham	Private	First, Longstreet	May 26, 1778-joined; May 1778-on furlough; June 1778.
Striker/ Stricke, John	Sergeant	First, Longstreet	May 24, 1778-joined; May-June 1778.
Strimple/ Strimel, John	Corporal	Fourth, Holmes	Dec 1777-Jan 1778-furlough; Feb-March 1778; April 1778-sick present; May 1778; June 1778-on guard.
Strope, George	Private	Third, Gifford	June 7, 1778-joined; June 1778.
Strowbridge/ Strobridge, Joseph	Private	First, Morrison	Dec 1777-April 1778; May 1778-sick Princeton; June 1778-bullock guard.
Stuart, David	Private	Fourth, Forman	May 20, 1778-joined; May 1778; June 1778-on guard.
Stuart/ Stewart, Hugh	Private	Spencer's, Wilkins/ Edsall	Dec 1777-March 1778; April 1778-on command at the lines; May 1778-sick camp; June 1778. In May he transferred to Edsall's Co.
Stuart, John	Private	Fourth, Mitchell	Dec 1777-on command at Rockaway; Jan-March 1778-on command; April-May 1778-attending sick at Trenton; June 1778.
Stull, Joseph	Private	First, Piatt	May 21, 1778-joined, May 1778-on command; June 1778-on guard.
Stutes, George	Private	Third, Mott	June 1778.
Suffy, William	Private	First, Polhemus	May 15, 1778-joined; May-June 1778.

Sullivan/ Sullevin, Cornelius	Private	Second, Luse	March 26, 1778-enlisted; April-June 1778.
Sullivan, Daniel	Private	Third, Mott	June 11, 1778-enlisted; June 12, 1778-joined; June 1778.
Sullivan, Joshua	Fifer	Forman's, Burowes	Dec 1777-June 1778.
Sullivan/ Sulivan, Patrick	Private	Second, Hollingshead	Dec 1777-June 1778.
Sullivan/ Sulivan, Timothy	Private	Third, Cox	Dec 1777-Feb 1778; March 1778-on command; April 1778; May 1778-on guard; June 1778.
Sutton, John	Private	First, Piatt	May 31, 1778-joined; June 1778.
Sutton, Jonas	Private	Third, Paterson	Dec 1777-Feb 1778; March-April 1778-on command; May-June 1778.
Sutton, Joseph	Private	Third, Paterson	June 1778.
Sutton, Peter	Private	First, Piatt	June 1778-on command.
Sutton, William	Private	First, Piatt	May 31, 1778-joined; May-June 1778.
Sutton, William	Private	Second, Luse	Dec 1777; Jan 1778-sick absent; Feb-April 1778; May 1778-sick absent; June 1778.
Swain, Jessy	Private	Third, Paterson	June 1778.
Swain/Swayn, Samuel	Private	Fourth, Forman	Dec 1777-March 1778-sick in hospital; April 1778-sick absent; May 1778-hospital Reading; June 1778-sick absent.
Swan, Joseph	Private	Second, Sparks	May 3, 1778-enlisted; June 1778.
Swany, Timothy	Private	Fourth, Mitchell	June 1778.
Sweden/ Sweeden, Casper	Private	Third, Holmes	Dec 1777-Feb 1778; March-April 1778-on command; May 1778; June 1778-on command.
Sweeden/ Sweeting Richard	Private	Third, Gifford	May 27, 1778-joined; May-June 1778.
Swift, James	Private	Third, Ballard	Dec 1777-April 1778; May 1778-on command Valley Forge; June 1778.
Swift, Richard	Corporal	Second, Bowman	Dec 1777; Jan 3, 1778-deserted.
Swim, Jesse	Private	Third, Paterson	June 26, 1778-joined; June 1778.

Name	Rank	Company	Service
Syren/Syran, John	Private	Spencer's, Brittin	Dec 1777-March 1778-on command; April-June 1778-sick Lancaster.
Sytes, Peter	Private	Third, Gifford	June 26, 1778-joined; June 1778.
Tallew/Tellew, Peter	Private	Third, Paterson	May 27, 1778-joined; May-June 1778.
Taylor, Abraham Clark	Private	First, Angel	May 31, 1778-joined; May-June 1778-on command.
Taylor, Christopher	Private	Fourth, Forman	Dec 1777-Feb 1778; March 1778-on command; April 1778-on command Lord Stirling's; May 1778-on command; June 1778-with Lord Stirling.
Taylor, David	Private	First, Morrison	May 27, 1778-joined; May-June 1778.
Taylor, John	Private	First, Mead	June 5, 1778-enlisted; June 1778.
Taylor, John	Private	Second, Cummings	April 6, 1778-joined; April-June 1778.
Taylor, Peter	Private	First, Piatt	Dec 1777-March 1778; April 1778-at the lines; May-June 1778.
Taylor, Robert	Private	First, Morrison	Dec 1777-March 1778; April 1778-sick present; May 20, 1778-died.
Taylor, Samuel	Private	First, Morrison	June 1778-furlough.
Taylor, William	Private	Forman's, Combs	Dec 1777-June 1778.
Teams, Absalom	Private	Second, Sparks	Dec 1777-April 1778; May 1778-on furlough; June 1778-on command.
Templeton, James	Private	First, Piatt	Dec 1777-April 1778; May 1778-sick absent; June 1778.
Tennant, William	Private	Fourth, Holmes	Dec 1777-Feb 1778-hospital; March 1778-sick in Glocester; April 1778-deserted.
Tharp, Benjamin	Private	Forman's, Burowes	Dec 1777-April 1778; May 10, 1778-taken prisoner.
Tharp, David	Private	Fourth, Lyon	June 1, 1778-joined; June 1778-on guard.
Tharp, Jacob	Private	First, Longstreet	Jan 1, 1778-enlisted; Jan 5, 1778-joined; Jan-May 1778; June 20, 1778-taken. The June 1778 payroll states he was "taken prisoner since exchanged."
Tharp, Peter	Private	Third, Cox	Dec 1777-June 1778.
Tharp/Thorp, Solomon/Saul	Private	Fourth, Forman	Dec 1777-Feb 1778; March-April 1778-on command; May-June 1778.
Tharp, Thomas	Private	Third, Cox	Dec 1777-June 1778.

Name	Rank	Company	Notes
Thomas, Alexander/ Elexander	Private	Spencer's, Brodrick	Dec 1777-Jan 1778; Feb 1778-sick present; March-April 1778; May-June 1778-sick in Sussex.
Thomas, Amos	Private	Fourth, Holmes	May 1778-deserted.
Thomas, Ebert	Private	Second, Cummings	May 20, 1778-enlisted; May 27, 1778-joined; May-June 1778.
Thomas, Edmund D.	1st. Lt.	Third, Ballard	Dec 1777-June 1778. Oath at Valley Forge on May 11, 1778.
Thomas/ Thoma, James	Private	First, Angel	Nov 1777-deserted; Jan 1778.
Thomas/ Tomas, John	Private	First, Angel	Dec 1777-April 1778; May 1778-sick Princeton; June 1778-sick absent.
Thomas, John	Corporal	Fourth, Anderson	Dec 1777-March 1778; April 1778-sick Yellow Springs; May-June 1778.
Thomas, Jonathan	Private	Second, Cummings	March 1, 1778-joined; March-April 1778; May 1778-on command; June 1, 1778-[deserted].
Thomas, Joseph	Private	Third, Paterson	December 9, 1777-deserted.
Thomas, Luke	Private	Spencer's, Brodrick	Dec 1777-on command; Jan 1778; Feb-March 1778-on command; April 1778; May 1778-on command lines; June 1778.
Thomas, Matthew	Private	Second, Cummings	June 1778-on command.
Thomas/ Tomas, Thomas	Private	Fourth, Holmes	March 23, 1778-enlisted, March 1778-sick present; April 1778; May 1778-sick absent; June 1778-hospital.
Thomas, Valentine	Private	Third, Anderson	May 1778 muster roll shows he joined on May 15, 1777; this is assumed to be 1778, as there are no earlier records; June 1778.
Thomas, William	Private	First, Polhemus	Dec 1777-Feb 1778; March 1778-sick present; April-June 1778.
Thompson, Amos	Private	Second, Hollingshead	May 26, 1778-enlisted; June 1778.
Thompson, Andrew	Private	First, Angel	Dec 1777-June 1778.
Thompson, Aron	Fifer	Fourth, Martin	Dec 1777-March 1778-sick absent; April 1778-sick Jersey; May 1778-sick absent; July 13, 1778-deserted.
Thompson, George	Corporal	Second, Helms	Dec 1777; Jan 24, 1778-[discharged].
Thompson, George	Private	Second, Phillips	May 28, 1778-enlisted; June 1778-sick absent.

Name	Rank	Company	Notes
Thompson/ Thomson, James	Private	Second, Helms	Dec 1777-June 1778.
Thompson, James	Private	Spencer's, Maxwell	Dec 1777-May 1778; June 1778-on guard.
Thompson, John	Private	Third, Paterson	Jan 19, 1778-enlisted; March 1, 1778-deserted.
Thompson, John	Corporal	Third, Ross	First appears on May 1778 payroll as "joined May 25, 1777" which must be an error for 1778; May-June 1778-on furlough
Thompson, Joshua	Private	Fourth, Kinsey	Nov 1777-sick hospital; Dec 1777-dead.
Thompson, Nathaniel	Private	Fourth, Mitchell	Dec 1777-March 1778; April 1778-sick in camp; May 4, 1778-died.
Thompson, Price	Private	Fourth, Mitchell	Dec 1777-sick at hospital; Jan-Feb 1778; March-April 1778-Commissary's guard; May-June 1778.
Thompson, Robert	Private	Second, Cummings	Dec 1777-April 1778; May 1778-sick absent; June 1778.
Thompson, Thomas	Private	First, Mead	Feb 5, 1778-enlisted; Feb 1778-deserted.
Thorn, Richard	Private	First, Angel	May 31, 1778-joined; May-June 1778.
Thornton/ Thornhill, Benjamin	Private	First, Piatt	May 26, 1778-joined; May-June 1778.
Thornton, Gilbert	Private	First, Baldwin	June 1778-sick absent.
Thornton, Joseph	Private	First, Baldwin	May 1778; June 1778-on command.
Thorp, Benjamin	Private	First, Mead	April 1778-not joined.
Throgmorton, James	Private	Third, Paterson	Dec 1777-Jan 1778; Feb 1778-on furlough; March 1778-sick present; April-May 1778-sick absent; June 1778.
Thursten/ Thirsten, Benjamin	Private	First, Mead	Dec 1777-Jan 1778-on furlough; Feb-April 1778-sick in Jerseys; May 1778; June 1778-sick absent.
Tilton, Joseph	Sergeant	First, Angel	Dec 1777-June 1778.
Tindal/ Tindall, Samuel	Private	Third, Hennion	Dec 1777-May 1778; June 1778-on command.
Tindal, William	Private	Third, Anderson	June 7, 1778-enlisted; June 1778.
Tindall/ Tidol, William	Private	First, Piatt	May 31, 1778-joined; May 1778; June 1778-on command.

Name	Rank	Company	Service
Tindoll/Tindall, Richard	Private	First, Piatt	May 31, 1778-joined; May-June 1778.
Tingley, Lemuel	Private	Third, Ballard	June 5, 1778-enlisted; June 1778.
Tipper/Typper, Christopher	Private	First, Baldwin	Dec 1777-Jan 1778-sick Morristown; Feb-March 1778-sick Jerseys; April 1778-deserted.
Tire, John	Private	Second, Helms	May 15, 1778-enlisted; June 10, 1778-joined; June 1778.
Titus, Shadrick	Private	Second, Bowman	March 4, 1778-enlisted; April 8, 1778-joined; April 1778; May-June 1778-sick absent.
Toby, Isaac	Drummer	Third, Paterson	Dec 1777-Jan 1778-sick absent; Feb 26, 1778-discharged.
Todd/Tod, John	Private	First, Angel	Dec 1777-April 1778; May 1778-on command; June 1778-wagoner.
Todd, William	Private	Second, Luse	May 10, 1778-enlisted; June 1778.
Tolin/Tolan, Hugh	Private	First, Longstreet	Dec 25, 1777-enlisted; Feb 1778; March 1778-sick in camp; April 10, 1778-dead.
Tompkins/Thompkins, Amos	Private	First, Morrison	May 1778; June 1778-sick [Newark Mountain].
Tompkins/Tomkins, Isaac	Private	Spencer's, Brittin	Dec 1777-Jan 1778; Feb-March 1778-sick present; April 3, 1778-died.
Tompkins, John	Private	Spencer's, Brittin	Dec 1777-March 1778-sick in hospital; April 1778-sick Trenton; May 1778-supposed to be dead or deserted.
Tompkins/Tomkins, Jonas	Sergeant	Spencer's, Brittin	Dec 1777-on furlough; Jan-March 1778-wounded absent; April-May 1778; June 1778-on furlough.
Tool, Patrick	Private	Second, Phillips	Dec 1777-June 1778.
Tone, Andrew	Private	Third, Ballard	Dec 1777-Feb 1778-driving wagon; March 18, 1778-deserted.
Toomy/Tumy, Samuel	Private	Third, Paterson	Jan 28, 1778-enlisted; Feb-March 1778; April 1778-on guard; May 1778-sick absent; June 1778-wagoner.
Tophey/Toffee, William	Private	Spencer's, Wilkins/Edsall	Dec 1777-Feb 1778; March-April 1778-on furlough; May 1778-sick camp; June 1778-sick absent. In May transferred to Edsall's Co.
Town, Joseph	Private	First, Piatt	Dec 1777-June 1778.

Name	Rank	Company	Service
Town, Timothy	Private/ Corporal	Spencer's, Brittin	Dec 1777; Jan 1, 1778-promoted to corporal; Jan 1778; Feb 1778-sick present. March 1778 muster roll shows he died on March 30, but the March payroll shows he died on March 28.
Townly/ Townley, Joshua	Private	First, Morrison	Dec 1777; Jan-Feb 1778-sick absent; March-sick in Jersey; April-June 1778.
Townsen, Roderick	Private	Second, Cummings	May 20, 1778-enlisted; June 1778.
Trapwell, William	Private	Second, Phillips	Feb 7, 1778-enlisted; March-April 1778; May 21, 1778-deserted.
Treligan/ Torligan, John	Private	First, Morrison	Dec 1777-Jan 1778; Feb 1778-sick absent; March-April 1778-sick in Pennsylvania; May 1778-sick present; June 1778.
Trout, Jacob	Private	Fourth, Mitchell	June 1778.
Truax, John	Corporal	Third, Paterson	Dec 1777-May 1778; June 1778-on furlough.
Truby, Sandy	Sergeant	First, Polhemus	Dec 1777; Jan-March 1778-on command; April 1778-deserted.
Trusdal/ Truisdal, Stephen	Private	Fourth, Lyon	June 15, 1778-joined; June 1778.
Tucker, Abraham	Private	First, Baldwin	May-June 1778.
Tumy/Toomy, Henry	Private	Third, Paterson	Dec 1777-June 1778.
Turner, William	Private	Second, Luse	May 5, 1778-enlisted; June 1778.
Turvey, Daniel	Private	Third, Cox	June 21, 1778-enlisted; June 26, 1778-joined; June 1778.
Tuttle, Caleb	Private	First, Mead	June 5, 1778-enlisted; June 1778.
Tuttle, Daniel	Private	First, Baldwin	Dec 1777-Feb 1778; March 1778-sick present; April-June 1778.
Tuttle, Daniel	Private	Fourth, Mitchell	Dec 1777-at Rockaway sick; Jan-Feb 1778-sick Rockaway; March 1778-deserted.
Tuttle, Isaiah	Private	Third, Ballard	Dec 1777-Feb 1778; March 1778-sick present; April 1778-sick in Jersey; May 1778-sick in M Town; June 1778-sick Morristown.
Tuttle, John	Sergeant	Third, Ballard	Dec 1777-March 1778; April 1778-sick present; May 10, 1778-died.
Tuttle, John Jr.	Private	Fourth, Forman	Dec 1777-June 1778.

Tuttle, John Sr.	Private	Fourth, Forman		Dec 1777-March 1778-sick in hospital; April 1778; May 1778-hospital Yellow Springs; June 1778-sick in hospital.
Tuttle, John	Private	Fourth, Mitchell		May 30, 1778-deserted.
Tuttle, William	Private	Third, Ballard		Dec 1777-Feb 1778; March 1778-on command; April 1778-sick present; May-June 1778.
Tway, John	Private	Third, Ballard		Dec 1777; Jan-Feb 1778-sick in hospital; March 1778-sick hospital; April 1778; May 1778-on command at lines; June 1778.
Tway, Timothy	Private	Fourth, Anderson		Dec 1777-March 1778; April 1778-on command at the lines; May 1778; June 1778-on guard.
Twining, John	Private	First, Mead		Jan 22, 1778-enlisted; Jan-Feb 1778; March 18, 1778-dead.
Underwood, George	Private	First, Baldwin		Dec 1777-Jan 1778-sick Newark; Feb-March 1778-sick in Jerseys; April 1778-deserted.
Updike, William	Sergeant	Third, Paterson		Dec 1777-Feb 1778; March 1778-on command; April-May 1778; June 1778-on furlough.
Uptegrave/ Uptegrove, Isaac	Private	Second, Helms		May 10, 1778-enlisted; June 19, 1778-joined; June 1778.
Vaid, John	Private	Third, Hennion		March 10, 1778 enlisted; March 15, 1778-deserted.
Valentine/ Volentine, Jacob	Private	Third, Paterson		May 1778-on guard; June 1778.
Van Allen, Richard	Private	First, Longstreet		May 26, 1778-joined; May 1778; June 1778-on command.
Vanarn, Barnabas/ Barney	Private	Second, Luse		March 3, 1778-enlisted; March-April 1778; May 1778-unfit for service.
Van Arsdalen, John	Private	Second, Luse		May 5, 1778-enlisted; June 1778.
Vance, Thomas	Private	Spencer's, Maxwell		Dec 1777-March 1778; April 1778-on furlough; May-June 1778.
Van Cleaf, Peter	Private	Forman's, Burowes		Dec 1777-June 1778.
Van Derbelt, Daniel	Private	Second, Helms		May 9, 1778-enlisted; June 26, 1778-joined; June 1778.
Van Derberry, Peter	Private	First, Piatt		May 21, 1778-joined: May-June 1778-on guard.
Vanderhide/ Vanderhule, Abraham	Sergeant	Fourth, Forman		Dec 1777-March 1778; April 1778-sick present; May 1778; June 1778-on guard.

Van Deventer/ Van DeVenter, Christopher	Private	First Longstreet	June 4, 1778-joined; June 1778.
Vandike, Henry	Private	Second, Reading	Jan 1778-on command; March 1778-sick absent; April 1778; May-sick absent; June 1778.
Vandike, John	Private	Second, Reading	Jan 1778-on command; Feb-June 1778.
Van Dorn, Hendrick	Private	Forman's, Burowes	Dec 1777-June 1778.
Van Droff, Cornelius	Private	First, Morrison	May 1778; June 1778-sick Newark.
Vaneman/ Vaniman, Abraham	Private	Second, Sparks	June 2, 1778-enlisted; June 1778.
Vaneman/ Vanneman, Richard	Private	Second, Hollingshead	Dec 1777-Jan 1778; Feb 15, 1778-discharged; May 8, 1778-enlisted; June 1778-on command.
Van Horn/Van Horne, Simon	Sergeant	First, Longstreet	Dec 1777; Jan-Feb 1778-sick in Jerseys; March 1778; April 1778-sick in Jerseys; May-June 1778-sick absent.
Van Horn/Van Horne, William	Private	First, Polhemus	Dec 1777-April 1778; May 1778-guard; June 1778-on command.
Van Kirk, Samuel	Private	First, Piatt	June 1778-on command.
Van Lue, Frederick	Private	Second, Phillips	May 14, 1778-enlisted; May 28, 1778-joined; May-June 1778.
Van Mater/Van Marter, John	Sergeant	Third, Paterson	Dec 1777-Feb 1778; March 1778-on furlough; April-May 1778; June 1778-on furlough.
Van Nest, Henry	Private	First, Longstreet	May 24, 1778-joined; May 1778; June 1778-on command.
Van Norstrant/ Van Norstrand, George	Private	First, Longstreet	Dec 1777-Feb 1778; March-1778-on command on the lines; April 1778-on the lines; May-June 1778.
Van Orman, James	Private	Third, Paterson	June 1778-on command.
Van Orton/ Vanorton, John	Private	First, Piatt	May 21, 1778-joined; May 1778; June 1778-sick absent.
Vanosdal/ Vanosale, Henry	Drummer	Spencer's, Edsall	Dec 1777-sick hospital; Jan 1778; Feb 1778-sick hospital; March 1778-sick absent; April 1, 1778-died.
Van Osdoll/ Vanosdol, John	Private	First, Piatt	May 21, 1778-joined; May-June 1778-on guard.
Van Pelt, Jacob	Private	First, Longstreet	May 1778-on command; June 1778.
Van Reed, Cornelius	Private	Second, Phillips	May 19, 1778-enlisted; May 28, 1778-joined; May 1778; June 1778-on command.

Name	Rank	Company	Service
Van Sciver/ Van Sciven, John	Private	First, Piatt	Dec 1777-Jan 1778; Feb 1778-wagoner; March 1778-wagoner for G. Washington; April 16, 1778-deserted.
Varrick/Vark, James V.	Private	Third, Gifford	Dec 1777-Feb 1778; March-April 1778-sick present; May 1778-sick at the Yellow Springs Hospital; June 1778-sick absent.
Vaughan, William	Private	Third, Paterson	Dec 1777-Feb 1778; March-April 1778-on command; May 1778-sick absent; June 1778.
Vaul, Samuel	Private	Spencer's, Pierson	Dec 1777-March 1778; April 1778-sick present; May 7, 1778-died.
Van Wye, Henry/ Hendrick	Private	Second, Luse	Dec 1777-March 1778; April 5, 1778-taken prisoner.
Venett/Vinett, John	Private	First, Longstreet	Dec 1777-Feb 1778; March 1778-on command on the lines; April 1778; May 1778-on command; June 1778.
Vent, John	Private	Second, Phillips	May 8, 1778-enlisted; May 28, 1778-joined; May-June 1778.
Vick, James	Private	Second, Bowman	Dec 1777; Jan 1778-furlough; Feb 1778; March 1, 1778-deserted to Enemy.
Vincell/ Wincell, Adam	Private	Second, Cummings	Dec 1777; Jan 1778-on command; Feb-June 1778.
Vincent, Levi	Private	First, Morrison	May 1778; June 1778-furlough.
Voorhees/ Vores, Albert	Private	Spencer's, Brittin	Dec 1777-June 1778.
Voorhees/ Voorres, Garret	Private	Fourth, Lyon	Dec 1777-March 1778; April 1778-on guard; May 1778-on command; June 1778.
Voorhees, Hendrick	Private	Forman's, Burowes	Dec 1777-June 1778.
Voorhies, James	Private	First, Longstreet	May 24, 1778-joined; May 1778; June 1778-on command.
Voorhies/Van Voorhies, Peter	1st. Lt./ Captain/ 1st. Lt.	First, Longstreet/ Polhemus/ Longstreet	Dec 1777-on command to Jersey; Dec 1777-Jan 1778 he was 1st. Lt. in Longstreet's Co. In February 1778 he became captain of Polhemus' Co. when Polhemus became a temporary Major; March 1778-on command; April 1778-no record; May 1778-reverted to 1st. Lt. in Longstreet's Co.; June 1778-sick absent.
Voorhies/Van Voorhies, Tunis/Thunis	Sergeant	First, Longstreet	Dec 1777-Jan 1778; Feb 1778-sick in Jersey; March-April 1778; May-June 1778-on command.

Name	Rank	Company	Notes
Voorhis/Voorhes, Abraham	Private	First, Piatt	May 1778-sick absent; June 1778.
Vories/Vorhouse, George	Private	Second, Helms	May 9, 1778-enlisted; June 26, 1778-joined; June 1778.
Vredenburgh, John	Sergeant	First, Longstreet	Dec 1777; Jan 1778-with Doctor Cochran.
Vredenburgh, William	Private	First, Longstreet	Dec 1777-Feb 1778; March 1778-on guard; April 1778; May 1778-on command; June 1778-sick present.
Vreeland/Freeland, Abraham	Fifer	Fourth, Forman	Dec 1777-June 1778.
Vreeland, James	Private	First, Morrison	May-June 1778.
Wade, Henry	Private	Third, Gifford	Dec 1777-March 1778; April 1778-on command; May-June 1778.
Wade, Thomas	Private	Second, Bowman	March 14, 1778-enlisted; April 8, 1778-joined; April 1778; May 10, 1778-deserted to enemy.
Wade, Timothy	Private	Third, Paterson	May 27, 1778-joined; May-June 1778.
Waggoner, Christopher	Private	Spencer's, Wilkins	Dec 1777-April 1778-on furlough.
Waggoner/Wagoner, George	Private	Second, Cummings	Dec-April 1778; May 1778-on command; June 1778.
Waggoner, John	Private	Second, Luse	May 10, 1778-enlisted; June 1778.
Wain, John	Private	Second, Cummings	Dec 1777-April 1778; May 1778-on command; June 1778.
Walker, Francis	Private	Fourth, Forman	Dec 1777-April 1778; May 1778-on command; June 1778-on guard.
Walker, John	Sergeant	Second, Reading	Jan-March 1778; April 5, 1778-taken prisoner.
Walker, John	Private	Second, Sparks	June 23, 1778-enlisted; June 1778.
Walker, John	Private	Spencer's, Wilkins	Dec 15, 1777-deserted.
Walker, Masheck/Meshech	Private	First, Morrison	Dec 1777-Feb 1778; March 1778-General. Maxwell's guard; April 1778-sick present; May-June 1778.
Walker, William	Fifer	First, Angel	Dec 1777-June 1778.
Wallace/Walas, John	Private	Spencer's, Weatherby	Dec 1777-Jan 1778-sick hospital; Feb 1778-deserted hospital.
Wallace/Wallas, William	Private	First, Flahavan	Dec 1777-Feb 1778; March-April 1778-sick present; May 1778-command; June 1778.

Walling/ Walin, James	Private	Spencer's, Brodrick	Dec 1777-March 1778-sick absent; April 1778-[ ]; May 1778-sick camp; June 1778-sick Morestown.
Walter, John	Private	Third, Anderson	Dec 1777-March 1778-wounded absent; April 1778 wounded absent New Jersey; May 1778-wounded absent Princeton Hospital; June 1778-wounded absent.
Walter, John	Private	Third, Ross	Dec 1777; Jan 1778-on command with Col. Dayton; Feb 1778; March 1778-on command; April 1778-on picket; May-June 1778.
Wandle/ Wandal, David	Private	Spencer's, Brodrick	Dec 1777-wounded; Jan 1778; Feb 1778-wounded; March-April 1778; May-June 1778-wounded in Sussex.
Wandle/ Wandal, Jacob	Sergeant	Spencer's, Brodrick	Dec 1777-Jan 1778-sick absent; Feb-March 1778-sick present; April 1778-sick in [Sussex]; May-June 1778.
Ward, Ebenezer	Private	First, Morrison	Dec 1777; Jan 1778-with the artificers; Feb 1778-on furlough; March 1778-artificer; April-June 1778-armorer.
Ward, Isaac	Private	Third, Ballard	Dec 1777-Feb 1778; March 1778-on command; April 1778; May-June 1778-sick in Princetown.
Ward, John	Private	Second, Bowman	Dec 1777-April 1778; May-June 1778-sick absent.
Ward, Jonas	Captain	Spencer's, Ward	Dec 1777; Jan 1778-on furlough; Feb-March 1778; April 10, 1778-resigned.
Ward, Thomas	Private	First, Angel	Dec 1777-Feb 1778-sick at Bethlehem; March 1778-dead.
Ward, William	Private	First, Longstreet	June 4, 1778-joined; June 1778.
Warmer/ Wormer, William	Private	Third, Ross	May 25, 1778-joined; May 1778-on guard; June 1778.
Warner, Cuff See Cuff, Negro			
Waters, Thomas	Private	Fourth, Mitchell	June 1778.
Watkins, Thomas	Private	Fourth, Kinsey	Dec 1777-June 1778.
Watson, Alexander/ Alec	Private	Spencer's, Brittin	Dec 1777-Jan 1778; Feb-March 1778-sick present; April 1778; May 1778-on guard; June 1778.
Watson, Daniel	Private	Fourth, Martin	Dec 1777-Feb 1778; March 1778-sick present; April 1778; May 1778-sick Princeton; June 1778.

135

Name	Rank	Company	Service
Watson/Wattson, William	Private	Second, Phillips	May 22, 1778-enlisted; June 1, 1778-joined; June 1778.
Watts/Wats, Bowen	Private	Fourth, Kinsey	Dec 1777-Feb 1778; March 1778-waiter at hospital; April 1778; May 1778-on command; June 1778.
Watts, Robert	Corporal	Second, Luse	Dec 1777; Jan 1778-sick absent; Feb-June 1778.
Weatherby, Benjamin	Captain	Spencer's, Weatherby	Dec 1777-June 1778. Oath at Valley Forge on May 11, 1778.
Weatherhawk/Witherhawk, John	Private	Spencer's, Brittin	Dec 1777-June 1778.
Weatherton/Weatherrington Benjamin	Private	Third, Mott	June 1778.
Weaver/Wever, Anthony	Private	Third, Mott	June 1778-on command.
Weaver, John	Private	Fourth, Forman	Dec 1777-March 1778-sick in hospital; April 1778-sick absent; May 1778-hospital Reading; June 1778-sick absent.
Weaverlin/Weverling, Peter	Sergeant	Fourth, Forman	Dec 1777-June 1778.
Webster/Weebster, Elihu	Private	First, Angel	Dec 1777-April 1778; May 1778-on command; June 1778-main guard.
Webster, Thomas	Private	First, Piatt	May 31, 1778-joined; May-June 1778.
Welch/Welsh, David	Private	Third, Paterson	Dec 1777-Feb 1778; March 1778-on command; April-June 1778.
Welch, James	Private	Second, Hollingshead	Dec 1777; Jan 1778-sick in hospital; Feb-April 1778; May 1778-on command; June 1778-sick hospital.
Welch/Wilch, Nathaniel	Sergeant	Fourth, Martin	Dec 1777-Feb 1778; March 1778-on furlough; April-June 1778.
Welch/Weltch, Thomas	Private	Second, Reading	Jan-April 1778; May 1778-on command; June 1778.
Welsh, James	Private	Third, Gifford	June 7, 1778-joined; June 1778.
Wessells, Joseph	Private	First, Angel	Dec 1777-deserted to Newark.
West, Joseph	Private	Third, Hennion	June 7, 1778-enlisted; June 1778.
Weston/Wheston, William	Drummer	First, Longstreet	April-May 1778. This man and the next one are probably the same individual.

Name	Rank	Company	Service
Weston, William	Drummer	First, Piatt	Dec 1777-March 1778.
Weyman/ Weymon, Abel	1st. Lt.	Fourth, Mitchell	Dec 1777-on furlough; Jan 1778-sick absent; Feb-April 1778; May 1778-on command; June 1778. Oath at Valley Forge on May 11, 1778.
Wheaton/ Wheton, Samuel	Private	First, Morrison	August 1, 1777-deserted; April 25, 1778-joined; April 1778; May 11, 1778-deserted.
Wherrey/Whorrey, Robert	Sergeant/ Private	First, Angel	Dec 1777-April 1778; May 1778-sick at Princeton; June 1778-reduced to private, sick absent.
Wheston, William	Fifer	First, Flahavan	May-June 1778.
Whitchel/ Witchell, Jacob	Private	Fourth, Forman	Dec 1777-sick in hospital; Jan-Feb 1778; March 1778-on command; April 1778; May 1778-guard; June 1778.
White, Caleb	Private	Spencer's, Lyon	Dec 1777-Jan 1778; Feb-March 1778-on furlough; April 1778-sick Jersey; May-June 1778.
White, David	Corporal	First, Mead	Dec 1777-June 1778.
White, Jacob	Private	First, Angel	Dec 1777-June 1778.
White, Jacob	Private	Third, Anderson	June 7, 1778-enlisted; June 1778.
White, John	Private	Third, Ballard	Dec 1777-Jan 1778-sick in Jersey.
White/Wite, John	Private	Spencer's, Brittin	Dec 1777-Jan 1778; Feb-March 1778-on command; April 1778-prisoner.
White, Joseph	Private	Second, Hollingshead	May 5, 1778-enlisted; June 1778.
White, Peter	Private	Second, Reading	Jan-April 1778; May 1778-on command; June 1778.
White, Thomas	Private	First, Morrison	Dec 1777; Jan 1778-sick absent; Feb 1778-left sick in Jerseys; March 1778-sick in Jersey; April-June 1778.
White, Thomas	Private	Second, Helms	May 21, 1778-enlisted; June 15, 1778-joined; June 1778.
White, Thomas	Private	Fourth, Kinsey	Dec 1777-March 1778; April 1778-on command; May-June 1778.
White, William	Private	Forman's, Combs	Dec 1777-June 1778.
Whitehead/ Whithead, James	Private	First, Angel	Dec 1777-March 1778; June 1778-on command.
Whitehead, James	Drummer	First, Flahavan	April 1778.

Name	Rank	Company	Service
Whitehead, Samuel	Private	First, Baldwin	May 1778; June 1778-on command.
Whitehead, Samuel	Private	Second, Luse	March 22, 1778-enlisted; April 1778; May 1778-on command; June 1778.
Whiteker/ Whittaker, John	Private	Third, Anderson	Dec 1777-June 1778.
Whitlock, Ephraim	2nd. Lt.	Fourth, Forman	Dec 1777-Feb 1778; March 1778-on furlough; April 1778; May 1778-sick absent; June 1778. Oath at Valley Forge on May 11, 1778.
Whitlock/ Whittlock, James	Private	Fourth, Forman	Dec 1777-May 1778; June 1778-on furlough.
Whitmore/ Whittimore, Amos	Private	First, Angel	Dec 1777-May 1778; June 1778-sick absent.
Whittmore/ Whittimore, Samuel	Private	Second, Luse	Dec 1777; Jan 1778-sick absent; Feb-May 1778.
Wicks, Cornelius	Private	First, Piatt	Dec 1777-March 1778-sick in Jersey.
Wigton/ Whigton, Samuel	Sergeant	Fourth, Lyon	Dec 1777-sick hospital; Jan 1778-sick present; Feb-March 1778-sick in hospital; April 1778-sick Bethlehem; May 1778; June 1778-sick hospital.
Wikoff, William	Captain	Forman's, Wikoff	Dec 1777-June 1778.
Willcox/ Woolcox, James	Private	First, Morrison	Dec 1777-April 1778; May 1778-sick at Princeton; June 1778.
Wilhelm/ Willhelm, Henry	Private	Fourth, Anderson	May 28, 1778-enlisted; June 1778-on guard.
Wilkins, Henry	Private	Second, Sparks	March 15, 1778-deserted.
Wilkins, John	Captain	Spencer's, Wilkins	Dec 1777-on furlough; Jan-Feb 1778-on command; March 1778-on furlough; April 8, 1778-resigned.
Wilkinson, Samuel	Private	First, Mead	June 5, 1778-enlisted; June 1778-sick absent.
Wilkison/ Wilkerson, Nathan	2nd. Lt.	Third, Ballard	Dec 1777-March 1778; April 1778-doing duty in Quartermaster's Department; May 1778-doing duty in the Quartermaster's Detachment; June 1778-doing duty in the Quartermaster's Department. Oath at Valley Forge on May 11, 1778.

Name	Rank	Company	Service
Williams/Wilson, Henry	Private	Spencer's, Brittin	April-May 1778; June 1778-sick Peekskill. He appears as Henry Wilson on the April 1778 muster roll, but as Henry Williams on all the other rolls.
Williams, Jesse	Private	Forman's, Forman	Dec 1777-June 1778.
Williams, John	Private	First, Polhemus	Dec 1777-April 1778; May 1778-furlough; June 1778-on command.
Williams, John	Private	Second, Cummings	Dec 1777-June 1778.
Williams, John	Corporal	Second, Reading	Jan 1777-April 1778; May 1778-on command; June 1778-on guard.
Williams/Williames, John	Private	Fourth, Mitchell	Dec 1777-Jan 1778; Feb-March 1778-General Maxwell's guard; April 1778; May 1778-on command; June 1778.
Williams, Moses	Private	Third, Paterson	May 27, 1778-joined; May 1778; June 1778-on command.
Williams, Thomas	Private	Fourth, Forman	Dec 1777-Feb 1778; March 1778-sick present; April 1778-on command; May-June 1778.
Williams, William	Private	Second, Sparks	Dec 1777-March 1778; April 5, 1778-taken prisoner; July 17, 1778-exchanged.
Williamson, Garrett	Private	First, Piatt	Dec 1777-April 1778; May 1778-sick absent; June 1778.
Williamson, Jacob	Private	Third, Ballard	May 28, 1778-enlisted; May-June 1778.
Williamson, John	Private	Third, Ross	Sept 11, 1777-taken prisoner; Jan-Feb, April 1778-prisoner with ye enemy; May-June 1778-sick absent.
Willis, Aaron	Private	First, Flahavan	Dec 1777-Feb 1778; March 1778-command; April 1778; May-June 1778-on furlough.
Willis, Joseph	Private	First, Baldwin	May-June 1778.
Williss/Willes, Isaac	Private	Second, Luse	Dec 1777-March 1778; April 5, 1778-taken prisoner.
Willoughby, William	Private	Third, Ross	May 1778-on guard; June 1778.
Willson, Andrew	Corporal	Fourth, Forman	Dec 1777-sick absent; Jan 1778-sick hospital; Feb-March 1778-sick absent; April 1778; May 1778-on command; June 1778.
Willson, Garrat	Private	First, Piatt	May 31, 1778-joined; May 1778; June 1778-on command.
Willson, James	Private	First, Piatt	June 1778.

Name	Rank	Company	Notes
Wilson/Willson, George	Private	Spencer's, Pierson	Dec 1777 payroll-"wounded the 4th." Dec 1777-Jan 1778-wounded; Feb 1778-sick hospital; March 1778-wounded October 4; April 1778-wounded absent; May 1778-Bethlehem Hospital; June 1778-wounded Bethlehem.
Wilson, Henry - see Williams, Henry			
Wilson/Willson, James	Private	Third, Paterson	Dec 1777-March 1778; April 1778-on command; May-June 1778-on command.
Wilson, Jeremiah	Private	First, Piatt	May 26, 1778-joined; May 1778; June 1778-sick absent.
Wilson/Willson, John	Private	First, Morrison	Dec 1777-March 1778; April-June 1778-wagoner.
Wilson/Willson, John	Private	First, Angel	Dec 1777-Feb 1778; March 1778-on command; April-June 1778.
Wilson/Willson, Moses	Private	First, Baldwin	Dec 1, 1777-enlisted; Dec 1777-June 1778.
Wilson/Whilson, Thomas	Private	First, Longstreet	Dec 1777-June 1778.
Wilson/Willson, Thomas	Private	Second, Bowman	Dec 1777; Jan 1778-sick absent; Feb-April 1778; May-June 1778-sick absent.
Wilts/Wiltits, Michael	Private	Third, Hennion	Dec 1777-March 1778; April 1778-on command; May 1778-sick Princeton Hospital; June 1778-sick absent.
Wincell - see Vincell			
Wind, Henry	Private	First, Polhemus	Dec 1777-June 1778.
Winfield/Windfield, Matthew	Private	Fourth, Anderson	Dec 1777-Feb 1778-sick in hospital; March-April 1778-Invalids.
Winslow, Jacob	Private	First, Piatt	May 1778-on command; June 27, 1778-deserted.
Winters/Winter, Jacob	Private	First, Angel	May 31, 1778-joined; May 1778-on command; June 1778.
Winters, Joseph	Private	Second, Phillips	May 15, 1778-enlisted; June 1, 1778-joined; June 1778-on command.
Witticar/Whiticar, Elnathan	Private	Second, Cummings	May 20, 1778-enlisted; May 24, 1778-joined; May 1778-on command; June 1778.
Woglum, Benjamin	Sergeant	Second, Phillips	Dec 1777-May 1778; June 1778-sick absent.

Name	Rank	Company	Service
Wolf, Henry	Private	Second, Cummings	Dec 1777-April 1778; May 1778-on command; June 1778.
Wood, Aaron	Private	Spencer's, Weatherby	Dec 1777-April 1778; May 1778-command driving wagons; June 1778-driving wagon.
Wood, Daniel	Private	Fourth, Anderson	May 28, 1778-enlisted; June 1778.
Wood, Francis	Private	Third, Paterson	June 5, 1778-joined; June 1778. The man listed below is probably the same individual.
Wood, Francis	Private	Spencer's, Brittin	April 1778; May 10, 1778-"taken as substitute to the Jersey Brigade."
Wood, George	Private/ Fifer	First, Baldwin	Dec 1777-sick at Bethlehem; Jan 1778-sick present; Feb-March 1778-sick absent; April 1778-promoted to fifer; April 1778; May-June 1778-on furlough.
Wood, Jacob	Private	First, Morrison	Dec 29, 1777-enlisted; April 1778 payroll-paid back to Dec 29, 1777; May 30, 1778-deserted.
Wood, Rheuben	Private	Third, Cox	June 1, 1778-enlisted; June 5, 1778-joined; June 1778-on guard.
Woddard/ Woodward, Asee	Private	Second, Hollingshead	May 26, 1778-enlisted; June 28, 1778-taken.
Woodcock, John	Private	Fourth, Mitchell	Dec 1777-at hospital sick; Jan-March 1778-sick hospital; April-May 1778-sick Allentown.
Wooden, Samuel	Private	Second, Hollingshead	March 30, 1778-enlisted; April-May 1778; June 1778-sick hospital.
Woodroff, Eliazer	Private	Third, Ballard	June 5, 1778-enlisted; June 1778.
Woodrow, Caleb	Private	Second, Hollingshead	July 9, 1777-deserted; March 30, 1778-returned; March-April 1778; May 15, 1778-deserted.
Woodruff/ Woodrof, Daniel	Corporal	Third, Hennion	Dec 1777-Jan 1778; Feb 1778-on furlough; March 1778; April 1778-sick present; May 1778; June 1778-on furlough.
Woodruff, Daniel	Private	Spencer's, Pierson	Dec 1777-Feb 1778; March 1778-General's guard; April 1778-on picket; May 1778-sick camp; June 1778-Yellow Springs sick.
Woodruff, Ephraim	Private	Spencer's, Ward	Dec 1777-June 1778.
Woodruff, Ichabod	Private/ Corporal	First, Angel	Dec 1777-Feb 1778; March 1778-command at Lancaster; April-June 1778; June 1778-promoted to corporal.

141

Name	Rank	Company	Notes
Woodruff, Job	Private	First, Baldwin	May 30, 1778-joined; May 1778-on guard; June 1778.
Woodruff/ Woodrif, John	Private	Fourth, Martin	Dec 1777; Jan-March 1778-on command; April 1778-Cloathier General; May 1778-on command; June 1778-sick present.
Woodruff, Jonathan	Private	First, Baldwin	May-June 1778.
Woodruff, Stephen	Private	Spencer's, Brittin	Dec 1777-on furlough; Jan 1778-wounded absent; Feb 1778-on furlough; March 1778-wounded absent; April-June 1778.
Woodruff, Usial/Usezal	Private	First, Baldwin	May 1778; June 1778-on guard.
Woods, Isaac	Private	First, Piatt	Dec 1777-Jan 1778-sick in Jersey; Feb-May 1778.
Woods/Wood, William	Private	Fourth, Forman	Dec 1777-March 1778-sick in hospital; April 1778-sick hospital Reading; May 1778-hospital Reading; June 1778-sick present.
Woodside/ Woodsides, Robert	Private	Fourth, Kinsey	March 11, 1778-enlisted; March 31, 1778-joined; March 1778; April 1778-sick present; May 1778-sick in hospital; June 1778.
Woolcox/ Willcox, Isaac	Private	First, Morrison	May 27, 1778-joined; May-June 1778.
Woolley/Wooley, Isaac	Private	First, Flahavan	Dec 1777-Feb 1778; March 1778-on guard; April-June 1778.
Woolley/ Wolle, Jacob	Private/ Drummer	First, Flahavan	Dec 1777-March 1778-sick in Jersey; March 1778-promoted to drummer; April-June 1778.
Woolley, Jedediah	Private	Forman's, Burowes	Dec 1777-June 1778.
Wooten/ Wooden, Maurice	Drummer/ Drum Major	Third, Ballard	Dec 1777-April 1778; April 9, 1778-promoted to drum major, May-June 1778-on command.
Worden, Samuel	Sergeant	Third, Cox	Dec 1777-Feb 1778-sick in Jersey; March sick absent; April 1, 1778-deserted.
Wortman, Samuel	Private	First, Piatt	Dec 1777-Feb 1778; March 1778-Washington's Guard.
Woulinger/ Woullinger, Jacob	Drummer	Fourth, Kinsey	Dec 1777-June 1778.
Wright, David	Private	First, Piatt	Dec 1777-April 1778; May 1778-sick absent; June 1778.

Name	Rank	Company	Notes
Wright, Jacob	Private	First, Polhemus	May 1778 muster roll shows he joined on May 25, but the May payroll shows he joined on May 29. June 1778-on command.
Wright, James	Private	Fourth, Anderson	Dec 1777-March 1778; April 1778-sick in camp; May 22, 1778-died.
Wright, John	Private	Fourth, Holmes	Dec 1777-Feb 1778-hospital; March 1778-died at hospital.
Wright, Joseph	Private	First, Piatt	Dec 15, 1777-enlisted; Feb 1778-with Doctor Barnet; March-June 1778.
Wright, Samuel	Private	First, Piatt	Dec 1777-April 1778; May 1778-sick present; June 1778.
Wright, Thomas	Private	Fourth, Anderson	Dec 1777; Jan-Feb 1778-missing on the lines; March 1778-deserted.
Wright, William	Private	Second, Cummings	Dec 1777-Feb 1778; March 1778 payroll-missing or deserted; April 5, 1778-prisoner.
Wroth, John	Sergeant/ Private	Forman's, Combs	Dec 1777; Jan 12, 1778-reduced to the ranks; Jan-April 1778.
Wynne, Josiah	Private	Fourth, Mitchell	Dec 1777-March 1778; April 12, 1778-deserted.
Yard, Thomas	Captain	Second, Phillips	He appears only on the Dec 1777 payroll as company captain but Jonathan Phillips was promoted to captain of this company on Dec 1, 1777 and is also on the roll.
Yater, John	Private/ Sergeant	Second, Phillips	March 27, 1778-enlisted; March-April 1778; May 1778-on command; June 1778-promoted to sergeant; June 1778.
Yates/Yeatys, John	Private	First, Mead	Jan 1, 1778-enlisted; Feb-April 1778; May 1778-on command; June 1778.
Yates/Yeats, William	Private	First, Polhemus	Dec 1777-Jan 1778; Feb 1778-on command; March-April 1778; May 1778-sick Princeton; June 1778.
Yencer, George	Private	Spencer's, Wilkins	Dec 1777-Feb 1778; March 26, 1778-deserted.
Yorty, Frederick,	Private	Second, Hollingshead	Dec 1777-April 1778; May 1778-on command; June 1778.
Young, Aaron	Private	Third, Ballard	Dec 1777-April 1778; May 1778-sick in Princetown; June 1778.
Young, David	Private	Third, Cox	Dec 1777-Feb 1778; March 1778-deserted.
Young, John	Corporal	Second, Bowman	Dec 1777-April 1778; May 1778-on furlough; June 1778.
Young/Yong, Lapole/Lepole	Private	First, Flahavan/ Angel	Dec 1777; Jan 1778; Feb 1778-sick absent; March-April 1778; May 1778-sick Princeton; June 20, 1778-dead; transferred to Angel's Co. in April.

Young, Philip	Private	Spencer's, Weatherby	Dec 1777-March 1778-on furlough; April 1778-deserted.
Young, Thomas	Private	Fourth, Holmes	Dec 1777-June 1778.
Yureson, Giles	Private	Second, Sparks	May 10, 1778-enlisted; June 1778.

BIBLIOGRAPHY

The following publications were not used in compiling the above list. However, they can provide additional information for researchers in the Valley Forge Encampment and New Jersey men in the Revolutionary War.

Adelberg, Michael S. *Roster of the People of Revolutionary Monmouth County*. Baltimore: Clearfield Co., 1997.

Barber, John W., and Henry Howe. *Historical Collections of New Jersey*. New York: S. Tuttle, 1844; reprint, Salem, Mass.: Higginson Book Co., 1992.

Barton, William. "Journal of Lieut. William Barton, of Maxwell's Brigade; Kept during General Sullivans's Expedition against the Six Nations of Indians." in *Journals of the Military Expedition of Major General John Sullivan Against the Six Nations of Indians in 1779 with Records of Centennial Celebrations.* ed. Frederick Cook. Auburn: N.Y: Knapp, Peck & Thomson, 1887, 3-14. Originally printed in *Proceedings of the New Jersey Historical Society* 2 (November 1846): 22-42.

Bernstein, David. "New Jersey in the American Revolution: The Establishment of A Government Amid Civil and Military Disorder, 1770-1781." Ph. D. diss., Rutgers University, 1969.

Bill, Alfred Hoyt. *New Jersey and the Revolutionary War*. Princeton: D. Van Nostrand Co., 1964.

Bloomfield, Joseph. *Citizen-Soldier: The Revolutionary War Journal of Joseph Bloomfield*. ed. Mark E. Lender and James Kirby Martin. Newark: New Jersey Historical Society, 1982.

Bockstruck, Lloyd DeWitt. *Revolutionary War Bounty Land Grants Awarded by State Governments*. Baltimore: Genealogical Publishing Co., 1996.

Bodle, Wayne K. *The Seat of War: Civilians, Soldiers and Society During the Valley Forge Winter*. New York: New York University Press, 1997.

Bowman, John Elliot. "Some Jersey Veterans of the American Revolution." *Proceedings of the New Jersey Historical Society*, 2d. ser., 13 (July 1928): 325-29.

Brace, Frederic R. *Brief Sketches of the New Jersey Chaplains in the Continental Army and in the State Militia, During the War of Independence*. Paterson: The

Press Printing and Publishing Co., 1909. Originally published in *Proceedings of the New Jersey Historical Society*, 3d ser., 6 (January-April 1909): 1-11.

Burrowes, John. "Major Burrowes' Journal of the Sullivan Expedition." *Genesee County Scrapbook* 3 (Winter 1953): 18-23.

_____. "Journal of John Burrowes," in *Journals of the Military Expedition of Major General John Sullivan Against the Six Nations of Indians in 1779 with Records of Centennial Celebrations*. ed. Frederick Cook. Auburn, NY: Knapp, Peck & Thomson, 1887, 43-51.

Campbell, James W. S. *Digest and Revision of Stryker's Officers and Men of New Jersey in the Revolutionary War - for the use of the Society of the Cincinnati in the State of New Jersey* New York: Williams Printing Co., 1911; reprint, Baltimore: Genealogical Publishing Co., 1997.

Campfield, Jabez. "Diary of Dr. Jabez Campfield," in *Journals of the Military Expedition of Major General John Sullivan Against the Six Nations of Indians in 1779 with Records of Centennial Celebrations*. ed. Frederick Cook. Auburn, N.Y: Knapp, Peck & Thomson, 1887, 52-61. Originally printed in *Proceedings of the New Jersey Historical Society*, 2d. ser., 3 (1872-74): 115-36.

Clark, Murtie June. *The Pension Lists of 1792-1795, With Other Revolutionary War Pension Records*. 1991; reprint, Baltimore: Genealogical Publishing Co., 1996.

Clayton, W. Woodford, ed. *Bergen and Passaic Counties, New Jersey*. Philadelphia: Everts and Peck, 1882; reprint, Salem, Mass.,: Higginson Book Co., 1992.

Clayton, W. Woodford, ed. *History of Union and Middlesex Counties, New Jersey, With Biographical Sketches of Many of Their Pioneers and Prominent Men*. Philadelphia: Everts & Peck, 1882; reprint, Salem, Mass.,: Higginson Book Co.

Cowan, David L. "Revolutionary New Jersey." Proceedings of the New Jersey Historical Society, 71 (January 1953), 1-23.

Cushing, Thomas, and Charles E. Sheppard. *History of the Counties of Gloucester, Salem, and Cumberland, New Jersey, With Biographical Sketches of Prominent Citizens*. Philadelphia: Everts & Peck, 1883.

Dayton, Elias. "Papers of General Elias Dayton." *Proceedings of the New Jersey Historical Society*, 9 (January 1864): 175-194.

Detwiler, Frederick C. *War in the Countryside - the Battle and Plunder of the Short Hills, New Jersey, June 1777*. Plainfield, N.J.: Interstate Printing Co., 1977.

Dickinson, Wharton. "Philemon Dickinson: Major-General, New Jersey Militia-Revolutionary Soldier." *Magazine of American History*, 7 (December 1881): 420-427.

East Amwell Bicentennial Commission. *A History of East Amwell, 1700-1800*. Ringoes, N.J., 1976.

Elizabeth, N.J., Sesqui-centennial Committee. *Revolutionary History of Elizabeth, New Jersey*. Elizabeth: n. p., 1926.

Ellis, Franklin. *The History of Monmouth, New Jersey*. Philadelphia: R. T. Peck and Co., 1885; reprint, Salem, Mass.,: Higginson Book Co., 1992.

Elmer, Ebenezer. "Extracts from the Journal of Surgeon Ebenezer Elmer of the New Jersey Continental Line, September 11-19, 1777." ed. John Nixon Brooks. *Pennsylvania Magazine of History and Biography*, 35 (1911): 103-107.

_____. "Journal Kept During an Expedition to Canada in 1776 by Ebenezer Elmer, Lieutenant in the Third Regiment of the New Jersey Troops in the Continental Service, Commanded by Colonel Elias Dayton." *Proceedings of the New Jersey Historical Society*, 2 (1846-1847): 43-50, 95-194; 3 (1848-1849): 21-56, 90-102.

_____. "Journal of Dr. Ebenezer Elmer." in *Journals of the Military Expedition of Major General John Sullivan Against the Six Nations of Indians in 1779 with Records of Centennial Celebrations* ed. Frederick Cook Auburn, NY: Knapp, Peck & Thomson, 1887,. 80-85. Originally printed in *Proceedings of the New Jersey Historical Society*, 2 (November 1846), 43-50.

_____. "The Lost Pages of Elmer's Revolutionary Journal." ed A. Van Doren Honeyman. *Proceedings of the New Jersey Historical Society*, 2d. ser. 10 (October 1925):410-424.

Ewing, George. *The Military Journal of George Ewing (1754-1824) a Soldier of Valley Forge*. Yonkers, N.Y. Privately printed, 1928.

Fithian, Philip Vickers. *Philip Vickers Fithian: Journal 1775-1776, Written on the Virginia-Pennsylvania Frontier and in the Army around New York*. ed. Robert G. Albion & Leonidas Dodson. Princeton: Princeton University Press, 1934.

_____. *Letters to His Wife, Elizabeth Beatty Fithian*. ed. Frank D. Andrews. Vineland, N.J. Smith Printing House, 1932.

Fleming, Thomas. *The Forgotten Victory: The Battle for New Jersey - 1780*. New York: Reader's Digest Press, 1973.

Folsom, Joseph F. "Manuscript Light on Chaplain James Caldwell's Death," *Proceedings of the New Jersey Historical Society*, New Ser., 1 (January 1916): 1-12.

____. "Revolutionary Pension Records of Morris County," *Proceedings of the New Jersey Historical Society*, New Ser., 1 (April, July 1916), 89-99, 147-159; 2 (January, April 1917): 27-32, 98-117.

Fowler, David J. "Egregious Villains, Wood Rangers, and London Traders: The Pine Robber Phenomenon in New Jersey during the Revolutionary War." Ph. D. Dissertation, Rutgers University, 1987.

Genealogical Magazine of New Jersey. This began publication in 1925.

Gerlach, Larry R. Prologue to Independence: *New Jersey in the Coming of the American Revolution*. New Brunswick: Rutgers University Press, 1976.

____ ed. *New Jersey in the American Revolution, 1763-1783: A Documentary History*. Trenton: New Jersey Historical Commission, 1975.

Giller, Sayde. *Corrections to the Index of Revolutionary War Pension Applications in the National Archives*. Baltimore, Genealogical Publishing Co., 1965.

Gilman, Charles Malcom B. *The Story of the Jersey Blues*. Red Bank, N.J.: Arlington Laboratory for Clinical and Historical Research, 1962.

Godfrey, Carlos E. *The Commander-in-Chief's Guard: Revolutionary War*. Washington, D.C.: Stevenson-Smith Co., 1904; reprint, Baltimore: Clearfield Co., 1995.

Gough, Robert J. "Black Men and the Early New Jersey Militia," *New Jersey History*, 88 (Winter 1970): 227-238.

Grant, George. "Journal of Serg't Major George Grant." in *Journals of the Military Expedition of Major General John Sullivan Against the Six Nations of Indians in 1779 with Records of Centennial Celebrations*. ed. Frederick Cook Auburn, NY:

Knapp, Peck & Thomson, 1887, 107-114. Original published in *Hazard's Register of Pennsylvania* 14 (1834): 72-76.

Griffith, J. H. "William Maxwell, of New Jersey, Brigadier General in the Revolution." *Proceedings of the New Jersey Historical Society*, 2d ser., 13 (May 1894): 109-123.

Harris, Thomas. "Memoir of a Revolutionary Soldier." *Vineland Historical Magazine* 41 (1957): 302-308, 317-319, 362-367.

Hatfield, Edwin Francis. *History of Elizabeth, New Jersey; Including the Early History of Union County.* New York: Carlton & Lanahan, 1868; reprint, Salem, Ma.: Higginson Book Co., 1990.

Hay, Clyde B., and Willard L. De Yoe. *New Barbadoes Neck in Revolutionary War Days.* Rutherford, N. J: Rutherford Committee of the New Jersey Tercentenary, 1964.

Hayward, Elizabeth M. *Soldiers and Patriots of the American Revolution; A List Compiled from Baptist Periodicals at the Shirk Library, Franklin College.* Ridgewood, N. J., 1947.

Heitman, Francis. *Historical Register of Officers of the Continental Army during the War of the Revolution, April 1777 to December 1783.* Washington, D. C: Rare Book Shop Publishing Co., 1932; reprint, Baltimore: Clearfield Co., 1997.

Historical Records Survey (WPA). *Gloucester County Series, Revolutionary War Documents.* Newark, N.J., 1941.

Honeyman, A. Van Doren, ed. "The Condict Revolutionary Record Abstracts." *Proceedings of the New Jersey Historical Society*, New Ser., 5 (1920): 236-240; 6 (1921): 89-100, 166-176; 7 (1922):. 25-32, 134-140, 227-232; 8 (1923): 30-35, 306-313; 9 (1924): 49-57; 10 (1925): 182-187, 312-316.

_____. "Half-Pay to Hunterdon County Families of the Revolution 1780-1796." *Proceedings of the New Jersey Historical Society*, new ser. 13 (1928): 190-199.

_____. *The History of Union County, New Jersey.* vol. 1. New York: Lewis Historical Publishing Co., 1923.

Jackson, John W. *Valley Forge: Pinnacle of Courage.* Gettysburg, Pa.: Thomas Publications, 1992.

Jackson, Ronald V. *Index to Military Men of New Jersey, 1775-1815.* Bountiful, Ut.: Accelerated Indexing Systems, 1977.

James, Edward J. "Some Additional Information Concerning Ephraim Martin, Esquire, Colonel of the Fourth New Jersey Regiment of the Continental Line. *Pennsylvania Magazine of History and Biography.* 36 (1912): 143-161.

Jones, Chester N. *List of Widows of Revolutionary Soldiers Living in New Jersey.* Genealogical Society of New Jersey.

Lee, Francis B. *Documents Relating to The Revolutionary History of the State of New Jersey.* Trenton: John J. Murphy, vol. 2, 1903

Lee, Francis Bazley,. ed. *Genealogical and Memorial History of the State of New Jersey.* 4 vols. New York: Lewis Historical Publishing Co., 1910.

Leiby, Adrian C. *The Revolutionary War in the Hackensack Valley; The Jersey Dutch and the Neutral Ground.* New Brunswick: Rutgers University Press, 1962.

Lender, Mark Edward. *The New Jersey Soldier.* Trenton: New Jersey Historical Commission, 1975.

____. "The Enlisted Line: The Continental Soldiers of New Jersey," Ph. D. Diss., Rutgers University, 1975.

____.*One State in Arms: Military History of the Revolutionary War* Trenton: New Jersey Historical Commission, 1991

____. "The Social Structure of the New Jersey Brigade: The Continental Line as an American Standing Army, " In Peter Karsten, ed., *The Military in America From the Colonial Era to the Present* (New York: Free Press, 1980), 27-44.

Livingston, William. *Selections from the Correspondence of the Executive, 1776-1786.* Newark: Daily Advertiser Office, 1848.

Lobdell, Jared C. "Paramus in the War of the Revolution," *Proceedings of the New Jersey Historical Society,* 78 (July 1960): 162-177.

Lundin, Leonard. *Cockpit of the Revolution: The War for Independence in New Jersey.* Princeton: Princeton University Press, 1940, reprint; New York: Octagon Books, 1972.

McCarthy, Callahan J. "Lieutenant-Colonel Francis Barber, Elizabethtown Patriot and Hero." *Union County Historical Society Proceedings*, 2 (1923-34): 127-136.

McCarty, Thomas. "The Revolutionary War Journal of Sergeant Thomas McCarty." *Proceedings of the New Jersey Historical Society* 82 (1964): 29-46.

McCluskey, Vincent Stanley, "The Life and Times of Philip Vickers Fithian, Revolutionary War Hero." Ph. D. Diss., New York University, 1991.

McMullin, Phillip W. ed. *Grassroots of America*. Salt Lake City: Gendex Corp., 1972. This indexes the thirty eight volumes of the *American State Papers*.

Maxwell, William. "General William Maxwell Correspondence." *Proceedings of the New Jersey Historical Society* 10 (1925): 176-80.

Mellick, Andrew D., Jr. "The Militia of New Jersey in the Revolution." *Magazine of American History*, 19 (April 1888), 340-341.

Metcalfe, Bryce. *Original Members and Other Officers Eligible to the Society of the Cincinnati, 1783-1938*. The Society of the Cincinnati.

Mickle, Isaac. *Reminiscences of Old Gloucester: or Incidents in the History of the Counties of Gloucester, Atlantic and Camden*. Philadelphia: T. Ward, 1845.

Miers, Earl Schenck. *Crossroads of Freedom: The American Revolution and the Rise of a New Nation*. New Brunswick: Rutgers University Press, 1971.

Murray, Nicholas. *Notes, Historical and Biographical, Concerning Elizabethtown, Its Eminent Men, Churches, and Ministers*. Elizabethtown: E. Sanderson, 1844.

_____. "A Memoir of the Rev. James Caldwell, of Elizabethtown." *Proceedings of the New Jersey Historical Society*, 3 (May 1848), 77-89.

National Genealogical Society. *Index of Revolutionary Pension Applications in the National Archives*. Washington, D.C., 1976.

Neagles, James C. and Lila L. Neagles. *Locating Your Revolutionary War Ancestor: A Guide to the Military Records*. Logan, Ut.: The Everton Publishers, 1983.

New Jersey. *Minutes of the Provincial Congress and Council of Safety 1774-1778*. 2 vols. Trenton and Jersey City: Naar, Day and J. H. Lyon, 1872-1879.

New Jersey Historical Record Survey. *Index to Stryker's Register of New Jersey in the Revolution*. 1941; reprint, Baltimore: Clearfield Co., 1995.

New Jersey Historical Society. *Documents Relating to the Colonial, Revolutionary and Post-Revolutionary History of the State of New Jersey*. [*Archives of the State of New Jersey*, 1st Ser.] 42 vols. Newark and Paterson: Various publishers, 1880-1949.

Newman, Debra S. *List of Black Servicemen, Compiled from the War Department Collections of Revolutionary War Records*. National Archives Special list No. 36 Washington, D.C.: National Archives, 1974.

Ogden, Aaron. *Autobiography of Col. Aaron Ogden, of Elizabethtown*. Paterson: The Press Printing and Publishing Co., 1893. [Originally published in *Proceedings of the New Jersey Historical Society*, 2d Ser., 12 (January 1892): 13-31.

Ogden, Matthias. *Journal of Major Matthias Ogden*. Morristown: Privately printed, 1928.

Orderly Book of the New Jersey Brigade, July 30 to October 8, 1780. Bergen County Historical Society Annual Report for 1921-1922, pp. Also in *Proceedings of the New Jersey Historical Society* 13 (1928): 17-30.

Owen, Lewis F. *The Revolutionary Struggle in New Jersey, 1776-1783*. Trenton: The New Jersey Historical Commission, 1975.

Pennington, William S. "Copy of Diary of William S. Pennington, of New Jersey (May 4, 1780-March 22, 1781)." *Journal of the Military Service Institute of the United States* 4 (1883): 324-29. Also in *Proceedings of the New Jersey Historical Society*, n. s. 63 (1945): 199-218; 64 (1946): 31-42.

Peterson, Clarence S. *Known Military Dead during the American Revolutionary War*. Baltimore, 1959; reprint, Baltimore: Clearfield Co., 1997.

Philhower, Charles A. *The History of Westfield, Union County, New Jersey*. New York: Lewis Historical Publishing Co., 1923.

Pierce's Register. Register of the Certificates Issued by John Pierce, Esquire, Paymaster General and Commissioner of Army Accounts for the United States, to Officers and Soldiers of the Continental Army Under Act of July 4, 1783. 1915; reprint, Baltimore: Genealogical Publishing Co, 1987.

"Proceedings of the Committees of Freehold and Shrewsbury In Monmouth Co., on the Opening of the Revolution." *Proceedings of the New Jersey Historical Society*, 1 (1846): 184-197.

Ralston, Louise Bird. "Captain Conway's Inventory and the Old Barracks at Trenton," *Proceedings of the New Jersey Historical Society*, 76 (April 1958): 79-83.

Raum, John O. *History of the City of Trenton, New Jersey, Embracing a Period of Nearly Two Hundred Years....* Trenton: W. T. Nicholson & Co., 1871; reprint, Salem, Ma.: Higginson Book Co., 1992.

Roberts, Thomas. "Journal of Sergeant Thomas Roberts." *Journals of the Military Expedition of Major General John Sullivan Against the Six Nations of Indians in 1779 with Records of Centennial Celebrations.* ed. Frederick Cook. Auburn, NY: Knapp, Peck &Thomson, 1887, 240-45.

Roster of the Officers of the New Jersey Continental Line in the Revolutionary War Who Were Eligible to Membership in the Society of the Cincinnati. The Society of the Cincinnati, 1911.

Ryan, Dennis P., editor. *New Jersey in the American Revolution, 1763-1783: A Chronology.* Trenton: New Jersey Historical Commission, 1974.

Salter, Edwin & George C. Beekman. *Old Times in Old Monmouth: Historical Reminiscences of Old Monmouth County, New Jersey, Being a Series of Historical Sketches relating to Old Monmouth County (Now Monmouth and Ocean).* 1887; reprint Bowie, Md: Heritage Books, 1999.

Schuyler, Hamilton. *A History of St. Michael's Church, Trenton.* Princeton: Princeton University Press, 1926.

Scott, Austin. *Documents Relating to the Revolutionary History of the State Of New Jersey.* Trenton: State Publishing Co., 1917.

Sedgewick, Theodore, Jr. *A Memoir of the Life of William Livingston.* New York: J. & J. Harper, 1833

Shelley, Fred. "Ebenezer Hazard's Diary: New Jersey During the Revolution," *New Jersey History*, 90 (Autumn 1972), 169-180.

Shreve, John. "Personal Narrative of the Services of Lieut. John Shreve of the New Jersey Line of the Continental Army." *Magazine of American History*, 3 September 1879): 564-579.

Shute, Samuel M. "Journal of Lieut. Samuel M. Shute." *Journals of the Military Expedition of Major General John Sullivan Against the Six Nations of Indians in 1779 with Records of Centennial Celebrations*. ed. Frederick Cook. Alburn: Knapp, Peck &Thomson, 1887): 267-274.

Sinclair, Donald Arleigh. *New Jersey Biographical Index Covering Some 100,000 Biographies and Associated Portraits in 237 New Jersey...Sources Published Through 1980*. Baltimore: Genealogical Publishing Co., 1993.

Sinclair, Donald Arleigh and Grace W, Schut. *The American Revolution and New Jersey: A Bibliography*. New Brunswick, N.J.: Rutgers University Libraries, Special Collections and University Archives, 1995.

Smith, Samuel S. *The Battle of Monmouth*. Monmouth Beach: Philip Freneau Press, 1964.

____. *Winter at Morristown 1779-1780 The Darkest Hour*. Monmouth Beach: Philip Freneau Press, 1979.

Society of the Cincinnati in the State of New Jersey. The Society of the Cincinnati, 1960.

"Some Unpublished Revolutionary Manuscripts." *Proceedings of the New Jersey Historical Society*, 2d ser., 13 (1894-1895): 17-24, 79-88, 149-160; 3d ser., 3 (1902, 1906): 85-92, 118-123, 180-184; 6 (1909): 12-16, 79-86.

Spear, John. "The Orderly Book of Lieutenant John Spear (July 17 to December 4, 1781)." ed. Joseph F. Folsom. *Proceedings of the New Jersey Historical Society*, new ser., 1 (July 1916): 129-146.

Stevens, Lewis T. "Soldiers from Cape May In The Revolutionary War," *Cape May County, New Jersey, Magazine of History & Genealogy*, 1 (June 1932): 43-52.

Stewart, Bruce. *Morristown: A Crucible of the American Revolution*. Trenton: New Jersey Historical Commission, 1977.

Stewart, Mrs. Frank Ross. *Black Soldiers in the American Revolutionary War*. Centre, Alabama: Stewart University Press, 1978.

Stratford, Dorothy Agans & Thomas B. Wilson. *Certificates and Receipts of Revolutionary New Jersey.* Westminster, Md.: Family Line Publications, 1996.

Stryker, William S. *General Maxwell's Brigade of the New Jersey Continental Line in the Expedition Against the Indians, in the Year 1779.* Trenton: W. S. Sharp Printing Co., 1885.

_____. *The New Jersey Continental Line in Virginia Campaign of 1781.* Trenton: John L. Murphy, 1882.

_____., compiler. *Official Register of the Officers and Men of New Jersey in the Revolutionary War, Compiled under Orders of His Excellency Theodore F. Randolph, Governor, by William S. Stryker, Adjutant General.* Trenton: Nicholson & Co., 1872; reprint, Baltimore: Genealogical Publishing Co., 1997.

_____, et al., eds. *Documents Relating to the Revolutionary History of the State of New Jersey.* Archives of the State of New Jersey, 2d Ser. 5 vols. Trenton: State of New Jersey, 1901-1917.

Stryker-Rodda, Kenn. *Revolutionary Census of New Jersey - An Index, Based on Rateables, of the Inhabitants of New Jersey During the Period of the Revolution.* Lambertville, N. J.: Hunterdon House, 1986.

Swan, Jedediah. "Jedediah Swan's Orderly Book." ed. Joseph F. Folsom. *Proceedings of the New Jersey Historical Society*, New Ser., 2 (January, April, July 1917), pp. 35-53, 118-123, 170-187; 3 (January 1918): 26-44.

Thayer, Theodore. *Colonial and Revolutionary Morris County.* Morristown: Morris County Heritage Commission, 1975.

_____. *As We Were: The Story of Old Elizabethtown.* Newark: New Jersey Historical Society, 1964.

_____. "The War in New Jersey: Battles, Alarums and the Men of the Revolution," *Proceedings of the New Jersey Historical Society*, 71 (April 1953): 83-110.

Thompson, Alexander B., ed. "Field and Staff Officers New Jersey Regiments in Revolution." *Proceedings of the New Jersey Historical Society*, 8 (May 1857): 65-68.

Thompson, William Y. *Israel Shreve, Revolutionary War Officer.* Ruston, La.: McGinty Trust Fund Publications, 1979.

Treese, Lorett. *Valley Forge: Making and Remaking a National Symbol.* University Park: Pennsylvania State University Press, 1995.

Trussell, John B. B. Jr. *Birthplace of an Army: A Study of the Valley Forge Encampment.* Harrisburg: Pennsylvania Historical and Museum Commission, 1976.

Tuttle, Joseph F. "Biographical Sketch of General William Winds, of Morris Co., New Jersey." *Proceedings of the New Jersey Historical Society,* 7 (May 1853): 13-37.

____. ed. "The Ford Family of Morristown, N.J.," *Historical Magazine,* 2d Ser., 10 (August 1871), 91-93.

U. S. Congress, Walter Lowrie and Walter S. Franklin, eds. *American State Papers; Documents, Legislative and Executive, on the Congress of the United States, from the First Session of the First to the Second Session of the Seventeenth Congress, inclusive; Commencing March 4, 1789, and Ending March 8, 1823. Class IX Claims.* Washington, D.C. 1834. Contains much information on thousands of Revolutionary War service claims filed in Congress. See McMullin, Phillip W. *Grassroots of America,* for a thorough index.

U. S. Congress. *Digested Summary and Alphabetical List of Private Claims, Which Have Been Presented to the House of Representatives from the First to the Thirty-first Congress.* 3 vols. House. Misc. Doc.; reprint, Baltimore, Genealogical Publishing Co., 1970.

U. S. Department of the Interior. *Report of the Secretary of the Interior, with a Statement of Rejected or Suspended Applications for Revolutionary War Pensions,* 1852. Sen. Exec. Doc. 37; reprint, Baltimore: Clearfield Co., 1998.

U. S. Department of the Interior. *Report of the Secretary of the Interior, with a Statement of Rejected or Suspended Applications for Revolutionary War Pensions,* 1852. Sen. Exec. Doc. 37; reprint, Baltimore: Genealogical Publishing Co., 1969.

U. S. House of Representatives. *Resolutions, Laws, and Ordinances, Relating to the Pay, Half Pay, Commutation of Half Pay, Bounty Lands...Officers and Soldiers of the Revolution...and to Funding Revolutionary Debt.* 1838; reprint, Baltimore: Genealogical Publishing Co., 1998.

U. S. War Department. *Letter from the Secretary of War, Communicating a Transcript of the Pension List of the United States - June 1, 1813.* Washington,

D.C., 1813; reprinted as *Revolutionary Pensioners; a Transcript of the Pension List of 1813*. Baltimore: Genealogical Publishing Co., 1959.

U.S. War Department. *Letter from the Secretary of War, Transmitting a Report of the Names, Rank and Line of Every Person Placed on the Pension List, in Pursuance of the Act of 18th March 1818*. Washington, D.C., 1820; reprint, Baltimore: Clearfield Co., 1998.

U. S. War Department. *Message from the Presidents of the United States, Transmitting a Report of the Secretary of War in Compliance "A list of the pensioners of the United States, the sum annually paid to each, and the state or territories in which the said pensioners reside*. Washington, D.C., 1818; reprinted as *Revolutionary Pensioners of 1818*. Baltimore: Southern Book Co., 1959.

U.S. War Department. *Letter From the Secretary of War, Transmitting a List of the Names of Pensioners Under the Act of 18th of March, 1818, Whose Names Were Struck Off the List by Act of 1st May, 1820, and Subsequently Restored*. Washington, D.C., 1836; reprinted as *Pensioners of Revolutionary War - Struck Off the Roll*. Baltimore: Genealogical Publishing Co., 1969.

U.S. War Department. *Report from the Secretary of War...in Relation to the Pension Establishment of the United States*, 3 vols. 1834, Sen. Doc. 514, reprinted as *The Pension Roll of 1835*. Baltimore: Genealogical Publishing Co., 1968.

U. S. War Department. *Revolutionary Pensioners: A Transcript of the Pension list for the United States for 1813*. 1813; reprint, Baltimore: Clearfield Co., 1997.

Vermeule, Cornelius C. "Some Revolutionary Incidents in The Raritan Valley." *Proceedings of the New Jersey Historical Society*, New Ser., 6 (April 1921): 73-86.

____. "Number of Soldiers in the Revolution," *Proceedings of the New Jersey Historical Society*, New Ser., 7 (July 1922), 223-227.

____. "Revolutionary Days in Old Somerset," *Proceedings of the New Jersey Historical Society*, New Ser., 8 (October 1923), 265-281.

____. "Service of the New Jersey Militia in the Revolutionary War," *Proceedings of the New Jersey Historical Society*, New Ser., 9 (July 1924), 234-248.

Waldenmaier, Nellie Protsman. *Some of the Earliest Oaths of Allegiance in the United States of America*. Lancaster, Pa.: privately printed 1944.

Wall, John Patrick. *New Brunswick in the Critical Period of the Revolution.* [New Brunswick]: The Times Publishing Co., 1908.

Wall, John Patrick & Harold E. Pickersgill, eds. *The History of Middlesex County, New Jersey, 1664-1920.* New York: Lewis Historical Publishing Co.: 1921

Ward, Harry M. *General William Maxwell and the New Jersey Continentals* Westport, CT: 1997.

White, Donald Wallace. *A Village at War: Chatham, New Jersey, and the American Revolution.* Rutherford, N.J. Fairleigh Dickenson University Press, 1979.

____. "A Local History Approach to the American Revolution: Chatham, New Jersey," *New Jersey History,* 96 (Spring-Summer 1978), 49-64.

____. "Census Making and Local History: In Quest of the People of a Revolutionary Village," *Prologue,* 14 (Fall 1982), 157-168.

Worley, Ramona Cameron. *Valley Forge...In Search of That Winter Patriot.* Louisville: The National Society Sons of the American Revolution, 1979.

Wright, William C., ed., *New Jersey in the American Revolution.* 3 vols. Trenton: New Jersey Historical Commission, 1973-1976.

Yesenko, Michael R. *General William Maxwell and the New Jersey Brigade During the American Revolutionary War* Union, New Jersey: MRY Publishing, 1996.

www.ingramcontent.com/pod-product-compliance
Lightning Source LLC
Chambersburg PA
CBHW052100230426
43662CB00036B/1710